The Dance Technique of Lester Horton

· · · · · · · · ·

The Dance Technique of
Lester Horton

Marjorie B. Perces

Ana Marie Forsythe

Cheryl Bell

Illustrated by Libby Yoakum

Photographs by Tom Caravaglia

A Dance Horizons Book
Princeton Book Company, Publishers
Princeton, NJ

THE DANCE TECHNIQUE OF LESTER HORTON. Copyright © 1992 by Princeton Book Company, Publishers. No portion of this book may be reproduced in any form or by any means without written permission of the publisher.

A Dance Horizons Book
Princeton Book Company, Publishers
P.O. Box 57
Pennington, NJ 08534

Cover and interior design by Anne O'Donnell
Front cover art based on photos by Tom Caravaglia
All text photos by Tom Caravaglia
Line drawings by Libby Yoakum

Library of Congress Cataloging-in-Publication Data

Perces, Marjorie B., 1921–
   The dance technique of Lester Horton / Marjorie B. Perces, Ana Marie Forsythe, Cheryl Bell ; illustrated by Libby Yoakum ; photographs by Tom Caravaglia.
      p.   cm.
   ISBN 0-87127-164-8
   1. Modern dance—Study and teaching.   2. Horton, Lester, 1906–1953.   I. Forsythe, Ana Marie, 1944–   . II. Bell, Cheryl, 1947–   .   III. Title.
GV1783.P46   1992
792.8—dc20   92-241

Contents

List of Illustrations

Acknowledgments

This is the first book to preserve the dance technique of Lester Horton. A book on the Horton technique was initially begun as a research project, funded by City College of New York under the aegis of the late Thelma Hill, Marjorie B. Perces, and Florence Waren.

We have covered the rich movement evolved by Horton, who dedicated his life to the dance and theater. The movement he devised fortifies, stretches, and reshapes the body to help produce an accomplished dancer. An experienced dance teacher who uses the movement in this book will build well-placed dancers capable of a broad range of expression and demonstrating impressive technical skills. Because of the diversity of the movement, the Horton technique trains dancers who can readily adapt to any other dance form.

The basis of the Horton technique is in the vocabulary. It is very important to absorb this material before proceeding with the rest of the text. We have included preparatory movements to enable beginning students as well as advanced students to develop a thorough knowledge of the foundation on which this technique is built. The movements listed as preparations will be useful to students at all technical levels.

An explanatory paragraph that offers comments and information vital to a deeper understanding of the technique introduces each section. The abbreviation B.P.M. stands for beats per minute. We selected this method indicating tempo because all it requires is a clock with a second hand. Other abbreviations are ct. for count, Beg. for beginners, Int. for intermediate, and Adv. for advanced. All Horton vocabulary terms have been capitalized in the text for easy identification.

The photographs by Tom Caravaglia and illustrations by Libby Yoakum enhance the written material by showing the correct line and shape of the body in space, as well as by defining the desired movement sequences.

The model for the photographs was Keith McDaniel, and the models for the illustrations were Ronald Brown, Adrienne Hurd, Ana Marie Forsythe, and Julio Rivera.

We are deeply grateful to the following people for their assistance, talent, energy, and generous support: the late Alvin Ailey, the late Douglas Bennett, Debi Elfenbein, Barbara Elman, Elaine Finsilver, Dall Forsythe, Jana Frances-Fisher, Lenore Latimer, Carmen de Lavallade, Bella Lewitzky, Madeline Nichols, Genevieve Oswald, Paul Perces, Julio Rivera, Louise Roberts, John Schlenck, the late Joyce Trisler, James Truitte, Karen Williamson, and Larry Warren. We thank Margery Hauser for her intelligent and exhaustive proofreading of the manuscript. We especially appreciate the support of the New York State Council on the Arts.

Marjorie B. Perces
Ana Marie Forsythe
Cheryl Bell
New York City

Foreword

Alvin Ailey

A fluke brought me to the Lester Horton school. A friend had shown me some Lester Horton movements and they seemed exciting and masculine. It was only after watching a number of classes that I finally got the courage to participate.

Lester Horton turned out to be the greatest influence on my career.

He was a genius at the theater, a major choreographer, and he designed a dance technique that is unique and so insightful that it is continuing to be used to train dancers and inspire teachers and choreographers today, thirty years after his death.

In addition to being a master teacher, Lester was also a wonderful costume designer, painter, and sculptor—he even wrote some of his own scores for percussion instruments. His choreography was ahead of its time, often dealing with social issues.

The Horton technique was developed over a period of years, with many changes. Occasionally a class would consist of only one original movement and embellishments on that movement. Lester's approach to anatomy was very logical and was very compatible with ballet.

The technique I learned from Lester has continued to affect and influence me and my work. It is an important part of the curriculum at the Alvin Ailey American Dance Center, and continues to be an inspiration for my choreography. He was an incredible man.

I am pleased that a book about the Lester Horton technique has finally been written. It is long overdue. The beauty of this rich and fluid technique has had a lasting impact on modern dance, and this book will make an excellent contribution toward preserving it.

New York City
December 1989

Part One

One

Reminiscences of Early Horton Technique

Bella Lewitzky

Bella Lewitzky was Lester Horton's instrument while he was developing his technique. She worked by his side for several decades, contributing inspiration, support, and cohesion to his limitless creativity. Around the Horton studio, they said, "If Bella can't do it, it can't be done." She now directs and choreographs for her own company, the Bella Lewitzky Dance Company, which is based in Los Angeles.

The Horton technique began to take shape concurrently with the development of his choreography. The method he used was typical of the day. Lester would start a movement pattern going. The dancers would pick it up and he would bounce back with an elaboration of the theme. Very often the whole class would be based on a single movement and its development.

Our entire vocabulary in those days was fashioned out of this kind of exploration on the part of the company. Lester would draw from what we had done, guiding us toward the things he felt were significant and welding them into technical studies.

It was decided that one precept, one viewpoint, was not adequate to encompass dance. The body itself was the determining factor, and that could be developed in as many ways as any choreographer might need.

So we set about to broaden the technique, rather than to limit or even define it. We would get out on the floor and ask, "How many ways from down to up?" We would ask similar questions about progressing across the floor.

Then there were Lester's explorations in defying gravity. Tipping off balance and holding as long as we possibly could. Falling to and holding just a hairbreadth off the floor. These were the kinds of things he would explore. He was extending the range of movement, forcing a resistance to gravity's pull. We would reach a point we knew we could not achieve, and we did it. This was his demand and this was part of his genius.

Two

The Life and Work of Lester Horton

Jana Frances-Fischer

Lester Horton is an important modern dance pioneer. He worked in California with many dancers who went on to make their own name. One of them, Alvin Ailey, relates:

> Lester Horton was the greatest influence of my career. He is the reason I do all this. He was a genius of the theatre. Besides being a major choreographer he was a master costume designer, master painter, master sculptor. An incredible man. When you came into the world of Lester Horton you came into a completely creative environment—people of all colors, music of all nations.[1]

Biographical Sketch and Artistic Influences of Lester Horton

Lester Horton was born into a working-class family in Indianapolis, Indiana, on January 23, 1906. As a child and adolescent, he was fascinated with Indian tribal dances, painting, and costume design. He studied Indian lore, wrote stories about Indians, and loved to visit Indian burial mounds. In 1922, at the age of sixteen, he saw his first professional dance performance. The Denishawn Dancers, directed by Ruth St. Denis and Ted Shawn, had come to Indianapolis, presenting modernized versions of Indian (American and Asian), Japanese, Siamese, and Javanese dances. The colorful costumes and exotic movements captivated Horton—seduced him into the decision to become a dancer.[2] He began studying ballet, aesthetic (Greek) dance, and modern dance.

In the mid-1920s Horton relocated temporarily in Chicago. He studied ballet with Adolf Bolm at the Pavley-Oukrainsky School, but was dissatisfied with the rigidity

[1]Clive Barnes, "Genius on the Wrong Coast," *Los Angeles Herald Examiner* 3 Dec. 1967:7.
[2]Don Martin, personal interview, 22 March 1987.

of the classic forms.[3] In 1926, Horton was back in Indiana, researching, choreographing, and performing Indian ritual dances for the Indianapolis Little Theatre.[4]

In 1929, Horton was invited to California to join Michio Ito's company, which produced "plays for dancers." It was here that Horton learned the organic use of props, which would later become an integral part of his own choreography.[5] He remained in California for the rest of his life.

•• •   •
Lester Horton: Teacher, Choreographer, and Founder of Dance Theater

Horton went off to dance, direct, teach, and produce choreographies. "Early he exhibited a theatrical flair, a natural talent for teaching, an ability to absorb ideas rapidly, and a facility for invention."[6] Horton became well known on the West Coast as the choreographer of more than forty concert stage pieces, eight films, and numerous nightclub acts and native Indian pageants.[7] Winthrop Palmer describes them thus: "The dances that Lester Horton choreographed were inspired by Mexican themes, by Paul Klee, by Garcia Lorca, by the music of Stravinsky and Duke Ellington."[8]

In 1946 Horton established his own school and founded his company, Dance Theater, in a small studio on Melrose Avenue in Hollywood, California. The Horton troupe was one of the first in the country to house an interracial company of dancers.[9] Winthrop Palmer asserts that "Horton's bold experiments with modern dance techniques interested new audiences and many students. His pupils were a league of cultures and nations, Mexican, Japanese, Spanish, Black, and white."[10]

Horton demanded a lot from his dancers. He required them to study ballet, learn to read music, sew, work the light board, and assist in making scenery and props. The company worked together as a "family" to maintain the theater. They spent hours without pay, running the studio, teaching classes, handling publicity, and participating in virtually all aspects of production, design, and execution.

[3]John Sturgeon, personal interview, 22 March 1987.
[4]Joyce Trisler, *Dance Perspectives*, Autumn 1967:59.
[5]Lelia Goldoni, telephone interview, 13 March 1987.
[6]James Truitte, telephone interview, 30 Nov. 1986.
[7]Terrill Maguire, "Lester Horton and California Dance: Reflections on a Book by Larry Warren," review of *Lester Horton, Modern Dance Pioneer,* by Larry Warren, *York Dance Review* Spring 1977:39.
[8]Joyce Trisler, *Dance Perspectives*, Autumn 1967:59.
[9]Carmen de Lavallade, telephone interview, 5 Jan. 1987.
[10]Agnes de Mille, *American Dances* (New York: Macmillan Publishing Company, Inc., 1980), 110.

Carmen de Lavallade, principal female dancer with Horton from 1950 to 1954, recalls:

> It was a very close relationship. He was like my father. He was a very incredible man and made you feel comfortable. . . . The company was very close; we were more like family. He knew how to handle everyone equally. . . . I don't know how he did it, but he did. He never played favorites and he never put himself on the throne.[11]

Larry Warren, writer of the only major biography of Lester Horton to date, explains:

> The roster of artists he trained should alone assure his place as a prime contributor to the mainstream of the field [of modern dance]. Among those were Bella Lewitzky, whose phenomenal career has spanned forty years of dancing, choreography, and innovative teaching; Carmen de Lavallade, who has had a distinguished career as a dancer; James Truitte, one of America's outstanding modern dance teachers; Rudi Gernreich, an innovator in the fashion industry; and Alvin Ailey, who leads one of the world's best-known dance companies. There are, of course, many others, including James Mitchell, Janet Collins, Carl Ratcliff and Joyce Trisler.[12]

On November 2, 1953, at the age of 47, Lester Horton passed away in his Hollywood home. He died of a heart attack. The company disbanded in 1960, and dancers like Joyce Trisler, James Truitte, and Alvin Ailey left to pursue their own interests and dance careers.[13]

•• • • •
Horton's Modern Dance Technique

Although Lester Horton produced many ingenious and creative choreographic works, he is more often recognized for his unique system of dance movement. Along with Cunningham, Humphrey-Weidman, Graham, and Limon, Lester Horton created one of the major codified modern dance techniques. Many important modern dancers, trained in the Horton technique, emerged from his company, among them Alvin Ailey, Bella Lewitzky, Carmen de Lavallade, James Truitte, and Joyce Trisler.

---

[11]Carmen de Lavallade, telephone interview, 5 Jan. 1987.

[12]James Truitte, telephone interview, 30 Nov. 1986.

[13]Larry Warren, *Lester Horton: Modern Dance Pioneer* (Princeton, NJ: Princeton Book Company, Publishers, 1991).

Lester Horton never worked in his company with any dancer not trained in his style. His company dancers were required to take two classes a day, and lengthy ten- to twelve-hour rehearsals were not at all uncommon.[14]

Horton developed a dance technique reputed to fortify, stretch, and strengthen the human body in preparation for its use as an instrument for expressive dance.[15] With Horton, every muscle of the body is lengthened, and each section of the body is isolated.[16] Ex-principal dancer Bella Lewitzky testifies to this fact: "We had exercises for our fingers, our wrists, our shoulders, our eyes, our necks, ribs and arm undulations—these came from his love of Oriental theatre."[17]

Horton is famous for producing dancers with long, lean thigh muscles and flexible but strong lower backs.[18] The technique utilizes all spatial planes and movement levels. "Lester's technique was spatial in its emphasis, so it tended to reach outside the body," explains Bella Lewitzky.[19]

In addition, all aspects of tempo, movement range, rhythmical patterns, and dynamic accents are explored.[20] Lewitzky calls the Horton style an "architectural technique," focusing on "joint mobility, developing, throwing, flinging, swinging, casting and off-balance movements,"[21] and his expressive use of the rounding and arching spine. The concept of the rounding and arching spine is similar to Martha Graham's contraction and release theory. "Lester developed a technique which tested the capacity of the body to move at its extremes."[22]

The torso, in Horton technique, is considered to be the origin of all motion.[23] This notion is similar to the Graham and Humphrey-Weidman concepts. Other impulses for movement emanate from the shoulder, the sternum, the diaphragm, and the pelvic girdle.[24]

Horton's slow movements were exaggeratedly slow—his fast, exaggeratedly fast—demanding incredible effort and control. Open posture and spread arms predominated—every body part stretched to its physical limit:

> the overall impression was one of sweep and grandeur. . . . The floor of the studio actually rested on springs which re-enforced jumps.

[14]Terrill Maquire, *York Dance Review,* Spring 1977.

[15]James Truitte, telephone interview, 30 Nov. 1986.

[16]Righard Philip, "Twenty Years Later: The Alvin Ailey American Dance Theatre," *Dance Magazine,* Oct. 1978:66.

[17]Bella Lewitzky, *Dance Perspectives,* Autumn 1967.

[18]Terrill Maguire, *York Dance Review,* Spring 1977.

[19]Bella Lewitzky, *Dance Perspectives,* Autumn 1967.

[20]Joyce Trisler, *Dance Perspectives,* Autumn 1967.

[21]Bella Lewitzky, *Dance Perspectives,* Autumn 1967.

[22]Bella Lewitzky, *Dance Perspectives,* Autumn 1967.

[23]Lelia Goldoni, telephone interview, 13 March 1987.

[24]James Truitte, telephone interview, 30 Nov. 1986.

> . . . The bodies themselves, like taut coils of spring, seemed to be in tension, had weight and volume. They never floated, but darted, lunged, or sneaked into space, or simply possessed it.[25]

James Truitte is one of the few Horton instructors in the United States today who worked closely with Lester Horton. Truitte has established a BFA curriculum in Horton technique at the University of Cincinnati. Truitte explains that Horton developed a syllabus for his movement studies similar to some that exist for classical ballet. Horton gave titles to all his movement sequences. Examples of these lengthy exercise patterns are Deep Floor Vocabulary, Dimensional Tonus, Swing Stimulation I and II, Lunge Series, and Preludes I through IV. These series are known for their flow and their choreographic polish; they are not simply presented and received as a random arrangement of stock dance steps.[26]

James Truitte explains:

> The marvelous thing about the Horton technique is that it explores every part of the body, and works from the joint out. It is a logical exploration of the anatomy . . . after you have studied it for year after year and walk into another technique—whether it be Graham, Holm, or whomever—nobody can put a label or stamp on you as to your technical background. This is one of the great identifying features about Lester's technique.[27]

• • • •
Dance Theater: A West Coast Phenomenon

It must be remembered that Dance Theater, which began performing for the public in Los Angeles in 1948, was the only troupe on the West coast housed in a facility exclusively devoted to dance. At the time of Horton's death, it was in its sixth season, with some twenty full-length works in the repertoire. In most instances, Horton was not only the choreographer but also the designer.[28]

Dancer Don Martin looks back:

> The theater over on Melrose was a lifestyle. You walked through those doors, and it was a world apart from Melrose Avenue. . . . You were taught theater. . . . costume room to on-stage performance. . . . We were consumed by it. We lived by it. Whether we were in class or not, we were still in the Horton technique.[29]

[25]Joyce Trisler, *Dance Perspectives,* Autumn 1967.
[26]Joyce Trisler, *Dance Perspectives,* Autumn 1967.
[27]James Truitte, telephone interview, 30 Nov. 1986.
[28]Terrill Maguire, *York Dance Review,* Spring 1977.
[29]Don Martin, personal interview, 22 March 1987.

The Lester Horton Dancers made only two appearances in New York: one in 1943, and again in the spring of 1953, a few months before Horton died. The troupe gave highly successful performances at the Folies Bergère restaurant nightclub in 1943 and at the YMHA in 1953.[30] Before these dates, few people outside of California were fortunate enough to have viewed the genius of Horton's choreography or of his technique.

In an interview in 1937, Horton stated:

> I am sincerely trying to create a dance technique based entirely upon corrective exercises, created with a knowledge of human anatomy; a technique which will correct physical faults and prepare a dancer for any type of dancing he may wish to follow, a technique having all the basic movements which govern the actions of the body, combined with a knowledge of the origin of movement and a sense of artistic design.[31]

Lester Horton did that, and so much more.

[30]Lelia Goldoni, telephone interview, 13 March 1987.
[31]Dorathi Bock Pierre, *American Dancer*, October 1937:37.

Part Two

Three

Vocabulary

The vocabulary describes and illustrates the positions and shapes used throughout the Horton technique. It should be used as a reference and introduced as needed to teach the studies. All Horton vocabulary terms have been capitalized in the text for easy identification.

Positions of the Feet

Parallel 1st   the feet parallel, approximately two inches apart.

Natural 1st   the feet at 45° angle, heels touching.

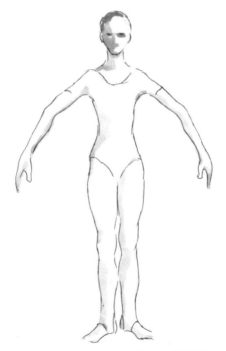

Figure 1. Natural 1st (feet); Demi-2nd (arms)

Figure 2. Natural 2nd (feet); 2nd (arms)

Parallel 2nd   the feet parallel and opened to the width of the pelvis.

Natural 2nd   the feet at 45° angle and opened to the width of the pelvis.

Wide Natural 2nd   the feet at 45° angle and opened wider than the shoulders.

Parallel 4th   the feet parallel approximately two inches apart, with one foot forward of the other and separated by one foot length.

Natural 4th   the feet at 45° angle, heels separated forward and back by one foot length.

> **Note:** *Several Horton studies simultaneously employ one naturally turned out foot and one parallel foot.*

•• • •   •
Positions of the Arms

Natural Low   the arms extended vertically downward, not touching the body, palms facing each other.

Middle Parallel   the arms extended horizontally forward, palms facing each other.

High Parallel   the arms extended vertically upward, palms facing each other.

2nd   the arms extended straight to the side, to shoulder level, palms facing downward.

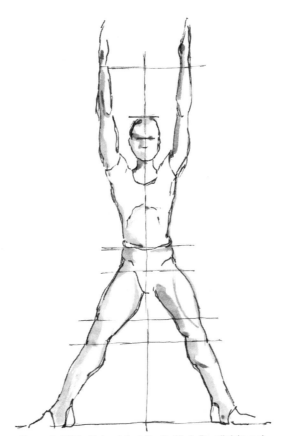

Figure 3. Wide Natural 2nd (feet); High Parallel (arms)

Demi-2nd   the arms rounded and extended to the side halfway between 2nd and Natural Low, palms inward.

Closed Egyptian   the arms raised forward to shoulder level, elbows bent at a 90° angle, palms facing inward.

Opened Egyptian   the arms raised to the side with the elbows at shoulder level, the forearms at a 90° angle, palms facing each other.

Diagonal Egyptian   the arms raised forward and diagonally upward, index fingers pointing toward each other, elbows bent to form a diamond shape, with the palms facing out; the head is tilted back with the focus on an upward diagonal, looking through the fingers.

Positions and Actions of the Body

Coccyx Balance   seated on the floor on both buttocks, both knees bent with lower legs raised forward and parallel to the ceiling; the feet pointed; the torso

Figure 4. Coccyx Balance

may tilt diagonally backward slightly, but the head remains erect, the arms in Middle Parallel even with the lower legs.

Figure 4 Positions

Standing   the outside of the left ankle is placed on the right thigh, just above the right knee, the left leg is fully turned out; the left foot may be either pointed or

Figure 5. Standing Figure 4; with plié

Figure 6. Seated Figure 4

flexed, the arms in Closed Egyptian; the torso is erect and the standing leg may be straight or in plié.

Squat   the outside of the left ankle is placed on the right thigh, just above the knee; the left leg is fully turned out, the right leg is fully bent to Primitive Squat position (see below); the torso is rounded slightly; and the arms are in Closed Egyptian with the elbows placed on the left shin.

Seated   the outside of the right leg from the hip down is lying on the floor, the left leg is bent, the left foot is placed on the floor parallel to the right leg, the left hip is pressing forward to the straightest line possible, the left arm is extended sideward and touching the top of the left knee, the right hand is on the floor with the right arm perpendicular to the floor.

Push-up   place the left hand on the floor shoulder width apart from the right hand and rotate the Seated Figure 4 position to face the floor, the left heel lifts off the floor and maintains contact with the right thigh, the right leg rotates parallel;

Figure 7. Figure 4 Push-up

Figure 8. Flat Back Back Bend

the ball of the right foot presses to the floor, the hands are directly under the shoulders; the arms are straight and the body forms a diagonal line.

Flat Back Back Bend   (pelvic press) stand with the feet in Parallel 2nd, the pelvis pressed diagonally forward; the torso tilted diagonally backward, the arms in High Parallel, the knees straight, the focus diagonally up.

Flat Back Forward   stand with the feet in Parallel 2nd, the torso tilted forward at a right angle (90°), the buttocks, calves, and heels in a straight line, the arms in Natural Low or High Parallel.

Flat Back Side   stand with feet in Wide Natural 2nd, the torso tilted forward at a right angle (90°), and as far to the side as possible; the sides of the torso should be parallel to the downstage and upstage wall; the arms in High Parallel, pointing perpendicularly to stage right or stage left.

High Lateral   the torso, the gesture leg, and the head are tilted sideward to form a diagonal line; the gesture leg straight and parallel, foot pointed and slightly off the floor; the standing leg straight and naturally turned out, the arms in High Parallel.

Hinge   stand with the feet in Parallel 2nd, the pelvis pressed diagonally forward, the torso tilted diagonally backward, but with the head remaining erect; both knees bent and approximately three inches from the floor, both heels raised to ¼ relevé; the arms in Natural Low or 2nd.

Figure 9. Flat Back Forward

Note: *A Hinge can also be done with both knees on the floor.*

Lateral   stand with the feet in Wide Natural 2nd, the arms in High Parallel, the torso tilted sideward at a 90° angle, the weight shifted into the opposite hip (the hip is off center).

Lunges

Deep Forward Lunge   deep plié with the right leg forward, the foot naturally turned out, the knee bent fully and aligned over the middle toes, the left leg extended straight back, the foot parallel on ¾ relevé, the pelvis over right heel, the torso erect with the arms in Middle Parallel, or the torso tilted diagonally forward with the palms on the floor, fingers pointing forward, and shoulder width apart.

Side Lunge   feet in Wide Natural 2nd; the left knee is bent, the knee over the middle toes, the pelvis over the left heel, the torso perpendicular to the floor, the arms either in Middle Parallel or 2nd.

Cross Lunge   the right leg bent and naturally turned out, the left leg extended sideward behind and beyond the right foot and parallel, the left foot flexed, the outside of the foot on the floor, both shoulders and hips face downstage, the body from the top of the head to the heel of the flexed foot forms a diagonal line; the right arm is in 2nd, the left arm is bent, the palm facing the ceiling, and the left elbow reaching across toward the center of the body.

Figure 10. Lateral

Figure 11. Deep Forward Lunge

Figure 12. Side Lunge

Figure 13. Cross Lunge

Figure 14. Pelvic Press

Pelvic Press   with the gesture leg in low attitude, the standing leg naturally turned out and straight, the pelvis is pressed diagonally forward, the torso tilted diagonally back, the arms in 2nd or Diagonal Egyptian.

Primitive Squat   the feet in either Parallel 1st or Parallel 2nd, the torso straight and erect, both knees fully bent and aligned over the middle toes, the heels remain on floor, the buttocks as close to the floor as possible, the arms in Middle Parallel.

Stag Positions

Standing   the right foot very slightly turned out, the right knee bent; the left leg parallel and lifted to the back with the knee bent, the thigh and the lower leg form a 90° angle, the toes pointed and reaching toward the ceiling; the right arm extended back at shoulder level, the left arm extended forward at shoulder level, both palms facing downward; the pelvis remains erect as the upper back arches, the head erect, the focus forward.

Kneeling   the right knee bent with the shin on the floor, the foot pointed; the left leg parallel to the back with the bent knee on the floor, the toes pointed and

Figure 15. Primitive Squat

reaching to the ceiling; the arms, torso, and head remain the same as in Standing Stag.

Strike Position   the standing leg straight and slightly turned out; the torso extended, the torso and the head inverted, the head reaching toward the shin of the standing leg; the gesture leg in high back attitude, the knee fully flexed and pointing to the ceiling, the foot pointed; the arms parallel to each other with the

Figure 16. Standing Stag

Figure 17. Kneeling Stag

palms facing each other; both arms reaching upward and parallel to the thigh of the gesture leg, fingers pointing to the ceiling.

Swings

Horizontal   the torso moves horizontally from Flat Back right side to Flat Back left side.

Release   the torso begins Flat Back right side, drops center, then pulls out to Flat Back left side.

Figure 18. Table

Table   stand with the supporting leg straight, the foot naturally turned out; the gesture leg raised laterally to hip level and the knee bent to form a 90° angle, the foot pointed; the outside surface of the leg parallel to the ceiling, the arms in 2nd.

Figure 19. Forward Table

Note: *Forward Table   the gesture leg raised to the front diagonal at hip level and the knee bent to form a 45° angle, the foot pointed, and the outside surface of the leg parallel to the ceiling; the supporting leg naturally turned out, the arms in 2nd.*

Figure 20. Back T

Figure 21. Front T

T Positions

Back T   the front of the torso, the gesture leg, and face form a straight line parallel to and facing the ceiling, the gesture leg slightly turned out, the standing foot is naturally turned out; the standing knee may bend slightly and the heel may raise to ¼ relevé, the arms in either High Parallel or 2nd.

Figure 22. Lateral T

Front T   the front of the torso, the gesture leg, and face form a straight line parallel to and facing the floor; the gesture leg parallel, the standing leg straight, the foot is naturally turned out, the arms in High Parallel.

Lateral T   the side of the torso, the gesture leg, and the head are tilted sideward to form a straight line parallel to both the ceiling and the floor; the gesture leg parallel, the standing leg straight, with the foot completely turned out, the arms in High Parallel.

Triangle   seated on the floor on both buttocks, the torso erect, the left leg bent with the shin parallel to the front, the foot pointed; the right leg inverted, the foot pointed and allowing the knee to touch the toes on the left foot, the arms either in 2nd or rounded with palms lightly touching the knees, fingers pointing forward.

Figure 23. Triangle

Four

Guide to Teaching

This chapter will cover descriptions and explanations of the material to be presented in this book. All of the Horton material has been graded to help teachers plan classes at the proper level for their students. The grading suggests an appropriate time in a student's development to introduce material, but does not imply that only students at that level should use the material. Advanced students must be familiar with all the material that beginner and intermediate students use.

Horton classes usually begin with *Flat Backs*. They stretch the hamstring muscles, prepare the back, and strengthen the abdominals. Since this technique calls upon the hamstring muscles frequently, these muscles must be slowly and thoroughly warmed up at the beginning of class. As a general rule, throughout all the *Flat Back* series the student must maintain the flat back line parallel to the floor to achieve maximum benefit and the correct line.

The *Primitive Squat* sequence lengthens the achilles tendons and the gastrocnemius (the calf muscles), stretches the gluteal muscles (the buttocks muscles), and releases the lower back muscles. It also activates the sheath of muscles just over the shin. With the correct alignment of the knees over the second toes, the *Primitive Squat Descent and Ascent* strengthens the muscles surrounding the knee joint, which helps prevent pronation and knee injury.

The *Laterals* are an important shape in the Horton technique. Both sides of the torso should be stretched and elongated in the execution of the laterals. The abdominal muscles must be activated to support the back each time the body is in any lateral position to prevent strain and injury to the body. In *Laterals* the stretch of the torso and the arms to the side results in a shift of weight and a pull of the hip to the opposite side. This muscular compensation enhances maximum sideward flexibility.

One of the least stressful ways to warm up the body is with the swinging action. The quality of the swing is integral to the movement, whether it is a leg swing, an arm swing, or a body release swing. In Horton *Leg Swings*, both legs remain parallel, encouraging the maximum muscular capability of the hamstring through the gluteus maximus. The torso maintains its center because the alignment of the pelvis does not change as the leg swings to the back.

The *Release Swings* can be done with plié or straight legs. Two actions are involved—the release, followed by an attenuation. Neither action should cause a cessation of the flow of energy or movement. The pendular action remains constant. It is essential that the head be inverted and the lower back, through the entire spine, be released each time. The action of the release swing frequently serves as momentum and as a preparation for a turn and occasionally for a jump. Some swing sequences should be included in every Horton class. The swings represent an important training aspect of the technique.

In the *Metatarsal Press* and in *Lunges,* the goal is to stretch and lengthen the muscles of the backs of the legs, from the heel through the buttocks. The achilles is a tendon which cannot be stretched, but these movements increase the blood flow to the surrounding muscles, thereby warming the tendon. This improves the demi-plié, which extends the potential for elevation. Both of these stretches make use of a consistent shape throughout the Horton technique—a turned-out leg working simultaneously with a parallel leg.

The parallel line, both in the arms and in the legs, is a fundamental aspect of the technique. In teaching and performing the Horton technique, the integrity of this line must be maintained. The parallel *Leg Swings* and the *Stag* position provide the opportunity to stretch and lengthen the quadriceps (thigh muscles). Parallel arms are a signature of the Horton technique, and help to enhance and define the line and expand the sense of space.

Dimensional Tonus was developed over a very long period of time. It was originally presented as the "Yawn Stretch" in the late forties, and was completed shortly before Horton's death. "Yawn Stretch" aptly describes the breath and quality that should be sustained throughout the study. It should only be given during the latter part of the warm-up. *Dimensional Tonus* needs to be taught in small sections over a period of several classes to enable the students to absorb the material correctly.

After completion of the warm-up, either floor work, which includes *Coccyx Balance* and other floor studies, or some *Stretches and Strengtheners* should be introduced. The selection should be determined by the progressions or combinations that will follow later in the class.

The next phase in a Horton class would include teaching a study. It is not always possible or even desirable to teach an entire study in one class session. Many of the studies are not only long, but also have complicated counts, tricky transitions, and varying dynamic qualities that require repetition and discussion. A few of the *Preludes, Fortifications,* and *Balance Studies* can be absorbed in one session. The level of the class plays a part in deciding how much to present.

A *Balance Study* usually begins the progressions. One of the outstanding features of the *Elementary Balance Study* is the accessibility of the design. Because of the simplicity of the movement and the clarity of the line, new beginning students are able to achieve immediate gratifying results. On the other hand, more advanced dancers are captured by the underlying complexity and the constant challenge to broaden their range of movement.

The *Progressions,* which include balance studies, leg swing series, turns, falls, elevations, and combinations of movements, are the culmination of the class, using the muscles warmed up earlier.

As in all dance classes, the lesson should work on more than one area of the body. Although it is important to maintain a theme for each class, it is equally important to avoid overworking one group of muscles. For example, the *Strike Stretch* and the *Hinge Studies,* if done to excess, could cause injury. They should be interspersed with other exercises over many classes where they would best function to strengthen the dancer and lengthen the muscles.

Five

The Warm-up

The following lesson plan of warm-up materials is a suggested sequence. Horton would often change the order not only of the warm-up but of the entire class.

The warm-up is designed to prepare the muscles of a dancer to execute demanding technical movements. The teacher must give a warm-up that works those parts of the body that will be called upon later in the class.

Horton believed the three weakest parts of the body are the abdominals, the back, and the feet. Therefore, careful attention was given to strengthening these areas of the body in the warm-up and throughout the class.

The necessary warm-up, limbering, and basic exercise vocabulary was condensed into short, flexible combinations.

> Flat Backs
>
> Primitive Squat Descents and Ascents
>
> Laterals
>
> Leg Swings (see Swings in chapter 6)
>
> Metatarsal Press (see Elevation in chapter 14)
>
> Lunges (see Stretches and Strengtheners in chapter 9)
>
> Dimensional Tonus (see Studies in chapter 7)
>
> **Note:** Dimensional Tonus was often used as part of the warm-up at the Horton Studio.

Flat Backs

To stretch the hamstring and back muscles and strengthen the abdominals

Beg., Int., Adv.; two 3's; count at 75 B.P.M.

Begin center, facing downstage, the feet in Parallel 2nd, the arms in Natural Low.

cts. 1-2-3 *Tilt the torso forward,* forming a right angle at the hip joint, keeping the arms close to the sides of the body. The fingers pull toward upstage.

cts. 2-2-3 *Lift the torso erect.*

Repeat at least four times.

Flat Back with Arm Reach

Beg., Int., Adv.; four 3's; count at 75 B.P.M.

Begin center facing downstage, the feet in Parallel 2nd, the arms in Natural Low.

cts. 1-2-3 *Tilt the torso forward* forming a right angle at the hip joint, keeping the arms close to the sides of the body. The fingers pull toward upstage, and the arms remain alongside the body.

cts. 2-2-3 Maintaining the Flat Back forward position parallel to the floor, *reach side and forward with both arms to High Parallel,* turning the palms gradually to face each other.

cts. 3-2-3 *Lift the torso erect.*

cts. 4-2-3 *Turn the palms to face outward, and press the hands down to Natural Low.*

Repeat at least four times.

Flat Back with Arms in High Parallel

Beg., Int., Adv.; two 3's; count at 75 B.P.M.

Begin center, facing downstage, the feet in Parallel 2nd, the arms in High Parallel.

cts. 1-2-3 *Tilt the torso forward* to form a right angle at the hip joint. The arms remain in High Parallel, and the head remains centered between the arms.

cts. 2-2-3 *Lift the torso erect,* keeping the arms in High Parallel.

Repeat at least four times.

Flat Back with Demi-Plié

Beg., Int., Adv.; four 3's; count at 75 B.P.M.

Begin center, facing downstage, the feet in Parallel 2nd, the arms in High Parallel.

cts. 1-2-3 *Tilt the torso forward,* forming a right angle at the hip joint, and keeping the arms in High Parallel and the head centered between the arms.

cts. 2-2-3 Maintaining the Flat Back line parallel to the floor, *demi-plié on* both legs, and press slightly outward with the knees, so the torso can lower between the legs.

cts. 3-2-3 *Straighten the legs,* and maintain the Flat Back line.

cts. 4-2-3 *Lift the torso erect.*

Repeat at least four times.

Flat Back Back Bend

Beg., Int., Adv.; two 3's; count at 85 B.P.M.

Begin center, facing downstage, the feet in Parallel 2nd, the arms in High Parallel.

cts. 1-2-3 In a simultaneous action, *press the pelvis diagonally forward, as the arms are pulling toward upstage.* The head remains centered between the arms, with the focus downstage.

cts. 2-2-3 Lift the torso erect.

Repeat at least twice.

Flat Back with Demi-Plié and Flat Back Back Bend

Beg., Int., Adv.; six 3's; count at 75 B.P.M.

Begin center, facing downstage, the feet in Parallel 2nd, the arms in High Parallel.

cts. 1-2-3 *Tilt the torso forward,* to form a right angle at the hip joint. The arms remain in High Parallel, and the head remains centered between the arms.

cts. 2-2-3 Maintaining the Flat Back line, demi-plié on both legs, and press the knees slightly outward, so the torso can lower between the legs.

cts. 3-2-3 *Straighten the legs,* and maintain the Flat Back line and the arms in High Parallel.

cts. 4-2-3 *Lift the torso erect.*

cts. 5-2-3 *Press the pelvis forward to Flat Back Back Bend,* keeping the head centered between the arms.

cts. 6-2-3 *Center the torso.*

Repeat at least four times.

Flat Back with Relevé

Beg., Int., Adv.; eight 3's; count at 75 B.P.M.

Begin center, facing downstage, the feet in Parallel 2nd, the arms in Natural Low.

cts. 1-2-3 *Tilt the torso forward,* forming a right angle at the hip joint, and keeping the arms close to the sides of the body. The fingers pull toward upstage.

cts. 2-2-3 *Reach to the side and forward with the arms to High Parallel,* turning the palms gradually to face each other.

cts. 3-2-3 *Relevé,* maintaining the Flat Back line and the arms in High Parallel.

cts. 4-2-3 *Lift the torso erect,* maintaining the relevé.
and 5-2-3

cts. 6-2-3 *Hold the erect position, with the arms in High Parallel.*

cts. 7-2-3 *Lower the heels,* holding the erect position and the arms in High Parallel.

cts. 8-2-3 Turn the palms outward, *and press the arms to Natural Low.*

Repeat at least three times.

Flat Back with Demi-Plié and Slide Stretch

Int., Adv.; eleven 3's; count at 75 B.P.M.

Begin center, facing downstage, the feet in Parallel 2nd, the arms in Natural Low.

cts. 1-2-3 *Tilt the torso forward,* to form a right angle at the hip joint, and keeping the arms close to the sides of the body. The fingers pull toward upstage.

cts. 2-2-3 *Reach to the side and forward with the arms to High Parallel,* turning the palms gradually to face each other.

cts. 3-2-3 *Demi-plié on both legs,* and press the knees slightly open to lower the torso between the legs.

cts. 4-2-3 *Straighten both legs, and simultaneously tilt the torso forward to form a diagonal line,* with the little fingers of each hand touching the floor. The head remains centered between the arms, and the back remains straight.

cts. 5-2-3 In a simultaneous action, *plié on both legs, and slide the little fingers along the floor, maintaining a flat back.* The head remains centered between the arms.

cts. 6-2-3 Keeping the little fingers where they are, *straighten both legs.*

cts. 7-2-3 *Lift the torso erect, keeping the arms in High Parallel, and the head*
and 8-2-3 *centered.*

cts. 9-2-3 *Flat Back Back Bend.*

cts. 10-2-3 *Center the torso.*

cts. 11-2-3 *Turn the palms outward, and press the arms to Natural Low.*

Repeat at least three times.

Round Back and Flat Back

Beg., Int., Adv.; two 3's; count at 75 B.P.M.

Begin center, facing downstage, the feet in Parallel 2nd, the arms in Natural Low.

cts. 1-2-3 In a consecutive sequence, drop the head forward, round the shoulders forward, and drop the back forward over the legs *until the body is lowered and completely rounded.*

cts. 2-2-3 Reach forward with both arms to High Parallel as the *torso straightens and lifts erect, passing through Flat Back Forward.*

Repeat at least four times.

Flat Back and Round Back

Beg., Int., Adv.; two 3's; count at 75 B.P.M.

Begin center, facing downstage, the feet in Parallel 2nd, the arms in High Parallel.

cts. 1-2-3 *Tilt the torso forward as far as possible maintaining a Flat Back.* The little fingers should touch the floor, and head should remain centered between the arms.

cts. 2-2-3 Drop the back, releasing the energy, and *roll up through the spine* until the torso is erect. The arms end in Natural Low.

"and" Reach side and up with both arms, palms facing up, and end with the arms in High Parallel.

Repeat at least four times.

Laterals

Beg., Int., Adv.; two 3's four times, two 2's four times, 2 cts. eight times; count at 85 B.P.M.

Begin center, facing downstage, the feet in Wide Natural 2nd, the arms in High Parallel.

cts. 1-2-3 In a simultaneous action, *reach sideward to the right with the body, and press the pelvis to the left, keeping the hips squared.* Both sides of the body should be elongated.

cts. 2-2-3 *Return the body, and the hip to center.* Repeat to the left side, and repeat the entire sequence again. Repeat with 2 counts for each movement. Repeat with 1 count for each movement.

Lateral with Flat Back

Beg., Int., Adv.; 8 cts.; count at 85 B.P.M.

Begin center, facing downstage, the feet in Wide Natural 2nd, the arms in High Parallel.

cts. 1-2 *Lateral right side*—as described above.

cts. 3-4 Rotate the body to *Flat Back to the right side.* The body is as far side as possible, with the left side of the torso parallel to downstage, the arms in High Parallel, and the head centered between the arms.

cts. 5-6 *Lateral right side.*

cts. 7-8 *Center the torso.*

Repeat to the other side.

> **Note:** *This phrase may be done with 1 count for each movement.*

Lateral with Horizontal Swing

Beg., Int., Adv.; 10 cts.; counts at 85 B.P.M.

Begin center, facing downstage, the feet in Wide Natural 2nd, the arms in High Parallel.

cts. 1-2 *Lateral right side.*

cts. 3-4 *Flat Back right side,* as described above.

cts. 5-6 Maintaining the established position, *move the torso horizontally to Flat Back left side.*

cts. 7-8 *Lateral left side.*

cts. 9-10 *Lift the torso erect.*

Repeat to the other side.

Repeat at least twice.

> **Note:** *This phrase may be done with 1 count for each movement.*

Lateral with Release Swing

Beg., Int., Adv.; 10 cts.; count at 85 B.P.M.

Begin center, facing downstage, the feet in Wide Natural 2nd, the arms in High Parallel.

cts. 1-2 *Lateral right side.*

cts. 3-4 *Flat Back right side.*

cts. 5-6 *Release Swing to Flat Back left side.*

cts. 7-8 *Lateral left side.*

cts. 9-10 *Lift the torso erect.*

Repeat to the other side.

> **Note:** *This phrase may be done with 1 count for each movement.*

> **Note:** *The Horizontal Swing and the Release Swing may be combined to form a longer phrase.*

•• • • •
Primitive Squat Descent and Ascent

Beg., Int., Adv.; 4 cts. twice; count at 85 B.P.M.

Begin center, facing downstage, the feet in Parallel 2nd, the arms in Middle Parallel.

cts. 1-2-3-4 Keeping the heels on the floor and the back straight, *lower the body to Primitive Squat position.*

cts. 2-2-3-4 *Lift the body erect.*

Repeat at least four times.

Six

Swings

Swinging is a natural body motion. Dance embellishes this natural motion by alternating a swing with other dance actions, like pulls, lifts, and turns. In a swing the body weight is shifted from one direction to another, almost giving in to gravity. The quality of a swing includes a release and an attenuation, with less time given to the release than to the attenuation. Therefore, on the simple Release Swing described below, the torso when it is in Flat Back side is permitted to lift *slightly* above the parallel line.

Release Swings

Beg., Int., Adv.; eight 3's twice; count at 60 B.P.M.

Begin center, facing downstage, the torso in Flat Back right side, the legs in Wide Natural 2nd, the arms in High Parallel.

    cts. 1-2-3 *Release Swing* to Flat Back left side.
    and 2-2-3
    cts. 3-2-3 *Release Swing* to Flat Back right side.
    and 4-2-3
    cts. 5-2-3 Repeat *Release Swing* to Flat Back left side.
     through
        8-2-3 *Release Swing* to Flat Back right side.

Repeat once more.

Release Swing into Lateral

Int., Adv.; eight 3's twice, count at 60 B.P.M.

Begin center, facing downstage, the torso in Flat Back right side, the legs in Wide Natural 2nd, the arms in High Parallel.

cts. 1-2-3 Release the torso as for a *Release Swing but do not open the torso* to Flat Back left side.

cts. 2-2-3 *Rotate the torso to Lateral left side.* On the 3rd beat, accented, rotate the torso to Flat Back left side.

cts. 3-2-3 Repeat to other side.
and 4-2-3

cts. 5-2-3 Repeat *Release Swing into Lateral left. Release Swing into Lateral*
through *right.* Repeat once more.
  8-2-3

Release Swing with Full Circle

Beg., Int., Adv.; eight 3's twice; count at 60 B.P.M.

Begin center, facing downstage, the torso in Flat Back right side, the legs in Wide Natural 2nd, the arms in High Parallel.

cts. 1-2-3 *Release Swing* to Flat Back left side.
and 2-2-3

cts. 3-2-3 *Release Swing* to Flat Back right side.
and 4-2-3

cts. 5-2-3 *Release* the body, but do not pull out to Flat Back left side.

cts. 6-2-3 *Describe a full vertical circle in space* by rotating the torso to face
and 7-2-3 downstage through Lateral left side, center the torso with arms in High Parallel, and moving through Lateral right side as low as possible.

cts. 8-2-3 *Release Swing* to Flat Back left side.

Repeat to the other side.

Variation No. 1

Beg., Int., Adv.; eight 3's twice; count at 60 B.P.M.

cts. 1-2-3 *Release Swing* to Flat Back left side.
and 2-2-3

cts. 3-2-3 *Release Swing* to Flat Back right side.
and 4-2-3

cts. 5-2-3 Release Swing to Flat Back left side and rotate the torso and lift the
and 6-2-3 right leg to *Lateral T position.*

cts. 7-2-3 Hold.
and 8-2-3

Repeat to the other side.

Variation No. 2

Beg., Int., Adv.; eight 3's twice; count at 60 B.P.M.

Repeat measures 1–6 of variation No. 1. In addition, on the sixth and seventh measure, turn one *Lateral T turn to the left* (see Turns in chapter 11) and on the 8th measure, hold. Repeat to other side.

Release Swing into Horizontal Attitude

Int., Adv.; eight 3's twice; count at 60 B.P.M.

Begin center, facing downstage, the torso in Flat Back right side, the legs in Wide Natural 2nd, the arms in High Parallel.

cts. 1-2-3 *Release Swing* to Flat Back left side.
and 2-2-3
cts. 3-2-3 Release Swing to Flat Back right side.
and 4-2-3
cts. 5-2-3 Release Swing to Flat Back left side, turn to face stage left, and *lift*
and 6-2-3 *the right leg to back attitude with the torso in Flat Back forward.*
　　　　　The arms lift to High Parallel.
cts. 7-2-3 Hold.
and 8-2-3

Repeat to other side.

Variation

Repeat measures 1–6. In addition, on the sixth and seventh measure, *turn one turn to the left in horizontal attitude position; and on the 8th measure, hold. Repeat to other side.*

Release Swing into Back Attitude

Beg., Int., Adv.; eight 3's twice; count at 60 B.P.M.

Begin center, facing downstage, the torso in Flat Back right side, the legs in Wide Natural 2nd, arms in High Parallel.

cts. 1-2-3 *Release Swing* to Flat Back left side.
and 2-2-3
cts. 3-2-3 *Release Swing* to Flat Back right side.
and 4-2-3
cts. 5-2-3 *Release Swing* to Flat Back left side and lift the body upright facing
and 6-2-3 stage left. *The right leg lifts to back attitude;* the arms lift to High
　　　　　Parallel. The left foot adjusts to natural turnout as the body lifts.
cts. 7-2-3 Hold.
and 8-2-3

Repeat to the other side.

Variation No. 1

Repeat measures 1–6. In addition, on measures 6 and 7, *double turn to the left in attitude position;* and on the 8th measure, hold. Repeat to the other side.

Variation No. 2

Repeat measures 1–6. In addition, on measures 6 and 7, *turn 1 ³⁄₄ to the left in back attitude position; the last ¹⁄₄ of the turn the torso and the right leg extend to Lateral T position, left side. The turn ends facing downstage;* and on the 8th measure, hold. Repeat to the other side.

Release Swing into Flat Back Back Bend

Int., Adv.; four 3's four times; count at 60 B.P.M

Begin center, facing downstage, the torso in Flat Back right side, the legs in Wide Natural 2nd, arms in High Parallel.

cts. 1-2-3 Release the torso as for a *Release Swing* but do not open the body to Flat Back left side.

cts. 2-2-3 Rotate the torso to *Lateral left side.*

cts. 3-2-3 Rotate the torso to *Flat Back Back Bend position.* The feet remain in Wide Natural 2nd.

cts. 4-2-3 Rotate the torso to *Flat Back left side.*

Repeat 3 more times.

Variation No. 1

Int., Adv.; three 3's; count at 60 B.P.M.

Repeat measures 1–3, except, on the *3rd beat of the 3rd measure, rotate the torso to Flat Back left side.* Repeat 2 more times.

• • • • 5/4 Swing

Preparation for 5/4 Swing

Beg., Int., Adv.; seven 3's twice; count at 60 B.P.M.

Begin center, facing downstage, the torso in Flat Back right side, the legs in Wide Natural 2nd, the arms in High Parallel.

cts. 1-2-3 Release the torso as in *Release Swing* but do not open the torso to Flat Back left side.

cts. 2-2-3 Rotate the torso to *Lateral left side.*

cts. 3-2-3 Rotate the torso to *Flat Back Back Bend position.* The feet remain in Wide Natural 2nd.

cts. 4-2-3 Turn out the right foot slightly as the body swings *to Strike position with both hands on the floor* (see Strike Stretch in Progressions, chapter 13).

cts. 5-2-3 Hold.

cts. 6-2-3 Return the left leg to Wide Natural 2nd (readjust the right foot to Wide Natural 2nd) and extend the torso to *Flat Back right side*. The arms move to High Parallel.

cts. 7-2-3 *Release Swing* to Flat Back left side.

Variation

Repeat measures 1–7, except that on the 5th measure, *both arms reach toward the left knee*. Both arms are parallel with the palms facing each other.

Repeat to the other side.

Preparation for 5/4 Swing with the Hands on the Floor

Int., Adv.; eight 3's twice; count at 60 B.P.M.

Begin center, facing downstage, the torso in Flat Back right side, the legs in Wide Natural 2nd, the arms in High Parallel.

cts. 1-2-3 *Release the torso as in Release Swing* but do not open the body to Flat Back left side.

cts. 2-2-3 Rotate the torso *to Lateral left side*.

cts. 3-2-3 Rotate the torso to *Flat Back Back Bend position*. The feet remain in Wide Natural 2nd.

cts. 4-2-3 Turn out the right foot slightly, as the body swings *to Strike position with both hands* on the floor.

cts. 5-2-3 *Turning ½ turn to the left* on the right leg, walk the hands on the floor, maintaining the Strike position.

cts. 6-2-3 Lower the left leg and place the feet in Wide Natural 2nd. *Release Swing with plié to the left into Forward Lunge position* facing stage right. The torso and the back leg are forming a diagonal. The arms move to High Parallel.

cts. 7-2-3 Straighten and brush the left leg back and lower the torso to *Forward T position*, keeping the right leg straight and the arms in High Parallel.

cts. 8-2-3 *Release Swing* to Flat Back left side.

Repeat to the other side.

5/4 Swing

Int., Adv.; 5 counts four times; count at 60 B.P.M.

ct. 1 Release the torso as in *Release Swing* but do not open the body to Flat Back left side.

Figure 24. Strike Position

and beat Rotate the torso through *Lateral left side.*

up beat *Flat Back Back Bend position.* The feet remain in Wide Natural 2nd.

ct. 2 *Turn ½ turn to the left on the right leg. The gesture leg is in Strike position* with the arms reaching upward and parallel to the left thigh, fingers pointing to the ceiling. Both arms are parallel with the palms facing each other.

cts. 3-5 Same as counts 6-2-3 through 8-2-3 as described above in preparation—*Forward Lunge, brush back to Forward T position, Release Swing.*

Repeat 3 more times.

12-Count Swing

Adv.; twelve 3's; count at 60 B.P.M.

ct. 1 *Release the torso as in Release Swing* but do not open the body to Flat Back left side.

ct. 2 Rotate the torso to *Lateral left side.*

ct. 3 Rotate the torso to *Flat Back Back Bend position*. The feet remain in Wide Natural 2nd.

cts. 2-2-3 *Turn ½ turn to the left in Strike position* with the arms reaching upward and parallel to the left thigh, fingers pointing to the ceiling. Both arms are parallel, with the palms facing each other.

cts. 3-2-3 Lower the left leg and place the feet in Wide Natural 2nd. *Release Swing with plié to the left into Forward Lunge position facing stage right*. The torso and the back leg are forming a diagonal line. The arms move to High Parallel.

cts. 4-2-3 Keeping the left leg in plié, lift the right leg back and move the torso to Flat Back Forward to *Forward T position*. The arms remain in High Parallel.

cts. 5-2-3 Straighten the left leg and rotate the body into *Lateral T position facing upstage*.

cts. 6-2-3 Hold counts 6-2; on the 3rd beat, *pull the rib cage to the right* (toward the ceiling), on a breath.

cts. 7-2-3 *Step on the right foot and turn 1 ½ turns to the right with the torso*
and 8-2-3 *in Flat Back Forward;* the left leg is lifted high in Parallel 2nd, the foot flexed. The right arm rounds slightly and swings across the body opening to 2nd. The left arm is in 2nd.

cts. 9-2-3 Lower the left foot to Wide Natural 2nd and lift the torso erect. In
and 10-2-3 a simultaneous succession of motions, *shift the weight onto the right leg, press the pelvis forward, describe a figure 8 with the arms, and complete the motion by pulling the torso out to Flat Back right side.*
The arms remain parallel and soften to describe a figure 8 in a vertical plane, starting to the right, and reach to High Parallel as the torso pulls out to Flat Back right side and the foot lowers to Wide Natural 2nd.

cts. 11-2-3 *Release Swing* to Flat Back left side.
and 12-2-3

Repeat to the other side, ending in Pelvic Press position, hands lifted in Diagonal Egyptian.

Preparation for Figure 8 Swing Study

Beg., Int.; 1 pattern in two 3's; count at 50 B.P.M.

Begin at the barre, the feet in Natural 1st, the left hand on the barre, the right arm side on an upward diagonal.

Variation No. 1

cts. 1-2-3 *The right arm describes a full clockwise circle on a vertical plane.* The right arm swings down, across the front of the body, and up, and opens side with the palm up. (There is an inward rotation of the

arm as it cuts across the front of the body.) The head and eyes
follow the motion of the hand.

cts. 2-2-3 Leading with the elbow, *the right arm describes a full circle
counterclockwise behind the body.* The right arm swings down,
behind the body, and up, and opens side on the upward diagonal.
(There is an outward rotation of the arm as it cuts across the back
of the body.) The head and eyes follow the motion of the hand.

Repeat four times.

Variation No. 2 with Plié

cts. 1 *Plié as the arm drops down* as described above.

2-3 *Rebound out of the plié and straighten both legs as the arm swings
overhead.*

cts. 2 *Plié as the arm circles behind the body and the pelvis presses
forward to Flat Back Back Bend.*

2-3 *Rebound out of the plié, straighten both legs, and center the body* as
the arm opens side.

Variation No. 3 with Relevé

ct. 1 *Plié as the arm drops down* as described above.

cts. 2-3 *Relevé on the rebound as the arm is on the upswing.*

ct. 2 *Plié as the arm circles behind the body and the pelvis presses to Flat
Back Back Bend.*

cts. 2-3 *Relevé on the rebound as the arm is on the upswing.*

Variation No. 4 with Jump

ct. 1 *Plié as the arm drops down* as described above.

cts. 2-3 *Jump with straight legs and pointed feet on the rebound as the arm
is on the upswing.*

ct. 2 *Plié as the arm circles behind the body and the pelvis presses to Flat
Back Back Bend.*

cts. 2-3 *Jump with straight legs and pointed feet on the rebound as the arm
is on the upswing.*

•• • • •

Figure 8 Swing Study

Beg., Int.; six phrases of four 6's; count at 50 B.P.M.

Begin center facing downstage, the feet in Natural 2nd, the arms in 2nd.

Phrase 1: four 6's

cts. 1-2-3 *Both arms drop and begin to describe a full circle on a vertical
plane.* There is an inward rotation of the arms as they cut across the

front of the body. As the arms cross at the wrist, the left arm is in front of the right arm, the arms lift upward and open side, with the palms facing up to complete the circle. The head and the eyes follow the motion of the hands.

cts. 4-5-6   In a continuous flowing action, *both arms drop behind the back, leading with the elbows.* There is an outward rotation of the arm as it cuts across the back of the body. The arms rotate inward as they return to 2nd slightly above shoulder height. The head drops back with the focus to the ceiling as the elbows cut across the back and lowers with the focus downstage as the arms return to 2nd.

Repeat 3 times.

Phrase 2: four 6's

cts. 1-2-3   As you continue the figure 8 arm swing described above, *the head and torso round forward slightly, the wrists cross at knee level.* The arms lift upward as the head and the torso lift erect and open to 2nd, with the palms facing up.

cts. 4-5-6   As you continue the figure 8 arm swing described above, the head drops back, *the chest lifts toward the ceiling and the pelvis presses slightly forward; the head and torso lift erect as the arms return to 2nd.*

Repeat 3 times.

Phrase 3: four 6's

cts. 1-2-3   As you continue the figure 8 arm swing described above, *the head and the torso release completely forward, the wrists cross at ankle level.* The arms lift upward as the head and the torso lift erect and open to 2nd, with the palms facing up.

cts. 4-5-6   As you continue the figure 8 arm swing described above, *the head drops back and the pelvis presses forward into Flat Back Back Bend. The head and the torso lift erect as the arms return to 2nd.*

Repeat 3 times.

Phrase 4: four 6's

cts. 1-2-3   Same as above in phrase 3—*figure 8 arm swing with complete torso release forward and lift erect.*

cts. 4-5-6   As you continue the *figure 8 arm swing* described *above, the pelvis presses to the left downstage diagonal.* Shift the weight onto the left foot and allow the right knee to bend into the low back attitude. The head drops back with the focus to the ceiling. The head and the torso center, the right leg lowers to Natural 2nd, as the arm returns to 2nd.

Alternate sides and repeat 3 times.

Phrase 5: four 6's

cts. 1-2-3   Same as in phrase 3—*figure 8 arm swing with complete torso release forward and lift erect.*

cts. 4-5-6   As you continue the figure 8 arm swing, *establish the low back attitude position described in the 4th phrase, and turn ½ turn to the left.* The head drops back with focus to the ceiling on the turn. The head and the torso center, the right leg lowers to Natural 2nd, as the arms return to 2nd.

Alternate sides and repeat 3 times.

Phrase 6: four 6's

cts. 1-2-3   Same as phrase 3—*figure 8 arm swing with complete torso release forward and lift erect.*

cts. 4-5-6   Same as in phrase 5—*with a full turn to the left.*

Alternate sides and repeat 3 times.

Leg Swings

Begin stage left, standing on a straight left leg, the foot in natural turnout, the right leg lifted behind in Stag position, the arms in 2nd.

No. 1 Basic Parallel Leg Swing

> **Note:** *The torso remains upright and the pelvis remains centered for this Leg Swing. The arms remain in 2nd.*

> **Note:** *In all the Leg Swing variations, continue alternating to progress across the floor.*

Beg., Int., Adv.; four 3's on each side; count at 65 B.P.M.

cts. 1-2-3   *Brushing the right foot on the floor, swing the right leg forward* until the shin is parallel to the ceiling. The right leg bends and is parallel.

cts. 2-2-3   *Brushing the right foot on the floor, swing the right leg back* until the thigh is parallel to the floor. The right leg bends and is parallel in Stag position.

cts. 3-2-3   Repeat 1-2-3, *swing the right leg forward.*

cts. 4-2-3   *Step forward on the right foot and lift the left leg behind in Stag position.*

Repeat to the other side.

No. 2 Parallel Leg Swing with Plié

Beg., Int., Adv.; four 3's on each side; count at 65 B.P.M.

Same as No. 1 Basic Parallel Leg Swing except that both legs plié as the foot is brushing on the floor. The standing leg straightens as the other leg swings off the floor.

No. 3 Parallel Leg Swing with Extension

Beg., Int., Adv.; four 3's on each side; count at 65 B.P.M.

Same as No. 1 Basic Parallel Leg Swing, except that on counts 3-2-3, after the right foot brushes on the floor, *the right leg extends and lifts accented,* as high as possible without tilting the pelvis.

No. 4 Parallel Leg Swing with Extension and Demi-Plié

Beg., Int., Adv.; four 3's on each side; count at 65 B.P.M.

Same as the No. 3 Leg Swing, except that as the right leg extends and lifts accented, *the left leg bends.*

No. 5 Parallel Leg Swing with Plié and Extension

Beg., Int., Adv.; four 3's on each side; count at 65 B.P.M.

Same as the No. 2 Leg Swing with demi-plié, but the leg extends and lifts accented on counts 3-2-3, as in the No. 3 Leg Swing with extension.

No. 6 Parallel Leg Swing with Round and Arch

Beg., Int., Adv.; four 3's on each side; count at 65 B.P.M.

> **Note:** The legs continue to do the No. 1 Basic Parallel Leg Swing. The arms remain in 2nd.

cts. 1-2-3 *The upper body rounds forward* as the right leg swings forward.
cts. 2-2-3 *The upper body arches back, opening the chest to the ceiling,* as the right leg swings back. The right foot and the head reach toward each other.
cts. 3-2-3 *The upper body rounds forward* as the right leg swings forward.
cts. 4-2-3 Same as the No. 1 Basic Parallel Leg Swing—*step forward on the right leg and lift the left leg behind in Stag position.*

Repeat to the other side.

No. 7 Parallel Leg Swing with Two ½ Turns

Beg., Int., Adv.; four 3's on each side; count at 65 B.P.M.

cts. 1-2-3 Same as the No. 1 Basic Parallel Leg Swing—*swing the right leg forward.*
cts. 2-2-3 As the right leg is brushing down, *turn on the left foot to the right ½ turn.* The torso faces stage left, and the right leg ends lifted forward and parallel in a simultaneous action.
cts. 3-2-3 *Repeat the swing of the right leg down, and the ½ turn to the right*

on the left foot, to face stage right. The right leg ends lifted forward and parallel in a simultaneous action.

cts. 4-2-3 Same as the No. 1 Basic Parallel Leg Swing—*step forward and lift the left leg behind in Stag position.* The arms remain in 2nd throughout this set.

Repeat to the other side.

No. 8 Parallel Leg Swing with Leg Fan

Beg., Int., Adv.; four 3's on each side; count at 65 B.P.M.

cts. 1-2-3 Same as the No. 1 Basic Parallel Leg Swing—*swing the right leg forward.*

cts. 2-2-3 Same as the No. 1 Basic Parallel Leg Swing—*swing the right leg behind.*

cts. 3-2-3 After the right foot brushes forward on the floor, *straighten and fan the right leg turned out by swinging it across the body to the left and opening it to the right.* Simultaneously, the left arm circles slightly curved, down, across the body, and up, and opens to 2nd. The right arm remains in 2nd.

cts. 4-2-3 Same as the No. 1 Basic Parallel Leg Swing—*step forward and lift the left leg behind in Stag position.*

Repeat to the other side.

No. 9 Parallel Leg Swing with ¼ Turn to Second

Beg., Int., Adv.; four 3's on each side; count at 65 B.P.M.

cts. 1-2-3 Same as the No. 1 Basic Parallel Leg Swing—*swing the right leg forward.*

cts. 2-2-3 Same as the No. 1 Basic Parallel Leg Swing—*swing the right leg behind.*

cts. 3-2-3 Brush the right foot forward on the floor, *and in a simultaneous action, turn ¼ turn to the left to face downstage, as the right leg straightens and kicks to 2nd position and both arms circle down, through Middle Parallel, to High Parallel.* The arms are straight on the circle. The legs, ¼ turn, and the arm circle are a coordinated action.

cts. 4-2-3 On the 4 and 2, *plié in 2nd on both legs, as both arms rotate outward and the palms press down to 2nd.* On the 3, *straighten the legs and shift the weight onto the right leg and turn ¼ turn to the right to face stage right, as the left leg lifts behind in Stag position. The arms remain in 2nd.*

Repeat to the other side.

Variation A

Beg., Int., Adv.; six 3's on each side; count at 65 B.P.M.

cts. 1-2-3 Same as above No. 9 Parallel Leg Swing with ¼ Turn to 2nd—*swing the right leg forward.*

cts. 2-2-3 Same as above No. 9 Parallel Leg Swing with ¼ Turn to 2nd—*swing the right leg behind.*

cts. 3-2-3 Same as above No. 9 Parallel Leg Swing with ¼ Turn to 2nd—*swing the right leg to 2nd position and turn ¼ turn to face downstage.*

cts. 4-2-3 Same as above No. 9 Parallel Leg Swing with ¼ Turn to 2nd—*plié on both feet in 2nd as both arms press to 2nd, for the full 3 counts.*

cts. 5-2-3 *Straighten the right leg and turn ¼ turn to the right to face stage right, as the left leg lifts behind in attitude.* Both arms raise to High Parallel.

cts. 6-2-3 *Hold the established position.* To repeat to the other side, lower the arms to 2nd on the upbeat and rotate the left leg to Stag position.

Variation A with Turn

Beg., Int., Adv.; six 3's on each side; count at 65 B.P.M.

cts. 1-2-3 Same as above in Variation A.
through
    4-2-3

cts. 5-2-3 *Turn 1 or 2 turns to the right in the position established in cts. 5-2-3 in Variation A.*

cts. 6-2-3 Same as above in Variation A—*hold the established position.* To repeat to the other side, lower the arms to 2nd on the upbeat and rotate the left leg to Stag position.

Variation B

Beg., Int., Adv.; six 3's on each side; count at 65 B.P.M.

cts. 1-2-3 Same as above No. 9 Parallel Leg Swing with ¼ Turn to 2nd—*swing the right leg forward.*

cts. 2-2-3 Same as above No. 9 Parallel Leg Swing with ¼ Turn to 2nd—*swing the right leg behind.*

cts. 3-2-3 Same as above No. 9 Parallel Leg Swing with ¼ Turn to 2nd—*turn ¼ turn to face downstage and kick the right leg to 2nd as the arms circle.*

cts. 4-2-3 Same as above No. 9 Parallel Leg Swing with ¼ Turn to 2nd—*demi-plié on both legs and press the palms down to 2nd.*

cts. 5-2-3 *Turn ¼ turn to the right to face stage right in Stag position.* The right leg remains in demi-plié. The arms move horizontally to Stag position.

cts. 6-2-3 *Hold the established position.* To repeat on the other side, on the upbeat, straighten the right leg and open the arms horizontally to 2nd.

Variation B with Turn

Beg., Int., Adv.; six 3's on each side; count at 65 B.P.M.

cts. 1-2-3 Same as above in Variation B.
through
4-2-3
cts. 5-2-3 *Turn 1 or 2 turns to the right in established Stag position.*
cts. 6-2-3 *Hold the established position.*

Variation C

Int., Adv.; six 3's on each side; count at 65 B.P.M.

cts. 1-2-3 Same as above No. 9 Parallel Leg Swing with ¼ Turn to 2nd—*swing the right leg forward.*
cts. 2-2-3 Same as above No. 9 Parallel Leg Swing with ¼ Turn to 2nd—*swing the right leg behind.*
cts. 3-2-3 Same as above No. 9 Parallel Leg Swing with ¼ Turn to 2nd—*turn ¼ to face downstage and kick the right leg to second as both arms circle.*
cts. 4-2-3 Same as No. 9 Parallel Leg Swing with ¼ Turn to 2nd—*plié on both legs and press both arms down to 2nd.*
cts. 5-2-3 *Turn ¼ turn to the right to face stage right, as the body moves to Lateral right side and the left leg lifts to back attitude.* Both arms are straight; the right arm is perpendicular to the floor, the left arm is perpendicular to the ceiling. The head turns to the right and looks down the right arm with the focus to the floor.
cts. 6-2-3 *Hold the established position.*

Variation C with Turn

Int., Adv.; six 3's on each side; count at 65 B.P.M.

cts. 1-2-3 Same as Variation C.
through
4-2-3
cts. 5-2-3 *Turn 1 or 2 turns to the right in the established position.*
cts. 6-2-3 *Hold the established position.* On the upbeat, center the torso and rotate the left leg to Stag position.

No. 10 Parallel Leg Swing with Front Stretch

Int., Adv.; eight 3's on each side; count at 65 B.P.M.

cts. 1-2-3 Same as No. 1 Basic Parallel Leg Swing—*swing the right leg forward.*

cts. 2-2-3 Same as No. 1 Basic Parallel Leg Swing—*swing the right leg behind.*

cts. 3-2-3 After the right foot brushes forward on the floor, *extend and lift the right leg forward and grab the right ankle with both hands, keeping the back straight.*

cts. 4-2-3 *Continue to lift and stretch the right leg.*
through
6-2-3

cts. 7-2-3 *Open both arms to 2nd without lowering the right leg.*

cts. 8-2-3 Same as No. 1 Basic Parallel Leg Swing—*step forward and lift the left leg behind* in Stag position.

No. 11 Parallel Leg Swing with Lateral T Hop

Beg., Int., Adv.; four 3's on each side; count at 65 B.P.M.

cts. 1-2-3 Same as No. 1 Basic Parallel Leg Swing—*swing the right leg forward.*

cts. 2-2-3 Same as No. 1 Basic Parallel Leg Swing—*swing the right leg behind.*

cts. 3-2-3 Brush the right foot forward on the floor, *plié on the left leg and, in a simultaneous action, hop on the left foot as the body turns ¼ turn to the left to face downstage and moves to Lateral T position. The arms circle down to stage right, and up to High Parallel.* The torso should be in Lateral T position in the air.

cts. 4-2-3 *Release swing to the right with plié.* The transition to the other side is a small jumping step (chassé in ballet terminology). After the demi-plié in 2nd from the Release Swing, jump and bring both feet to Natural 1st in the air. Land in plié and slide the right foot forward to stage right. Straighten the right leg and lift the left leg behind in Stag position. The arms move through Natural Low and lift to 2nd.

No. 12 Leg Swing in Lateral T Position

Adv.; four 3's on each side; count at 65 B.P.M.

cts. 1-2-3 Turn the body ¼ turn to the left to face downstage *as the right leg and torso swing to Lateral T position.* The left arm is down and pointing perpendicular to the floor, and the right arm is up and pointing perpendicular to the ceiling.

cts. 2-2-3 Maintaining the torso as far over in Lateral as possible and the arms in the perpendicular position established above, *swing the right leg down through Natural 1st, and up to Lateral T position again, as the body turns ½ turn to the left to face upstage.*

cts. 3-2-3 *Repeat the swing as described above in counts 2-2-3 to face downstage.*

cts. 4-2-3 *Chassé to the right facing downstage* (see counts 4-2-3 in No. 11 Leg Swing with Lateral T Hop). Omit the Release Swing.

No. 13 Figure 8 Leg Swing with Leg Fan

Beg., Int., Adv.; four 3's on each side; count at 65 B.P.M.

Note: *This Leg Swing is executed with turned-out legs.*

cts. 1-2-3   *Brush the right foot on the floor and across and in front of the body, and swing a bent, turned-out right leg to 2nd,* completing the first loop of the Figure 8.

cts. 2-2-3   *Brush the right foot on the floor, across, and behind the body to complete the second loop of the Figure 8.* Keep the right leg bent and turned out as it swings.

cts. 3-2-3   Brush the right foot on the floor and across the *front of the body; swing the right leg into a leg fan.*

cts. 4-2-3   *Step to the upstage right diagonal on the right foot and lift the left leg behind in attitude.* Arms remain in 2nd. (For a variation, the opposite arm may circle on the leg fan.)

No. 14 Leg Swing with Strike

Adv.; eight 3's twice; count at 65 B.P.M.

The arms remain in 2nd throughout.

Phrase 1

cts. 1-2-3   Same as No. 1 Basic Parallel Swing.
through
4-2-3

5-2-3   Same as No. 1 Basic Parallel Swing with the left leg.
through
8-2-3

Phrase 2

cts. 1-2-3   With the right leg turned out, *brush the right foot on the floor and swing the right leg forward to front attitude as the pelvis presses forward to Flat Back Back Bend.*

cts. 2-2-3   Brush the right foot on the floor, and *swing the right leg back to back attitude, and swing the torso forward into Strike position.*

cts. 3-2-3   Same as counts 1-2-3 described above—*swing the right leg forward to front attitude and press the pelvis forward to Flat Back Back Bend.*

cts. 4-2-3   Step forward onto the right foot *and lift the left leg back in back attitude.*

cts. 5-2-3   Repeat counts 1-2-3 through 4-2-3 on the left side.
through
8-2-3

Seven

Studies

In the last five years of his life, Horton recodified the technique into a series of studies, each of which had a clear and logical motivation. The movement in this section has enormous diversity. Horton designed some studies for strengthening, some for stretching, and some just for psychic stimulation. The studies move through space on all possible levels—on the floor, standing, and in the air. This diversity enables the dancer to become spectacularly proficient and gives this technique a rich, dramatic quality.

Fortification Studies

The following seventeen Fortification studies were designed to follow each other consecutively. Transitional phrases have been included to facilitate this. A starting position has also been included for each Fortification, making it possible to teach each one individually.

Fortification No. 1 (Achilles Tendon Stretch)

Int., Adv.; (five 4's and 10 cts.) twice; count at 60 B.P.M.

Begin center, facing downstage, the feet in Parallel 1st, the arms in Natural Low.

cts. 1-2 *Relevé.*

cts. 3-4 *Slide the right foot forward; gradually lower the heels in* Parallel 4th position. Simultaneously, raise the left arm forward to shoulder level, raise the right arm to 2nd. The arms form a 90° angle; both palms face the floor.

cts. 2-2-3-4 *Flat Back Forward* as the arms change to the opposite right angle (90°).

cts. 3-2-3-4 *Raise the torso erect* as the arms change to the original right angle.

cts. 4-2-3-4 *Repeat the Flat Back Forward* and arm change in 2 counts; *raise the torso erect* and change arms to the original right angle in 2 counts.

cts. 5-2-3-4 *Flat Back Forward,* the arms reach to the back heel (the left arm passes through 2nd, both arms are parallel, on the outside of the legs and reaching diagonally back), the head as close to the right ankle as possible.

10 cts.

cts. 1-2 Lift the arms to High Parallel and *Lateral to the left,* shifting the weight into the right hip. Do not bring the torso erect.

cts. 3-4 *Simultaneously Flat Back Forward and pivot on the balls of both feet to the left,* to end in Flat Back Forward facing upstage, the feet in Parallel 4th position; the arms remain in High Parallel.

cts. 5-6 *Raise torso erect and relevé* simultaneously; the arms lift to High Parallel.

cts. 7-8 Pivot to the right on both feet (in relevé) to *face downstage in Parallel 4th.*

cts. 9-10 *Lower the heels* and *slide the right foot back to Parallel* 1st, the arms lower through 2nd to Natural Low. Repeat the entire study to other side.

Fortification No. 1 Variation

Int., Adv.; seven 4's on each side; count at 60 B.P.M.

Begin center, facing downstage, the feet in Parallel 1st, the arms in Natural Low.

cts. 1-2 *Relevé.*

cts. 3-4 *Slide the right foot forward,* turning it out gradually, lowering the heels in 4th position with the left foot remaining parallel and the right foot naturally turned out. Simultaneously, the left arm raises forward to shoulder level, the right arm raises to 2nd, the arms form a right angle (90°); both palms face the floor.

cts. 2-2-3-4 *Flat Back Forward* as the arms change to the opposite right angle (90°).

cts. 3-2-3-4 *Raise the torso erect,* as the arms change to the original right angle.

cts. 4-2-3-4 Repeat the *Flat Back Forward* and arm change in 2 counts, *raise the torso erect* and change arms to the original right angle in 2 counts.

cts. 5-2-3-4 *Flat Back Forward, the arms reach to the back heel* (the left arm passes through 2nd, both arms are parallel, on the outside of the legs and reaching diagonally back), the head as close to the right ankle as possible.

ct. 6 Lightly accented, *Lateral to the left,* shifting weight into the right hip; the arms lift to High Parallel position.

2 Lightly accented, simultaneously Flat Back Forward and pivot on the balls of both feet to the left into Natural 2nd to *end in Flat Back Forward position facing stage left;* the arms remain in High Parallel.

3-4 *Raise the torso erect and relevé* simultaneously; the arms remain in High Parallel.

cts. 7-2 Pivot on both feet (in relevé) to face upstage in Natural 4th.
   3 *Lower the heels;* the arms remain in High Parallel.
   4 *The right foot moves forward* to join the left; both feet *end in Parallel 1st;* the arms lower through 2nd to Natural Low. Repeat on the left side, facing upstage.

Fortification No. 2 (Plié Study)

Beg., Int., Adv.; nineteen 3's, four 2's, three 3's, four 2's, eight 3's, four 4's, 12 cts., two 4's; count at 70 B.P.M.

Begin center, facing downstage, the feet in Parallel 1st, the arms in Natural Low.

Nineteen 3's

"and" Strongly accented, *turnout, the feet to Natural 1st,* the arms lift to demi-2nd.
   ct. 1 *Contract the metatarsal arch;* the pads of all the toes and the heels maintain contact with the floor.
   ct. 2 *Release the metatarsal arch* as all the toes lift off the floor as high as possible.
   ct. 3 *Contract the metatarsal arch,* the pads of all the toes and the heels maintain contact with the floor.

> **Note:** The above 3 count foot action *is repeated throughout this study. The feet remain contracted on the descent of the plié, and the feet release on the ascent of the plié.*

cts. 2-2-3 *Smoothly demi-plié* as upper torso inclines and slightly rotates to the left, head follows the contour of the spine, right arm remains rounded and moves in a diagonal line across the body to a point halfway between front and side; left arm remains in demi-2nd.
cts. 3-2-3 *Straighten the legs;* the arms return to demi-2nd and center the torso and the head.
cts. 4-2-3 Repeat *3 count foot action.*
cts. 5-2-3 Repeat the 2nd and 3rd measures to other side—*demi-plié,* and
   and straighten the legs.
cts. 6-2-3
   "and" Strongly accented, *point and open the right foot sideward to Natural 2nd,* arms lift to 2nd.
cts. 7-2-3 Repeat the *3 count foot action.*
cts. 8-2-3 *Grand plié in 6 counts;* the right arm rounds and moves diagonally
   and 9-2-3 upward as the head inclines slightly to the left. The right arm frames the head; the left arm remains in 2nd.
cts. 10-2-3 *Straighten the legs* and center the torso and the head; the right arm
   and 11-2-3 retraces the path described above and returns to 2nd.
cts. 12-2-3 Repeat the *3 count foot action.*

Figure 25. Fortification No. 2

cts. 13-2-3 Repeat measures 8 through 11 to the other side—*grand plié* and
through straighten the legs with arm circling.
16-2-3
"and" Strongly accented, *point and cross the right foot forward to Natural
4th.* The arms remain in 2nd.
cts. 17-2-3 Repeat the *3 count foot action.*
cts. 18-2-3 *Demi-plié,* the arms round and wrap around the body, the right arm
to the back, the left arm to the front, the hands midway across and
close to the body, both palms facing up.
cts. 19-2-3 *Straighten the legs;* the arms remain wrapped around the body.
"and" *Open the arms to 2nd.*

Four 2's faster tempo; count at 80 B.P.M.

cts. 1-2   *Demi-plié on count 1; straighten the legs on count 2.*
cts. 2-2   Repeat counts 1-2.
cts. 3-2   Repeat counts 1-2.
cts. 4-2   *Pivot on the balls of both feet to the left to face upstage.*

Three 3's; count at 70 B.P.M.

cts. 1-2-3   Repeat the *3 count foot action.*
cts. 2-2-3   Repeat measures 18 and 19 to the other side—*demi-plié* with the
and   arms wrapping around the body and *straighten the legs;* the arms
3-2-3   remain wrapped around the body.

Four 2's faster tempo

cts. 1-2   Open the arms to 2nd on the upbeat and repeat the four 2's as
through   described above—*demi-plié* and *straighten the legs* three times,
4-2   pivot to the right to face downstage, the feet in Natural 2nd, the
arms in Natural Low.

Eight 3's; count at 70 B.P.M.

cts. 1-2-3   *Grand plié,* the arms lift to 2nd.
cts. 2-2-3   *Lift the heels off the floor* with forced arches (¾ relevé).
cts. 3-2-3   *Lower the heels and increase the plié.*
cts. 4-2-3   *Straighten the legs,* the arms lower to Natural Low.
cts. 5-2-3   Repeat the above four 3's; the arms remain in 2nd on the last
through   measure.
8-2-3

Four 4's; count at 70 B.P.M.

cts. 1-2-3-4   Relevé on count 1; lower the heels on count 2; relevé on count 3;
lower the heels on count 4.
"and"   Open the right leg to Wide Natural 2nd.
cts. 2-2-3-4   Repeat the above 4 count movement (open the right leg to increase
3-2-3-4   the Wide Natural 2nd) three more times.
4-2-3-4

Twelve cts. double time

12 cts.   *Shimmy the whole body,* including the heels, as both arms round
and circle down, and then forward, and end overhead.

Two 4's half-time

cts. 1-2-3-4   With a breath, *the hands burst open, and the arms open* to 2nd and
grand plié.
cts. 2-2-3-4   *Straighten the legs;* the arms remain in 2nd.

Fortification No. 3 (Lateral Study)

Adv.; (eight cts. and twelve cts.) twice; count at 60 B.P.M.

Begin in the position established at the end of Fortification No. 2, facing downstage, the feet in Natural 2nd, the arms in 2nd.

ct. 1 Strongly accented, *move the right hip sideward.*

ct. 2 Open the right foot into Wide Natural 2nd position and *Lateral to the left;* the right arm moves to High Parallel, the left arm is straight, and the hand is pointing down to the left ankle. The focus is front.

cts. 3-4 *Flat Back to the left side;* the left arm moves to High Parallel.

cts. 5-6 *Lateral to the left;* the arms remain in High Parallel.

cts. 7-8 *Return the body to the center;* the arms remain in High Parallel.

12 cts.

cts. 1-2 *Lateral to the right* without accent; the arms remain in High Parallel through count 11.

ct. 3 Move the right foot and pivot on the left foot to 2nd position to face stage left.

ct. 4 *Flat Back to the right side.*

ct. 5 On an accented beat, *rotate the torso to face the ceiling* in Flat Back Back Bend.

ct. 6 *Hold.*

ct. 7 On an accented beat, *rotate the torso back into Flat Back* to the right side.

ct. 8 *Hold.*

ct. 9 *Swing the torso horizontally* to Flat Back left side.

ct. 10 Move the left foot and pivot on the right foot to 2nd position to face downstage as the torso laterals to the right.

ct. 11 Return the body to the center and lift the left leg to 2nd as high as possible.

ct.12 The left leg lowers to Natural 2nd; the arms lower sideward to Natural Low.

Repeat the entire study to the other side.

Fortification No. 4 (Lunge Study)

Beg., Int., Adv.; (four 8's and two 12 cts.) twice; count at 60 B.P.M.

Begin in the position established at the end of Fortification No. 3 facing downstage, the feet in Parallel 1st, the arms in Natural Low.

Phrase 1

cts. 1-2 *Point and slide the right foot forward;* both arms begin to reach forward to Middle Parallel.

cts. 3-4   The pointed right foot *continues to slide forward;* the pelvis begins to shift forward over the right heel as the right heel lowers and the right knee bends; both arms continue to reach forward to Middle Parallel.

cts. 5-6   Continue to slide forward until you are in a *Deep Forward Lunge* with the torso erect, the arms in Middle Parallel.

cts. 7-8   Return to the starting position by pulling *the right foot back into Parallel 1st,* the arms lower to Natural Low.

Repeat to the other side.

Phrase 2

Eight cts.; count at 50 B.P.M.

ct. 1   *The right foot steps forward into Deep Forward Lunge,* the arms in Middle Parallel.

ct. 2   Lightly accent the body as it rotates to face stage left, and *the torso tilts forward into Flat Back Forward position,* low to the floor; the right foot pivots ¼ turn to the left and turns out, the right knee stays bent and aligned over the middle toes; the right heel stays on the floor with the weight remaining over the turned-out right foot. The left foot flexes and rotates so that the heel is on the floor and the left knee is facing the ceiling; the arms move to 2nd, elbows slightly bent.

ct. 3   *Lightly accent* the body as it returns to a *Deep Forward Lunge,* facing downstage but with the upper body in Lateral right side, the arms in Opened Egyptian.

ct. 4   *Hold.*

ct. 5   In a smooth and continuous flow, center the torso and *pivot ¼ turn to the left,* going through deep 2nd position plié (facing stage left); the right arm moves to 2nd, the left arm moves to Middle Parallel rounded and opens to 2nd.

ct. 6   Continue to pivot to the left to face upstage in a Deep Forward Lunge with the left foot forward, the arms in Middle Parallel.

Figure 26. Fortification No. 4, Phrase 2, ct. 2

cts. 7-8 *Return to Parallel 1st by pulling the right foot forward* and lower the arms to Natural Low.

Repeat to the other side, facing upstage.

Phrase 3

12 cts.; count at 60 B.P.M.

cts. 1-2 *The right foot steps forward into Deep Forward Lunge,* the arms in Middle Parallel.

cts. 3-4 Turn to face stage left and, keeping the back erect, sit in *Side Lunge position* on the floor as close to the right heel as possible. The right foot pivots ¼ turn to the left and turns out; the right knee stays bent and aligned over the middle toes; the right heel stays on the floor. The left foot flexes and rotates so that the heel is on the floor and the left knee is facing the ceiling. The arms stay in Middle Parallel.

cts. 5-6 *Continue to turn to the left* to face upstage; allow the right leg to invert and the inside of the right leg to touch the floor; the left leg rotates out fully with a flexed foot; arms open to 2nd. The back is held erect.

cts. 7-8 Return to the *Side Lunge sit position* in counts 3 and 4.

cts. 9-10 Return to the *Deep Forward Lunge* position in counts 1 and 2.

cts. 11-12 Return to *starting position* by pulling the left foot forward into Parallel 1st, arms lower to Natural Low.

Repeat to the other side.

Note: *This phrase may also be done with one count for each movement.*

Repeat the entire study to the other side.

Transition from Fortification No. 4 into Fortification No. 5

After counts 7-8 (Side Lunge sit position), turn the torso to face downstage as the legs fold to Triangle position on counts 9-10. Hold counts 11 and 12; the arms remain in 2nd.

Fortification No. 5 (Hip Propulsion Study)

Int., Adv.; (five 2's and transition in 3 cts.) twice; count at 60 B.P.M.

Begin center facing downstage, in Triangle position, the right leg inverted, the arms in 2nd.

cts. 1-2 *Press the right hip forward toward the left knee and circle the torso forward to Flat Back, left to Lateral left side, then back to Flat Back Back Bend.* The right arm moves forward, left, and circles the head.

The left hand places on the floor close to the left hip with shoulder pressed down.

Simultaneously extend the left leg as far side as possible. The torso leans slightly toward the inverted leg. After the completion of the circle of the torso, release the right hip to the floor, flex the left foot, accent the right elbow toward the side of the body with the focus to the palm of the hand.

ct. 2   Press the right hip forward by contracting the right buttock and *point the left foot.*

2   *Release the right buttock and flex the left foot.*

cts. 3-2   *Repeat measure 2-2*—press the hip, point, release the hip, and flex.

cts. 4-2   *Extend and raise the right arm up to High Parallel as the torso stretches to Flat Back Forward over the extended left leg.* The right hip continues to press forward.

cts. 5-2   *Return the torso to Flat Back Back Bend and the right elbow to the right hip.* Bend the left leg to return to Triangle position.

Transition in 3 Counts

ct. 1   *Contract the buttocks and lift the hips off the floor and raise onto both knees.* The legs should form a triangle from the front.

ct. 2   *Turn the left lower leg parallel to the right lower leg* with the pelvis aligned over the knees.

ct. 3   *Lower to Triangle position with the left leg inverted.*

Repeat the entire study to the other side.

Transition from Fortification No. 5 to Fortification No. 6 in 3 Counts

ct. 1   *Extend both legs forward on the floor, keeping the back straight.* The arms reach to Middle Parallel.

cts. 2-3   *Roll the body down to the floor prone, as the arms lower to the sides of the body.*

Fortification No. 6 (Abdominal Study)

Int., Adv.; (two 3's, 5 cts., one 3, 5 cts., two 3's, six 3's) twice; 60–70 B.P.M.

Begin with the body prone, feet pointed toward downstage, arms at the sides of the body.

cts. 1-2-3   Lift the torso and bend both legs gradually until the body is in *Coccyx Balance position.* The torso lift is initiated by pulling in the abdominal wall. The head tilts forward by lowering the chin slightly as the feet lift slightly off the floor; both legs continue to bend until the body is in Coccyx Balance position.

cts. 2-2-3   Maintaining the Coccyx Balance position, *continue to pull up.*

5 cts.

cts. 1-2-3-4 Lower the body to the right in the *Pietà position* by lifting the left hip so the left buttock leaves the floor. This causes the weight to shift to the right side. Begin to lower the body, turning the head to the right and dropping it diagonally back, until it touches the floor. Both arms are parallel and reaching diagonally to the left so that only the head and the right buttock are on the floor. The legs extend and lower only enough to counterbalance the weight of the head.

ct. 5 On a strong breath, *return to Coccyx Balance position.*

One 3

cts. 1-2-3 Maintaining the Coccyx Balance position, *pull up.*

5 cts.

cts. 1-2-3-4 Repeat the head touching the floor on the left side.

ct. 5 On a strong breath, *return to Coccyx Balance position.*

Two 3's

cts. 1-2-3 Maintaining the Coccyx Balance position, *pull up.*

cts. 2-2-3 Lower the body to the starting position.

Six 3's

cts. 1-2-3 Turning the body onto the right side and maintaining the right foot perpendicular to downstage, *arch the body to shape a wide X.*

cts. 2-2-3 On a breath, *swing the arms forward to Middle Parallel, and bring the body back to Coccyx Balance position* facing downstage. Continue to pull up on counts 2-3 of the measure.

cts. 3-2-3 Lower the body to the starting position.

cts. 4-2-3 and 5-2-3 Repeat to the other side—*arch the body to shape a wide X, swing to Coccyx Balance position, and continue to pull up.*

cts. 6-2-3 Lower the body to the starting position.

Repeat the entire study to the other side.

Transition from Fortification No. 6 to Fortification No. 7 in 6 Counts

cts. 1-2-3 *Sit up,* keeping the legs extended forward on the floor, and reach forward with both arms to Middle Parallel.

cts. 4-5-6 Invert the right leg and bend the left leg into *Triangle position.* The arms open to 2nd on counts 4 and 5. On count 6, gently rest one hand on each knee with the elbows slightly bent and lifted.

Fortification No. 7

Int., Adv.; twelve 3's, three 2's, one 3 and 6 cts.; count at 60 B.P.M.

Begin center facing downstage, the legs in Triangle position with the right leg inverted. The right hand rests gently on the right knee and the left hand rests gently on the left knee.

Twelve 3's

cts. 1-2-3   *Lift the right knee* as high as possible (the right big toe remains on the floor); resist the lift with the hand on the knee.

cts. 2-2-3   *Lower the right knee back to the floor,* pressing down with the hand on the knee and the knee resisting the action.

cts. 3-2-3   Repeat the 1st measure—*lift the right knee.*

cts. 4-2-3   Repeat the 2nd measure—*lower the right knee.*

cts. 5-2-3   *Lift the buttocks off the floor;* the forward leg rotates outward onto the shin, the inverted leg remains stationary, arms lift to 2nd.

cts. 6-2-3   *Lower the buttocks,* returning to Triangle position; the arms remain in 2nd.

ct. 7   *Strongly accent and move the right pelvic joint diagonally to the left;* the upper torso and arms remain still. The right buttock remains off the floor until the end of the fortification study.

2-3   *Left leg opens to 2nd, the leg on the floor;* arms lift to High Parallel.

cts. 8-2-3   *Lateral* to the right.

cts. 9-2-3   *Return upper torso to center.*

cts. 10-2-3   *Lateral* to the left.

cts. 11-2-3   *Return upper torso to center.*

cts. 12-2-3   *Strongly accent and turn the torso* to face the left leg, Flat Back Forward as far as possible, ending with both hands holding the flexed left foot.

Three 2's

cts. 1-2   Keeping both hands on the foot, *arch the back.*

cts. 2-2   *Round the back.*

cts. 3-2   *Arch the back.*

One 3

cts. 1-2   *Reach out an up through Flat Back* over the left leg until the torso is erect, still facing the diagonal; the arms lift to High Parallel.

ct. 3   *Turn the torso to face downstage.*

Six cts. faster tempo; count at 85 B.P.M.

cts. 1-2-3   Round and *circle upper body sequentially forward* (count 1), sideward to the left (count 2), left shoulder touches floor and backward (count 3), right shoulder and back touch the floor; arms stay in High Parallel.

Note: *The circle to the back and return is a full, sweeping movement.*

cts. 4-5   *Reverse the movement* and circle the upper body sideward (count 4) and forward (count 5), ending with the torso erect and the arms in High Parallel.

ct. 6 Close the left leg to Triangle position, the right buttock returns to the floor, the hands lower sideward to return to knees.

Transition from Fortification No. 7 to Fortification No. 8 in 6 Counts

cts. 1-2-3- Slowly turn the torso to face stage left and round the body over the
4-5-6 left knee. Place both palms on the floor near the left knee, the fingers pointing toward each other, and the elbows bent.

Fortification No. 8 (Hinge Study)

Int., Adv.; (two 3's, 8 cts., 6 ct. transition) twice; (5 cts, 3 cts., 3 ct. transition) four times; count at 55 B.P.M.

Begin center, facing downstage, in Triangle position with the right leg inverted. Both palms are placed on the floor near the left knee, the fingers pointing toward each other and the elbows bent.

Phrase 1

cts. 1-2-3 Straighten the torso and turn to face stage right. Both knees lift, with the feet flat on the floor in Parallel 2nd. The left hand moves close to the left buttock and the right elbow bends and moves close to the right hip bone with the palm facing downstage. *Press the pelvis forward and the knees downward into a deep Hinge position with the right arm extended forward into Middle Parallel.* The knees should be approximately two inches from the floor.

cts. 2-2-3 *Retrace the path described above to return to Triangle position.*

8 cts.

cts. 1-2-3 Repeat counts 1-2-3 from above—*press into a deep Hinge facing stage right.*

ct. 4 While reaching forward with the right arm *lift the left hand off the floor and reach back.*

ct. 5 *Replace the left hand on the floor.*

cts. 6-7-8 *Retrace the path described above to return to Triangle position* with two hands on the floor.

Transition in 6 Counts

cts. 1-2-3 *Press to a deep Hinge position as described above.*

"and" *Lift the left hand off the floor.* Reach forward with the right arm.

ct. 4 *Maintaining the deep Hinge position, carry both arms to 2nd smoothly.*

cts. 5-6 Place the right hand on the floor and *lower the body to Triangle position as described in the beginning position, except face upstage* with the left leg inverted.

Repeat to the other side with the transition in 6 counts.

Phrase 2

cts. 1-2-3 *Press into a deep Hinge position* facing stage right as described above.

ct. 4 *Maintaining the deep Hinge position, lift the left hand off the floor.*

ct. 5 *Maintaining the deep Hinge position, carry the arms to 2nd position.*

3 cts.

cts. 1-2-3 *Retrace the path described above; return to Triangle position* facing downstage with the right leg inverted.

Transition in 3 Counts

cts. 1-2-3 *Press into a deep Hinge position* facing stage right, carry the arms through 2nd and lower the body to *Triangle position* facing upstage with the left leg inverted.

Repeat to the other side with the transition in 3 counts.

Phrase 3

cts. 1-2-3 *Press into a deep Hinge position* facing stage right with the right arm reaching forward and the left hand on the floor.

cts. 4-5 Continuing to *press the pelvis forward, lift to standing.* The left hand leaves the floor and moves through Natural Low and Middle Parallel to lift to High Parallel. The right arm lifts to High Parallel simultaneously as the left arm lifts.

3 cts.

ct. 1 With a strong accent, *drop with a hinging action, placing the left hand on the floor.*

cts. 2-3 Retrace the path described above to *return to Triangle position* with the right leg inverted.

Transition in 3 Counts

cts. 1-2-3 *Press into a deep Hinge position* facing stage right, carry the arms through 2nd, and lower the body to Triangle position, facing upstage with the left leg inverted.

Repeat to the other side with the transition in 3 counts.

Transition from Fortification No. 8 into Fortification No. 9 in 3 Counts

cts. 1-2 Remain in Triangle position and bring the torso erect facing downstage and the arms lifting to 2nd.

ct. 3 *Gently place the left hand on the left knee and the right hand on the right knee.*

Fortification No. 9 (Split Stretch)

Int., Adv.; (12 cts. twice, 4 ct. transition) twice; 12 cts, 3 cts., 12 cts., 3 cts.; count at 70 B.P.M.

Begin center, facing downstage in Triangle position, the right leg inverted. The left hand is gently placed on the left knee and the right hand is gently placed on the right knee.

> **Note:** If students have difficulty maintaining this hand position during the Fortification study, the left hand may be placed on the floor near the left hip.

Phrase 1

cts. 1-2-3 Maintaining the torso erect and squared off, *extend the right leg to the rear.* The right arm extends forward to Middle Parallel, palm down.

ct. 4 *Flex the right foot.*

cts. 5-6-7-8 *Extend the left leg and rotate both legs outward as the body turns ¼ turn to the right to face stage right.* The arms open to 2nd.

cts. 9-10 As the right foot points, *rotate the right leg inward as the body turns ¼ turn to the left to face downstage in a split.* The arms remain in 2nd.

cts. 11-12 Bend both legs and *return to Triangle position with the left hand on the left knee and the right hand on the right knee.*

Repeat once more.

Transition in 4 Counts

cts. 1-2-3-4 *Extend both legs as the body turns ¼ turn to the right with both feet pointed.* Open the arms to 2nd, and *continue to turn ¼ turn to the right to face upstage in a split. Bend both legs to Triangle position with the left leg inverted and the hands placed on the knees as described above.*

Repeat to the other side with the transition in 4 counts.

Phrase 2

cts. 1-2-3 With both feet pointed, *extend both legs and turn ¼ turn to the right to face stage right* as the legs rotate open. The arms open to 2nd.

cts. 4-5-6 *Turn ¼ turn to face upstage into a split.* The arms remain in 2nd.

cts. 7-8-9 Place both hands on the floor on either side of the legs, pull the hips up toward the ceiling and the head toward the right knee, and draw the legs toward each other to 4th position with natural turnout.

cts. 10-11-12 *Slide the feet into a split and raise the arms to 2nd.*

cts. 1-2-3 *Bend both legs to Triangle position facing upstage with the left leg inverted.*

cts. 1-2-3 *Turn ¼ turn to the left to face stage right as both legs extend and rotate outward. The arms open to 2nd.*

cts. 4-5-6 *Turn ¼ turn to the left to face downstage with both legs extended in split position. The arms remain in 2nd.*

cts. 7-8-9 Place both hands on the floor on either side of the legs and *pull the hips up toward the ceiling; the head pulls down toward the left knee, and the legs are drawn toward each other into 4th position with natural turnout.*

cts. 10-11-12 *Slide the feet into a split* and raise the arms to 2nd.

cts. 1-2-3 Bend both legs to *Triangle position with the right leg inverted facing downstage,* the hands are placed on the knees as described above.

Transition from Fortification No. 9 to Fortification No. 10 in 4 Counts

cts. 1-2-3-4 *Extend the body prone and lower the arms to the sides of the body in 4 counts smoothly.*

Fortification No. 10 (Incorporates the Front Fall)

Beg., Int., Adv.; (four 4's, two 6's, 12 counts) twice; count at 65 B.P.M.

Begin facing downstage supine, the arms in High Parallel, the legs straight and parallel, the feet pointed.

Four 4's

ct. 1 Strongly accented, *raise the torso to sitting position,* back slightly rounded, the arms in Middle Parallel but rounded, with palms facing in toward the body; the legs rotate out as the knees bend, the toes point and the big toes touch each other, heels raise off the floor.

ct. 2 *Hold.*

cts. 3-4 In a sustained motion, *return to the starting position* by first placing the lower back on the floor.

cts. 2-2-3-4 Repeat the 1st measure—*sit up, hold, roll down.*

ct. 3 Strongly accented, raise the torso to sitting position, the back straight, the arms in Middle Parallel; the legs stay parallel, as the right knee bends, the right foot places flat on the floor.

2 *Hold.*

3-4 *Return to the starting position* by first placing the lower back on the floor.

cts. 4-2-3-4 Repeat the 3rd measure to the other side, except that on counts 3 and 4 the *arms lower to the sides of the body on the floor.*

Two 6's slower tempo; count at 55 B.P.M.

ct. 1 Keeping the legs parallel, bend the right leg and *place the metatarsal (ball) of the right foot on the floor,* near the right buttock.

2-3-4 *Push the pelvis toward the ceiling* as high as possible, keeping the hips level.

5-6 Slide the right foot forward and straighten the right knee; keeping the pelvis lifted, *slowly lower the body down to the floor;* the buttocks touch first, then the lower back touches.

cts. 2-2-3- Repeat to the other side—*place the metatarsal on the floor, press*
4-5-6 *the pelvis toward the ceiling, lower the body.*

12 cts.

ct. 1 Keeping the legs straight, *raise the torso to sitting position,* the back straight, the arms in Middle Parallel.

ct. 2 Bend the left leg and *invert the right leg to sit in Triangle position,* the arms open to 2nd.

ct. 3 *Raise up onto both knees* by bringing the pelvis forward over the knees and moving the left foreleg back. The legs should be parallel and hip width apart.

ct. 4 *Circle the arms down, forward, and up* to High Parallel.

"and" *Flex the toes.*

cts. 5-8 *Tilt the torso back with a hinging action.*

"and" *Press the pelvis forward as the upper body arches back.*

ct. 9 Both arms reach back in a circular motion and come down to the sides. As the pelvis continues to press forward, *Front Fall,* bracing the fall with bent arms, elbows close to the body. As the palms touch the floor, the right arm straightens and slides forward on the side of the hand, little finger on the floor, the head turns to the left.

ct. 10 *Pull back the pelvis so that the buttocks lift toward the ceiling* and the knees bend slightly; the toes remain flexed.

ct. 11 Return the pelvis to the floor and straighten the legs; the toes remain flexed and the head remains turned to the left.

ct. 12 Extend the left arm downstage as you turn left and *roll onto your back.*

Repeat the whole study facing upstage on the left side.

Note: *In this study, the Front Fall is done with the right hand sliding forward both times.*

*Transition from Fortification No. 10 to Fortification No. 11
in 4 Counts*

cts. 1-2   *Sit up, keeping the legs extended, and reach forward with both arms to Middle Parallel.*

cts. 3-4   *Bend the left knee and invert the right leg to Triangle position.* The torso leans to the left in order to place the left forearm on the floor with the palm up. The right arm curves and frames the head. The right buttock is off the floor.

Fortification No. 11 (Basic Rise and Fall)

Int., Adv.; four 3's five times; count at 80 B.P.M.

Begin center, facing downstage, in Triangle position, the right leg inverted. The left forearm is on the floor, with the elbow bent at a right angle. The elbow should be in the center of the back, with the fingers pointing perpendicular to upstage and the left palm on the floor. The right arm is rounded over the head. The torso is arched and looks as if it were "wrapping around a column," with the head reaching toward the inverted leg.

> **Note:** The rise out of the floor (and the fall back into it) gets its impetus from a large burst of energy on the first beat. The body acts like a coil, unwinding on the ascent and winding on the descent.

Phrase 1

cts. 1-2-3   *Ascent: Swing the body and the right arm to the right,* push off the floor with the left hand, to face stage right, into *Primitive Squat position,* by count 1. The arms reach to Middle Parallel. Sustain the position for the 2nd and 3rd beats.

cts. 2-2-3   *Descent: Retrace the movement back to the starting position,* and sustain the Triangle position for the 2nd and 3rd beats. On the descent, the arms and the upper torso must pull into lateral right side to lower the body and help facilitate the descent.

cts. 3-2-3   Repeat the *ascent* as described above in counts 1-2-3—swing the body to Primitive Squat position.

cts. 4-2-3   Repeat the *descent* as described above in counts 2-2-3, except change to Triangle position with the left leg inverted, facing upstage. The right elbow is on the floor, and the left arm is rounded over the head.

Phrase 2

cts. 1-2-3   *Ascent: Swing the body and the left arm to the left,* and push off with the right hand to Flat Back Forward position, with the legs in Parallel 2nd plié. The body should be between the knees, as low as possible. The arms are in High Parallel. Sustain the Flat Back Forward position for the 2nd and 3rd beats.

cts. 2-2-3 *Descent:* Retrace the movement to Triangle position with the left leg inverted, facing upstage.

cts. 3-2-3 *Ascent:* Repeat the *ascent* as described above in phrase 2 in counts 1-2-3; swing the body to Flat Back Forward position.

cts. 4-2-3 *Descent:* Retrace the movement to Triangle position with the right leg inverted, facing downstage.

Phrase 3

cts. 1-2-3 *Ascent: Swing the body and the right arm to the right,* and push off with the left hand to face stage right into *plié in Wide Natural 2nd,* with the torso erect. Maintain the lowest possible level. The arms are in 2nd. Sustain the position on the 2nd and 3rd beats.

cts. 2-2-3 *Descent:* Retrace the movement to Triangle position with the right leg inverted, facing downstage.

cts. 3-2-3 *Ascent:* Repeat the ascent as described above in phrase 3 in counts 1-2-3—swing the body into plié in Wide Natural 2nd.

cts. 4-2-3 *Descent:* Retrace the movement to Triangle position with the left leg inverted, facing upstage.

Phrase 4

cts. 1-2-3 *Ascent: Swing the body and the left arm to the left,* to face stage right, and raise the body erect, and relevé in Wide Natural 2nd, with the arms in High Parallel. Sustain the position for the 2nd and 3rd beats.

cts. 2-2-3 *Descent:* Retrace the movement back to Triangle position, with the left leg inverted, facing upstage.

cts. 3-2-3 *Ascent:* Repeat the ascent as described above in phrase 4 in counts 1-2-3—swing the body to relevé in Wide Natural 2nd.

cts. 4-2-3 *Descent:* Retrace the movement back to Triangle position, with the right leg inverted, facing downstage.

Phrase 5

cts. 1-2-3 *Ascent: Swing the body and the right arm to the right,* to face stage right, to a jump with the legs straight, and in Wide Natural 2nd. The torso is erect and the arms are in High Parallel.

cts. 2-2-3 *Descent:* Retrace the movement back to Triangle position, with the right leg inverted, facing downstage.

cts. 3-2-3 *Ascent:* Repeat the ascent as described above in phrase 5, in counts 1-2-3—swing the body to a jump with the legs straight, and in Wide Natural 2nd.

cts. 4-2-3 *Descent:* Retrace the movement back to Triangle position, with the left leg inverted, facing upstage.

> **Note:** While executing the descent the arms and the torso pull toward stage right to resist the lowering of the body.

*Transition from Fortification No. 11 to Fortification No. 12
in 4 Counts*

> ct. 1 Repeat the ascent as described above in phrase 4 of counts 1-2-3.
>
> ct. 2 Lower the heels and *turn ¼ turn to the left to face downstage.* Close the right foot to Natural 1st.
>
> cts. 3-4 *Turn, press the palms, and lower the arms to Natural Low.*

Fortification No. 12

Int., Adv.; eight 2's twice; count at 65 B.P.M.

Begin center, facing downstage, the feet in Natural 1st, the arms in Natural Low.

> cts. 1-2 *Parallel the right leg and lift the right knee forward until the right thigh is parallel to the ceiling.* The right foot is pointed directly below the right knee. (The thigh and shin are forming a right angle.) Simultaneously lift the right arm forward, with the palm facing the floor.
>
> cts. 2-2 Keeping the right leg at a right angle, *open the leg to 2nd.* The right arm also opens to 2nd and the left arm lifts to 2nd.
>
> cts. 3-2 Continue to lift out of the pelvis and *open and extend the right leg to arabesque.* The arms remain in 2nd.
>
> cts. 4-2 *Relevé.*
>
> ct. 5 *Turn ¼ turn to the left on relevé in the established position to face stage left.*
>
> 2 *Lower the heel and pull up.*
>
> ct. 6 *Plié on the standing leg, as the right leg reaches diagonally downward.*
>
> 2 *Step back on a straight right leg and lift the left leg forward, parallel and bent at a right angle.* The left arm remains in 2nd and the right arm moves forward to the center of the body with the palm facing the body. *Both arms round.*
>
> ct. 7 *Turn the head sharply to look downstage.*
>
> 2 Maintaining the established position, *turn ¼ turn to the right to face downstage.*
>
> cts. 8-2 *Lower the left leg to Natural 1st and the arms to Natural Low.*

Repeat to the other side.

Transition from Fortification No. 12 to Fortification No. 13

On the upbeat, *close the toes from Natural 1st to Parallel 1st.*

Fortification No. 13

Int., Adv.; (12 cts. and 8 cts.) twice; count at 60 B.P.M.

Begin center, facing downstage, the feet in Parallel 1st, the arms in Natural Low.

12 cts.

ct. 1 As the arms are raising sideward to 2nd, *lift the right leg forward smoothly to hip height.*

ct. 2 *Continue to move the leg smoothly through High 2nd position to arabesque.*

cts. 3-4 Turn the body ¼ turn to the right to face stage right, and simultaneously *stretch the body out to Lateral T position* with the arms in High Parallel.

cts. 5-6 Maintaining the leg in Lateral T position, *reach both arms and the head and torso between the legs.*

ct. 7 Maintaining the position described above in counts 5-6, *plié.*

ct. 8 *Take a small hop onto the right foot,* making a ¼ turn to the right to face upstage; and center the torso, raise the left leg to Parallel 2nd hip high, and extend the arms to 2nd.

cts. 9-10 As the left leg continues to lift, *reach toward the left foot with both arms parallel to each other and the palms facing toward downstage.* The torso and the focus will turn slightly to the left.

cts. 11-12 *Return to the position established on count 8*—the torso erect, the left leg lifted to Parallel 2nd, and the arms in 2nd.

8 cts.

cts. 1-4 *Bend the left knee to Table position,* as the right hand lightly touches the left shoulder, and the left hand lightly touches the left knee. The head lifts to face the ceiling.

cts. 5-6 As the arms move to 2nd, *the left leg straightens and turns out, staying as high as possible.* The head returns to center.

cts. 7-8 Simultaneously, *the arms lower to Natural Low and the left leg lowers to Parallel 1st.*

Repeat to the other side, facing upstage.

Transition from Fortification No. 13 to Fortification No. 14 in 2 Counts

cts. 1-2 *Rotate both legs outward to Natural 1st and place the ball of the left foot on the floor behind the right foot.*

Fortification No. 14 (Dimensional Turn Preparation)

Beg., Int., Adv.; two 8's, one 8, two 8's, two 8's, two 8's; count at 65 B.P.M.

Begin center stage, facing downstage standing on the right foot, which is extremely turned out. The left foot is in ¾ relevé placed directly behind the right ankle; both knees are bent. The arms remain in Natural Low.

Basic Foot Action

upbeat	Keeping both knees bent, *shift the weight to the ball of the left foot and pick the right foot off the floor slightly. Turn ¼ turn to the right.*
ct. 1	*Shift the weight and place the turned-out right foot on the floor.* Accent the down beat.
"and"	Repeat the upbeat above—*shift the weight to the ball of the left foot,* but remain facing stage right.
ct. 2	Repeat count 1 above—*shift the weight and place the turned-out right foot on the floor.*
cts. 3-4-5-6-7-8	Repeat the ¼ pivotal turns with two beats per direction to complete one full turn.
cts. 2-2-3-4-5-6 7-8	Repeat ¼ pivotal turn with two beats per direction to the left side. The transition to the left side is straighten the right leg, relevé on the right foot, and bring the left foot forward to the starting position.
cts. 1-2-3-4-5-6-7-8	Repeat the ¼ pivotal turns with one beat per direction to complete one full turn and the upbeat transition to repeat to the other side.
cts. 1-2-3-4-5-6 7-8 and 2-2-3-4-5-6-7-8	Repeat the ¼ pivotal turns with the two beats per direction to the right. *The front foot moves from 4th position to 5th position, with a slight forward hip movement that causes a rocking motion.* Repeat the upbeat transition to repeat to the other side.
cts. 1-2-3-4-5-6-7-8 and 2-2-3-4-5-6-7-8	Repeat the same pivotal turns described above with the rocking motion; with ½ *turns to the right on two beats per direction.* Complete two full turns. Repeat the upbeat transition to repeat to the other side.
cts. 1-2-3-4-5-6-7-8	Repeat the same pivotal turns described above with the rocking motion with ½ turns to the right with one beat per direction. Repeat 4 full turns. Repeat the upbeat transition to repeat to the other side.
cts. 2-2-3-4-5-6-7-8	Repeat to the other side.

Note: *See Pivotal Turns in chapter 11 for additional variations.*

Fortification No. 15 (Elevation Preparation)

Int., Adv.; (two 3's, one 6, one 3) twice, 5 cts. twice, 4 cts. twice, 3 cts. twice; count at 85 B.P.M.

Begin center, facing downstage, the right leg extended back and parallel, with the ball of the foot on the floor. The left knee bent, the left foot naturally turned out; the right arm in Middle Parallel, the left arm in 2nd, both palms facing the floor.

cts. 1-2-3 *Press the right heel toward the floor, and increase the plié in the left knee.* Maintain the weight on the left leg.

cts. 2-2-3 *Straighten the front knee and pull up the thigh to avoid hyperextending the knee.*

cts. 1-6 With a driving movement, *lower the right heel as the left knee bends six times.*

cts. 1-2-3 *Pass the left pointed foot close to the right ankle, bending the left knee to change to the other side.* The arms lower to Natural Low and lift to opposition on the other side.

Repeat to the other side with the transition.

cts. 1-5 On a down beat, *lower the right heel five times* as described above.

upbeat With a small jump, *bring the pointed left foot backward as described above to change to the other side.* The arms lower to Natural Low and lift to opposition on the other side. Land on the down beat on count 1 to begin the other side.

Repeat to the other side with the transition on the upbeat. Repeat with 4 counts and repeat with 3 counts.

Fortification No. 16 (Elevation Preparation)

Beg., Int., Adv.; four 4's, four 2's, 8 cts.; count at 65 B.P.M.

Begin center, facing downstage, feet in Parallel 1st, the arms in Natural Low.

Phrase 1

cts. 1-2-3-4 *Pulse the knees gently four times.*

cts. 2-2-3-4 *Pulse the knees raising the heels off the floor.* With each pulse the heels raise progressively higher. The arms lift to Demi-2nd with the arms straight.

cts. 3-2-3-4 *Jump off the floor four times with the knees bent in the air* and the feet relaxed. Be sure to land correctly. The arms remain in Demi-2nd, arms straight.

cts. 4-2-3-4 *Jump higher off the floor four times with the knees bent and the feet lifted to the buttocks.* The feet are pointed.

Phrase 2

cts. 1-2 *Jump with the knees bent and the feet lifted to the buttocks and turn ¹/₂ turn to the right to face upstage.* The feet are pointed. The arms remain in Demi-2nd, arms straight.

cts. 2-2 *Jump with the knees bent and the feet lifted to the buttocks and turn ¹/₂ turn to the left to face downstage.* The feet are pointed. The arms remain in Demi-2nd, arms straight.

cts. 3-2 Repeat counts 1-2—*jump and turn ¹/₂ turn to the right.*

cts. 4-2 Repeat counts 2-2—*jump and turn ¹/₂ turn to the left.*

Phrase 3

cts. 1-2- *Vibrate the heels as the legs straighten and the arms lower to*
3-4-5-6- *Natural Low.*
7-8

> **Note:** Beginner students require a slightly faster tempo than more advanced dancers.

Fortification No. 17

Int., Adv.; count at 55 B.P.M.

Begin center, facing downstage, the feet in Natural 1st, the hands placed on the front of the thighs, the fingers pointing straight down, the arms bent, the elbows pointing sidewards.

Section A

Four 3's twice, two 3's, 4 cts.

cts. 1-2-3 *Lift both heels and rotate them to pigeon-toe the feet.* The hands angle inward, the elbows outward while they remain placed on the thighs.
cts. 2-2-3 *Return to the starting position.*

Repeat once more.

cts. 1-2-3 *Contract the metatarsal arch in the feet and pull the knuckles of the hand upward.*
cts. 2-2-3 *Curl the toes upward and arch the fingers upward, keeping the palms on the thighs.*

Repeat once more.

ct. 1 *Open the arms to Demi-2nd, palms facing downstage and the fingers distended.*
ct. 2 *Contract the metatarsal arch in the feet and make a fist with each hand.* The fingers move into a fist beginning with the little finger and going to the thumb consecutively.
ct. 3 *Bring the feet to Parallel 1st by moving the toes inward and lower the arms to Natural Low as the hands uncurl.*

Repeat once more by opening the feet to Natural 1st on count 1 as the arms open to Demi-2nd.

ct. 1 *Contract the buttocks and turn out the feet to Natural 1st.*
ct. 2 *Open the right leg to 2nd as the arms lift to 2nd.*
ct. 3 *Contract the metatarsal arch of the feet.*
"and" *Release the feet.*
ct. 4 *Close the left leg to Natural 1st and lower the arms to Natural Low.*

Section B

4 cts., two 6's, four 6's twice, 4 cts.

cts. 1-2-3-4 *Plié in Natural 1st, and lift the arms to 2nd.*
- ct. 1 *Lift the right heel, rotate it outward, and lower the right heel, placing the foot in a pigeon-toed position.* The legs remain in plié.
- ct. 2 *Lift the right heel and replace it in Natural 1st.*
- ct. 3 Repeat count 1—*pigeon-toe the right foot.*
- ct. 4 Repeat count 2—*return to Natural 1st.*
- ct. 5 Repeat count 1—*pigeon-toe the right foot.*
- ct. 6 Repeat count 2—*return to Natural 1st.*

Repeat to the other side.

cts. 1-2-3- Alternating pigeon-toed and turned out, *move the right foot away*
4-5-6 *from the left heel.* (The heel moves on count 1, the toe on count 2, etc.) The arms remain in 2nd throughout.
cts. 2-2-3- Alternating pigeon-toed and turned out, move the right foot back to
4-5-6 Natural 1st.

Repeat to the other side.

cts. 1-2-3- Repeat the four 6's directly above *with arm rotation.* As the right
4-5-6 foot pigeon-toes, *the right shoulder rotates forward and the palm*
through *rotates backward to face the ceiling.* The arm has a space hold. Only
4-2-3- the shoulder rotates in the joint. As the right foot turns out, *the right*
4-5-6 *shoulder rotates outward in the shoulder joint to enable the palm of the right hand to face the ceiling.*

Repeat on the other side.

- ct. 1 *Turn the left palm down.*
- cts. 2-3 *Lower the arms to Natural Low and straighten the legs.*
- ct. 4 *Rotate the heels outward to Parallel 2nd.*

Section C

Four 3's twice, four 2's twice, 4 cts. twice, 6 cts. twice, five 6's

cts. 1-2-3 *Relevé.* The right arm reaches forward as the left arm reaches sideward. Both palms are facing the floor.
cts. 2-2-3 Staying in relevé, *rotate both legs outward until the heels touch in Natural 1st.* The arms fold in front of and touching the body, with the left arm on top of the right arm. The hands are cupped and the palms face the ceiling.
cts. 3-2-3 Staying in relevé, *rotate both legs back to Parallel 2nd, as the arms lower to lift sideward to 2nd,* with the palms facing the floor.
cts. 4-2-3 *Lower the heels,* as the arms lower to Natural Low.

Repeat the phrase above on the other side.

Four 2's twice

Repeat the above phrase with 2 counts for each movement, on the right and left side.

4 cts. twice

Repeat the above phrase with 1 count for each movement, on the right and left side. On the upbeat, lower the heels to Natural 1st, the arms in Natural Low.

6 cts. twice

cts. 1-6   *Relevé* 3 counts and lower the heels 3 counts. Simultaneously circle the right arm diagonally back, straight up, forward, and down to Natural Low. At the same time, the left arm reaches forward, side, and down to Natural Low.

Repeat to the left side.

On the upbeat, bring the toes inward to end with the feet in Parallel 2nd, arms in Natural Low.

Five 6's

ct. 1   *Relevé and lift the arms to 2nd.*
ct. 2   Keeping the heels off the floor, *squat with the buttocks on the heels.* Keep the spine erect. The arms swing down and forward to Closed Egyptian.
ct. 3   Keeping the heels off the floor, *move the torso to Flat Back Forward.* The arms retrace the path down and sideward to 2nd.
ct. 4   Repeat count 2—*squat with the arms in Closed Egyptian.*
ct. 5   *Straighten the legs and lift to relevé with the body erect.* The arms swing down and sideward to 2nd.
ct. 6   *Lower the heels and lower the arms to Natural Low.*

Repeat the above 6 counts two more times.

Repeat the above 2 counts, relevé on ct. 1, squat on ct. 2. On ct. 3, relevé and hold cts. 4-5-6.

cts. 1-2-3-   *Lower the heels slowly as the arms lower to Natural Low.*
4-5-6

•• • •   •
Balance Studies

> **Note:** *The following balance studies can be done in a stationary position, or as progressions across the floor.*

Elementary Balance

Beg., Int., Adv.; Eight 3's on each side; count at 55 B.P.M.

Begin stage left, facing stage right, the feet in Natural 1st, the arms in Natural Low.

cts. 1-2-3 Parallel the right leg, and *lift the right knee forward until the right thigh is parallel to the ceiling.* The right foot is pointed directly below the right knee. (The thigh and the shin are forming a right angle.) The arms lift forward to Middle Parallel, palms facing down.

cts. 2-2-3 Keeping the right leg at a right angle, *open the leg to 2nd.* The arms gradually rotate inward, the palms face outward, and, as if opening a curtain, the arms move to 2nd.

cts. 3-2-3 Press the pelvis forward and tilt the upper torso back into *Flat Back Back Bend position.* The arms remain in 2nd, and the focus is forward on an upward diagonal.

cts. 4-2-3 Accenting count 1 of the measure, rotate the arms outward, palms facing the ceiling. On counts 2 and 3 of the measure, and "on a breath," pull the abdominal wall in and up, and *lift the torso to an upright position. The arms lift up to High Parallel.*

cts. 5-2-3 Keeping the arms in High Parallel, *Table the right leg.*

cts. 6-2-3 *Tilt the torso forward to Flat Back position,* parallel to the floor only, and extend the right leg in arabesque, lifting it as high as possible.

cts. 7-2-3 Accenting count 1 of the measure, *parallel the extended right leg, maintaining the height of the leg.* The hips will now be squared off or level. On count 2 of the measure, *bend both knees.* The extended leg lowers until the shin is parallel to the floor. The arms bend and the elbows pull in toward the knee, the forearms parallel to the floor, palms facing the ceiling. The torso rounds over, and the head drops, with the focus between the legs to the opposite wall. On count 3 of the measure, *straighten the left leg, lift the torso erect, and bring the right leg forward* to the right-angle position described above in counts 1-2-3. The arms straighten to Natural Low.

cts. 8-2-3 *Walk forward,* stepping right, left, right, or in the stationary variation, *lower and straighten the right leg to Natural 1st.*

Repeat to the other side. When progressing across the floor, draw the left leg forward, with the shin leading, to begin the left side.

> **Note:** *For advanced students, on counts 4-2-3, "on a breath," relevé as the torso lifts to upright position. The heel lowers on the first count of counts 7-2-3.*

Table Balances

Table Balance

Beg., Int., Adv.; seven 3's on each side; count at 55 B.P.M.

Begin stage left, facing stage right, the feet in Natural 1st, the arms in Natural Low.

cts. 1-2-3   *Parallel the right leg and lift the right knee forward* until the right thigh is parallel to the ceiling. The right foot is pointed and directly below the knee. (The thigh and the shin are forming a right angle.) The arms lift forward to Middle Parallel, palms facing down.

cts. 2-2-3   Keeping the right leg at a right angle, *open the leg to 2nd.* The arms open to 2nd.

cts. 3-2-3   *Rotate the right leg to Table position.* The standing leg remains naturally turned out.

cts. 4-2-3   On a sustained breath, *pull up.*

cts. 5-2-3   *Lift and rotate the right leg out* by dropping the right hip to level the pelvis. The right leg remains bent and the knee lifts.

cts. 6-2-3   Keeping the right leg bent, bring it forward. The arms move forward to Middle Parallel, palms facing down.

cts. 7-2-3   *Walk forward,* stepping right, left, right. The palms rotate to face each other and the arms lower slowly to Natural Low.

Repeat to the other side.

Table Balance with Relevé

Int., Adv.; Nine 3's on each side; count at 55 B.P.M.

Begin stage left, facing stage right, the feet in Natural 1st, the arms in Natural Low.

cts. 1-2-3   *Parallel the right leg and lift the right knee forward* until the right thigh is parallel to the ceiling. The right foot is pointed directly below the knee. (The thigh and the shin are forming a right angle.) The arms lift forward to Middle Parallel, palms facing down.

cts. 2-2-3   Keeping the right leg at a right angle, *open the leg to 2nd.* The arms open to 2nd.

cts. 3-2-3   Lift and rotate the right leg to *Table position.* The standing leg remains naturally turned out.

cts. 4-2-3   On a sustained breath, *pull up.*

cts. 5-2-3   *Relevé.*

cts. 6-2-3   *Lower the heel.*

cts. 7-2-3   *Lift and rotate the right leg out* by dropping the right hip to level the pelvis. The right leg remains bent and the knee lifts as high as possible.

cts. 8-2-3   Keeping the right leg bent, bring it forward. The arms move forward to Middle Parallel, palms facing down.

cts. 9-2-3   *Walk forward,* stepping right, left, right. The palms rotate to face each other and the arms lower slowly to Natural Low.

Repeat to the other side.

Table Balance with Flat Back

Beg., Int., Adv.; Nine 3's on each side; count at 55 B.P.M.

Begin stage left, facing stage right, the feet in Natural 1st, the arms in Natural Low.

cts. 1-2-3 *Parallel the right leg and lift the right knee forward* until the right thigh is parallel to the ceiling. The right foot is pointed directly below the knee. (The thigh and the shin are forming a right angle.) The arms lift forward to Middle Parallel, palms facing down.

cts. 2-2-3 Keeping the right leg at a right angle, *open the leg to 2nd. The arms open to 2nd.*

cts. 3-2-3 Lift and rotate the right leg to *Table position.* The standing leg remains naturally turned out.

cts. 4-2-3 On a sustained breath, *pull up.*

cts. 5-2-3 *Tilt the torso forward into Flat Back position.* The right leg remains in Table and the arms remain in 2nd.

cts. 6-2-3 Keeping the right leg in Table position, *return the torso to an upright position.* The arms remain in 2nd.

cts. 7-2-3 *Lift and rotate the right leg out* by dropping the right hip to level the pelvis. The right leg remains bent and the knee lifts as high as possible.

cts. 8-2-3 *Keeping the right leg bent, bring it forward.* The arms move forward to Middle Parallel, palms facing down.

cts. 9-2-3 *Walk forward,* stepping right, left, right. The palms rotate to face each other and the arms lower slowly to Natural Low.

Repeat to the other side.

Table Balance with Flat Back, Plié, and Relevé

Int., Adv.; Thirteen 3's on each side; count at 55 B.P.M.

Begin stage left, facing stage right, the feet in Natural 1st. The arms in Natural Low.

cts. 1-2-3 *Parallel the right leg and lift the right knee forward* until the right thigh is parallel to the ceiling. The right foot is pointed directly below the knee. (The thigh and the shin are forming a right angle.) The arms lift forward to Middle Parallel, palms facing down.

cts. 2-2-3 Keeping the right leg at a right angle, *open the leg to 2nd.* The arms open to 2nd.

cts. 3-2-3 Lift and rotate the right leg to *Table position.* The standing leg remains naturally turned out.

cts. 4-2-3 On a sustained breath, *pull up.*

cts. 5-2-3 *Tilt the torso forward into Flat Back position.* The right leg remains in Table and the arms remain in 2nd. The Table position must be maintained parallel to the floor and as high as possible through counts 10-2-3.

cts. 6-2-3 Staying in the Flat Back/Table position, *demi-plié on the left leg.*

cts. 7-2-3 Staying in the Flat Back/Table position, *straighten the left leg.*

cts. 8-2-3 Staying in the Flat Back/Table position, *relevé on the left leg.*

cts. 9-2-3 Staying in the Flat Back/Table position, *lower the left heel.*

cts. 10-2-3 Keeping the right leg in Table position, *return the torso to an upright position.* The arms remain in 2nd.

cts. 11-2-3 *Lift and rotate the right leg out* by dropping the right hip to level the pelvis. The right leg remains bent and the knee lifts as high as possible.

cts. 12-2-3 Keeping the right leg bent, *bring the leg forward.* The arms move forward to Middle Parallel, palms facing down.

cts. 13-2-3 *Walk forward,* stepping right, left, right. The palms rotate to face each other and the arms lower slowly to Natural Low.

Repeat to the other side.

Table Balance with Flat Back and Extension

Beg., Int., Adv.; Ten 3's on each side; count at 55 B.P.M.

Begin stage left, facing stage right, the feet in Natural 1st, the arms in Natural Low.

cts. 1-2-3 *Parallel the right leg and lift the right knee forward* until the right thigh is parallel to the ceiling. The right foot is pointed directly below the knee. (The thigh and the shin are forming a right angle.) The arms lift forward to Middle Parallel, palms facing down.

cts. 2-2-3 Keeping the right leg at a right angle, *open the legs to 2nd.* The arms open to 2nd.

cts. 3-2-3 Lift and rotate the right leg to *Table position.* The standing leg remains naturally turned out.

cts. 4-2-3 On a sustained breath, *pull up.*

cts. 5-2-3 *Tilt the torso forward into Flat Back position.* The right leg remains in Table and the arms remain in 2nd.

cts. 6-2-3 Keeping the right leg parallel, *extend the leg to the side* as high as possible. The torso remains in Flat Back and the arms remain in 2nd.

cts. 7-2-3 Bend the right leg and *return to Table position.*

cts. 8-2-3 *Return the torso to an upright position* and *lift and rotate the right leg out* by dropping the right hip to level the pelvis. The right knee remains bent and the knee lifts as high as possible.

cts. 9-2-3 Keeping the right leg bent, *bring the leg forward.* The arms move forward to Middle Parallel, palms facing down.

cts. 10-2-3 *Walk forward,* stepping right, left, right. The palms rotate to face each other and the arms lower slowly to Natural Low.

Repeat to the other side.

Table Balance with Flat Back, Extension, Relevé, and Plié

Int., Adv.; Thirteen 3's on each side; count at 55 B.P.M.

Begin stage left, facing stage right, the feet in Natural 1st, the arms in Natural Low.

cts. 1-2-3 Parallel the right leg and *lift the right knee forward* until the right thigh is parallel to the ceiling. The right foot is pointed directly below the knee. (The thigh and the shin are forming a right angle.) The arms lift forward to Middle Parallel, palms facing down.

cts. 2-2-3 Keeping the right leg at a right angle, *open the leg to 2nd.* The arms open to 2nd.

cts. 3-2-3 Lift and rotate the right leg to *Table position.* The standing leg remains naturally turned out.

cts. 4-2-3 On a sustained breath, *pull up.*

cts. 5-2-3 Tilt the torso forward into *Flat Back position.* The right leg remains in Table and the arms remain in 2nd.

cts. 6-2-3 Keeping the right leg parallel, *extend the leg to the side* as high as possible. The torso remains in Flat Back and the arms remain in 2nd.

cts. 7-2-3 Maintaining the position, *relevé on the left leg.*

cts. 8-2-3 Maintaining the position, *lower the left heel and demi-plié on the left leg.*

cts. 9-2-3 Maintaining the position, *straighten the left leg.*

cts. 10-2-3 Bend the right leg and *return to Table position.*

cts. 11-2-3 *Return the torso to an upright position* and *lift and rotate the right leg out* by dropping the right hip to level the pelvis. The right knee remains bent and the knee lifts as high as possible.

cts. 12-2-3 Keeping the right leg bent, *bring the leg forward.* The arms move forward to Middle Parallel, palms facing down.

cts. 13-2-3 *Walk forward,* stepping right, left, right. The palms rotate to face each other and the arms lower slowly to Natural Low.

Repeat to the other side.

Table Balance with Flat Back and Extension (Variation)

Int., Adv.; Ten 3's on each side; count at 55 B.P.M.

Begin stage left, facing stage right, the feet in Natural 1st, the arms in Natural Low.

cts. 1-2-3   Parallel the right leg and *lift the right knee forward* until the right thigh is parallel to the ceiling. The right foot is pointed directly below the knee. (The thigh and the shin are forming a right angle.) The arms lift forward to Middle Parallel, palms facing down.

cts. 2-2-3   Keeping the right leg at a right angle, *open the leg to 2nd*. The arms open to 2nd.

cts. 3-2-3   Lift and rotate the right leg to *Table position*. The standing leg remains naturally turned out.

cts. 4-2-3   On a sustained breath, *pull up*.

cts. 5-2-3   Simultaneously *tilt the torso forward* into Flat Back position.

and 6-2-3   Keeping the right leg parallel, *extend the leg to the side* as high as possible.

cts. 7-2-3   *Return the torso to an upright position* and *lift and rotate the extended right leg out* by dropping the right hip to level the pelvis. The extended leg lifts as high as possible.

cts. 8-2-3   Keeping the leg lifted, *bend the right leg* until the right foot is pointed directly below the knee.

cts. 9-2-3   Keeping the right leg bent, *bring the leg forward*. The arms move forward to Middle Parallel, palms facing down.

cts. 10-2-3   *Walk forward*, stepping right, left, right. The palms rotate to face each other and the arms lower slowly to Natural Low.

Repeat to the other side.

Table Balance with Flat Back, Extension, and Promenade

Int., Adv.; Twelve 3's on each side; count at 55 B.P.M.

Begin stage left, facing stage right, the feet in Natural 1st, the arms in Natural Low.

cts. 1-2-3   Parallel the right leg and *lift the right knee forward* until the right thigh is parallel to the ceiling. The right foot is pointed directly below the knee. (The thigh and the shin are forming a right angle.) The arms lift forward to Middle Parallel, palms facing down.

cts. 2-2-3   Keeping the right leg at a right angle, *open the leg to 2nd*. The arms open to 2nd.

cts. 3-2-3   Lift and rotate the right leg to *Table position*. The standing leg remains naturally turned out.

cts. 4-2-3   On a sustained breath, *pull up*.

cts. 5-2-3   Tilt the torso forward into *Flat Back position*. The right leg remains in Table and the arms remain in 2nd.

cts. 6-2-3   Keeping the right leg parallel, *extend the leg to the side* as high as possible. The torso remains in Flat Back and the arms remain in 2nd.

cts. 7-2-3 Maintaining the position, *promenade one full turn* to the left.
 and
 8-2-3

cts. 9-2-3 Bend the right leg and *return to Table position.*

cts. 10-2-3 *Return the torso to an upright position* and *rotate the right leg out* by dropping the right hip to level the pelvis. The right knee remains bent and the knee lifts as high as possible.

cts. 11-2-3 Keeping the right leg bent, *bring the leg forward.* The arms move forward to Middle Parallel, palms facing down.

cts. 12-2-3 Walk forward, stepping right, left, right. The palms rotate to face each other and the arms lower slowly to Natural Low.

Repeat to the other side.

Table Balance with Lateral

Int., Adv.; Nine 3's on each side; count at 55 B.P.M.

Begin stage left, facing stage right, the feet in Natural 1st, the arms in Natural Low.

cts. 1-2-3 Parallel the right leg and *lift the right knee forward* until the right thigh is parallel to the ceiling. The right foot is pointed directly below the knee. (The thigh and the shin are forming a right angle.) The arms lift forward to Middle Parallel, palms facing down.

cts. 2-2-3 Keeping the right leg at a right angle, *open the leg to 2nd.* The arms open to 2nd.

cts. 3-2-3 Lift and rotate the right leg to *Table position.* Slightly lift and rotate the standing heel outward so the toes point directly sideward and the standing leg is completely turned out, as the right leg is rotating to Table position. Lower the left heel.

cts. 4-2-3 On a sustained breath, *pull up.*

cts. 5-2-3 Keeping the right leg in Table position, *tilt the torso* to Lateral left side. The right arm reaches toward the ceiling and continues until it meets the left arm in High Parallel.

cts. 6-2-3 Keeping the right leg in Table position, *return the torso to an upright position.* Both arms return to 2nd. The right arm reaches toward the ceiling and lowers to 2nd. The left arm continues to reach out.

cts. 7-2-3 *Lift and rotate the right leg out* by dropping the right hip to level the pelvis and raise the left heel to readjust the standing leg to natural turn out. The right leg remains bent and the knee lifts as high as possible.

cts. 8-2-3 Keeping the right leg bent, *bring the leg forward.* The arms move forward to Middle Parallel, palms facing down.

cts. 9-2-3 *Walk forward,* stepping right, left, right. The palms rotate to face each other and the arms lower slowly to Natural Low.

Repeat to the other side.

•• • • •
T Balance Studies

Lateral T Balance

Int., Adv.; Ten 3's on each side; count to 55 B.P.M.

Begin stage left, facing stage right, the feet in Natural 1st, the arms in Natural Low.

cts. 1-2-3 Parallel the right leg and *lift the right knee forward* until the right thigh is parallel to the ceiling. The right foot is pointed directly below the knee. (The thigh and the shin are forming a right angle.) The arms lift forward to Middle Parallel, palms facing down.

cts. 2-2-3 Keeping the right leg at a right angle, *open the leg to 2nd*. The arms open to 2nd.

cts. 3-2-3 Rotate the right leg to *Table position*. Slightly lift and rotate the standing heel outward so the toes point directly sideward and the standing leg is completely turned out as the right leg is rotating to Table position. Lower the left heel.

cts. 4-2-3 On a sustained breath, *pull up*.

cts. 5-2-3 Extend the right leg and tilt the torso to *Lateral T position*. The
and right arm reaches toward the ceiling and continues until it meets the
6-2-3 left arm in High Parallel.

cts. 7-2-3 *Return the torso to an upright position and* return the right leg to *Table position*. Both arms return to 2nd. The right arm reaches toward the ceiling and lowers to 2nd; the left arm continues to reach out.

cts. 8-2-3 *Lift and rotate the right leg out* by dropping the right hip to level the pelvis, and raise the left heel to readjust the standing foot to natural turn out. The right leg remains bent and the knee lifts as high as possible.

cts. 9-2-3 Keeping the right leg bent, *bring the leg forward*. The arms move forward to Middle Parallel, palms facing down.

cts. 10-2-3 *Walk forward*, stepping right, left, right. The palms rotate to face each other and the arms lower slowly to Natural Low.

Repeat to the other side.

Front T Balance

Int., Adv.; Thirteen 3's on each side; count at 55 B.P.M.

Begin stage left, facing stage right, the feet in Natural 1st, the arms in Natural Low.

cts. 1-2-3 Parallel the right leg and *lift the right knee forward* until the right thigh is parallel to the ceiling. The right foot is pointed directly below the knee. (The thigh and the shin are forming a right angle.) The arms lift forward to Middle Parallel, palms facing down.

cts. 2-2-3 Keeping the right leg at a right angle, *open the leg to 2nd.* The arms open to 2nd.

cts. 3-2-3 Lift and rotate the right leg to *Table position.* Slightly lift and rotate the standing heel outward so the toes point directly sideward and the standing leg is completely turned out as the right leg is rotating to *Table position.* Lower the left heel.

cts. 4-2-3 On a sustained breath, *pull up.*

cts. 5-2-3 Extend the right leg and tilt the torso to *Lateral T position.* The
and right arm reaches toward the ceiling and continues until it meets the
6-2-3 left arm in High Parallel.

cts. 7-2-3 Rotate the right hip inward ¼ so that the body is in *Front T*
and *position.* The action of the hip causes the torso to face the floor,
8-2-3 with the right leg remaining parallel. The left foot remains stationary. The arms remain in High Parallel.

cts. 9-2-3 Return to *Lateral T position* by rotating the right hip outward.

cts. 10-2-3 *Return the torso to an upright position and* return the right leg to *Table position.* The right arm reaches toward the ceiling and both arms return to 2nd.

cts. 11-2-3 *Lift and rotate the right leg out* by dropping the right hip to level the pelvis and raise the left heel to readjust the standing foot to natural turn out. The right leg remains bent and the knee lifts as high as possible.

cts. 12-2-3 Keeping the right leg bent, *bring the leg forward.* The arms move forward to Middle Parallel, palms facing down.

cts. 13-2-3 *Walk forward,* stepping right, left, right. The palms rotate to face each other and the arms lower slowly to Natural Low.

Repeat to the other side.

Back T Balance

Adv.; Thirteen 3's on each side; count at 55 B.P.M.

Begin stage left, facing stage right, the feet in Natural 1st, the arms in Natural Low.

cts. 1-2-3 Parallel the right leg and *lift the right knee* forward until the right thigh is parallel to the ceiling. The right foot is pointed directly below the knee. (The thigh and the shin are forming a right angle.) The arms lift forward to Middle Parallel, palms facing down.

cts. 2-2-3 Keeping the right leg at a right angle, *open the leg to 2nd.* The arms open to 2nd.

cts. 3-2-3 Lift and rotate the right leg to *Table position.* Slightly lift and rotate the standing heel outward so the toes point directly sideward and the standing leg is completely turned out as the right leg is rotating to *Table position.* Lower the left heel.

cts. 4-2-3 On a sustained breath, *pull up.*

cts. 5-2-3 Extend the right leg and tilt the torso to *Lateral T position.*

and 6-2-3 The right arm reaches toward the ceiling to meet the left arm in High Parallel.

cts. 7-2-3 Rotate the right hip outward ¼ so that the body is in *Back T*
and *position.* The action of the hip causes the torso to face the ceiling,
8-2-3 with the right leg remaining parallel. The left foot is permitted to adjust to establish the Back T position. The arms remain in High Parallel.

cts. 9-2-3 Return to *Lateral T position* by rotating the right hip inward and adjusting the standing foot to fully turned out position.

cts. 10-2-3 *Return the torso to an upright position and* return the right leg to *Table position.* Both arms return to 2nd. The right arm reaches toward the ceiling and lowers to 2nd.

cts. 11-2-3 Lift and *rotate the right leg out* by dropping the right hip to level the pelvis and raise the left heel to adjust the standing leg to natural turn out. The right leg remains bent and the knee lifts as high as possible.

cts. 12-2-3 Keeping the right leg bent, *bring the leg forward.* The arms move forward to Middle Parallel, palms facing down.

cts. 13-2-3 *Walk forward,* stepping right, left, right. The palms rotate to face each other and the arms lower slowly to Natural Low.

Repeat to the other side.

Advanced T Balance

Adv.; Sixteen 3's on each side; count at 55 B.P.M.

Begin stage left, facing stage right, the feet in Natural 1st, the arms in Natural Low.

cts. 1-2-3 Parallel the right leg and *lift the right knee forward* until the right thigh is parallel to the ceiling. The right foot is pointed directly below the knee. (The thigh and the shin are forming a right angle.) The arms lift forward to Middle Parallel, palms facing down.

cts. 2-2-3 Keeping the right leg at a right angle, *open the leg to 2nd.* The arms open to 2nd.

cts. 3-2-3 Lift and rotate the right leg to *Table position.* Slightly lift and rotate the standing heel outward so the toes point directly sideward and the standing leg is completely turned out as the right leg is rotating to *Table position.* Lower the left heel.

cts. 4-2-3 On a sustained breath, *pull up.*

cts. 5-2-3 Extend the right leg and tilt the torso to *Lateral T position.* The
and right arm reaches toward the ceiling and continues until it meets the
6-2-3 left arm in High Parallel.

cts. 7-2-3 Rotate the right hip inward ¼ so that the body is in *Front T*
and *position.* The action of the hip causes the torso to face the floor,
8-2-3 with the right leg remaining parallel. The left foot remains
stationary. The arms remain in High Parallel.

cts. 9-2-3 Return to *Lateral T position* by rotating the right hip outward.

cts. 10-2-3 Rotate the right hip outward ¼ so that the body is in *Back T*
and *position.* The action of the hip causes the torso to face the ceiling,
11-2-3 with the right leg remaining parallel. The left foot is permitted to
adjust to establish the *Back T position.* The arms remain in High
Parallel.

cts. 12-2-3 Return to *Lateral T position* by rotating the right hip inward and
adjusting the standing foot to a fully turned out position.

cts. 13-2-3 *Return the torso to an upright position and* return the right leg to
Table position. The right arm reaches toward the ceiling and both
arms return to 2nd.

cts. 14-2-3 *Lift and rotate the right leg out* by dropping the right hip to level the
pelvis and raise the left heel to readjust the standing foot to natural
turn out. The right leg remains bent and the knee lifts as high as
possible.

cts. 15-2-3 Keeping the right leg bent, *bring the leg forward.* The arms move
forward to Middle Parallel, palms facing down.

cts. 16-2-3 *Walk forward,* stepping right, left, right. The palms rotate to face
each other and the arms lower slowly to Natural Low.

Repeat to the other side.

Lateral T Balance with Promenade

Adv.; Twelve 3's on each side; count at 55 B.P.M.

Begin stage left, facing stage right, the feet in Natural 1st, the arms in Natural
Low.

cts. 1-2-3 Parallel the right leg and *lift the right knee forward* until the right
thigh is parallel to the ceiling. The right foot is pointed directly
below the knee. (The thigh and the shin are forming a right angle.)
The arms lift forward to Middle Parallel, palms facing down.

cts. 2-2-3 Keeping the right leg at a right angle, *open the leg to 2nd.* The arms
open to 2nd.

cts. 3-2-3 Lift and rotate the right leg to *Table position.* Slightly lift and rotate
the standing heel outward so the toes point directly sideward and
the standing leg is completely turned out as the right leg is rotating
to *Table position.* Lower the left heel.

cts. 4-2-3 On a sustained breath, *pull up.*

cts. 5-2-3 Extend the right leg and tilt the torso to *Lateral T position.* The
and right arm reaches toward the ceiling and continues until it meets the
6-2-3 left arm in High Parallel.

cts. 7-2-3 Maintaining the position, *promenade one full turn* to the left.
and
8-2-3

cts. 9-2-3 *Return the torso to an upright position and* return the right leg to *Table position*. The right arm reaches toward the ceiling and both arms return to 2nd.

cts. 10-2-3 *Lift and rotate the right leg out* by dropping the right hip to level the pelvis. The right leg remains bent and the knee lifts as high as possible.

cts. 11-2-3 Keeping the right leg bent, *bring the leg forward*. The arms move forward to Middle Parallel, palms facing down.

cts. 12-2-3 *Walk forward,* stepping right, left, right. The palms rotate to face each other and the arms lower slowly to Natural Low.

Repeat to the other side.

Lateral T Balance with Side Fall

Int., Adv.; Ten 3's on each side; count at 55 B.P.M.

Begin center, facing downstage, the feet in Natural 1st, the arms in Natural Low.

cts. 1-2-3 Parallel the right leg and *lift the right knee forward* until the right thigh is parallel to the ceiling. The right foot is pointed directly below the knee. (The thigh and the shin are forming a right angle.) The arms lift forward to Middle Parallel, palms facing down.

cts. 2-2-3 Keeping the right leg at a right angle, *open the leg to 2nd*. The arms open to 2nd.

cts. 3-2-3 Lift and rotate the right leg to *Table position*. Slightly lift and rotate the standing heel outward so the toes point directly sideward and the standing leg is completely turned out as the right leg is rotating to *Table position*. Lower the left heel.

cts. 4-2-3 On a sustained breath, *pull up*.

cts. 5-2-3 Extend the right leg and tilt the torso to *Lateral T position*. The
and right arm reaches toward the ceiling and continues until it meets the
6-2-3 left arm in High Parallel.

cts. 7-2-3 Maintaining the position, *plié on the left leg*.

cts. 8-2-3 Maintaining the position, straighten the left leg and *turn ½ turn* to
and the right in ¼ relevé. Then bend the right leg and lower it to
9-2-3 parallel passé as the left leg bends and the body lowers to *Side Fall* to the right (see Side Fall in chapter 10).

cts. 10-2-3 *Front Recovery:* Lift the torso off the floor and center the weight onto both buttocks. The right knee bends with the right leg turned out, and the left leg is turned out and extended diagonally forward. Lift the pelvis upward and forward over the right knee, keeping the left leg straight and at hip level. Both arms reach to *Middle Parallel*. Bend the left leg and place the left foot forward on the floor, both arms open to 2nd, and shift the pelvis forward and simultaneously flex the right foot; place the ball of the right foot on the floor. Lift the torso erect and pull the left foot back to *Parallel 1st* as the arms lower to *Natural Low*.

Repeat to the other side, facing upstage.

•• • • •
Coccyx Balance Studies

Coccyx Balance

Beg., Int., Adv.; Three 3's four times; count at 60–70 B.P.M.

Begin lying prone on the floor face up, with the legs straight ahead, and the arms at the sides of the body.

cts. 1-2-3   Lift the torso and bend both legs gradually until the body is in *Coccyx Balance position;* the arms lift to Middle Parallel (see Vocabulary in Chapter 3). The torso lift is initiated by pulling in the abdominal wall. The head tilts forward by lowering the chin slightly as the feet lift slightly off the floor; both legs continue to bend until the body is in Coccyx Balance position.

cts. 2-2-3   Maintaining the Coccyx Balance position, *continue to pull up.*

cts. 3-2-3   *Lower the body to the starting position.* Initiate the lowering of the body by exhaling and pulling in the abdominal wall, which causes the lower back to touch the floor first. Both legs begin to lower and straighten gradually as the spine lowers sequentially to the floor. Then the feet and the head touch the floor at the same time and the arms lower to the sides of the body. Repeat three more times.

Coccyx Balance with Extended Legs

Beg., Int., Adv.; Seven 3's four times; count at 60–70 B.P.M.

Begin lying prone on the floor, face up, with the legs straight ahead, the arms at the sides of the body.

cts. 1-2-3   Lift the torso and bend both legs gradually until the body is in Coccyx Balance position; the arms lift to Middle Parallel.

cts. 2-2-3   Maintaining the Coccyx Balance position, *continue to pull up.*

cts. 3-2-3   *Extend both legs* until they are straight, with pointed feet reaching on an upward diagonal. The back remains straight. The torso and legs form a V.

cts. 4-2-3   Maintaining the V position, *continue to pull up.*

cts. 5-2-3   *Bend both legs* and return to Coccyx Balance position.

cts. 6-2-3   Maintaining the Coccyx Balance position, *continue to pull up.*

cts. 7-2-3   *Lower the body to the starting position.* Repeat three more times.

Coccyx Balance with Single Leg Extensions

Beg., Int., Adv.; Eight 3's twice, count at 60–70 B.P.M.

Begin lying prone on the floor, legs straight ahead, arms at sides.

cts. 1-2-3   Lift the torso and bend both legs gradually until the body is in *Coccyx Balance position*. The arms lift to Middle Parallel.

cts. 2-2-3   Maintaining the Coccyx Balance position, *continue to pull up*.

cts. 3-2-3   *Extend the left leg* until straight, with pointed foot reaching on an upward diagonal. The back remains straight.

cts. 4-2-3   *Extend the right leg* until straight, with pointed foot reaching on an upward diagonal. The back remains straight.

cts. 5-2-3   *Bend the right leg* to the previous position.

cts. 6-2-3   *Bend the left leg* to the previous position.

cts. 7-2-3   Maintaining the Coccyx Balance position, *continue to pull up*.

cts. 8-2-3   *Lower the body to the starting position*. Repeat once more except on counts 3-2-3 extend the right leg; extend the left leg on counts 4-2-3; bend the left leg on counts 5-2-3 and bend the right leg on counts 6-2-3.

Coccyx Balance with ½ Descent (Lower Back Press) and Full Descent with Straight Legs

Int., Adv.; Ten 3's four times; count at 60–70 B.P.M.

Begin lying prone on the floor, legs straight ahead, arms at sides.

cts. 1-2-3   Lift the torso and bend both legs gradually until the body is in *Coccyx Balance position;* the arms lift to Middle Parallel.

cts. 2-2-3   Maintaining the *Coccyx Balance position, continue to pull up*.

cts. 3-2-3   *Extend both legs* until they are straight, with pointed feet reaching on an upward diagonal. The back remains straight. The torso and legs form a V.

cts. 4-2-3   Maintaining the V position, *continue to pull up*.

cts. 5-2-3   *½ Descent:* Initiate the lowering of the body by exhaling and pulling in the abdominal wall, which causes the lower back to touch the floor. The legs remain straight as they lower to an inch from the floor and the arms remain in Middle Parallel.

cts. 6-2-3   Maintaining the ½ Descent position, *continue to press the lower back into the floor.*

cts. 7-2-3   *Return to Coccyx Balance position with extended legs.*

cts. 8-2-3   Maintaining the Coccyx Balance position with the legs straight, *continue to pull up.*

cts. 9-2-3 and 10-2-3   *Lower the body to the starting position.* The legs remain straight as the spine and the legs lower to the floor. Repeat three more times.

Note: *The Descent with straight legs is not recommended for beginning students. Also, special attention should be paid so that the lower back touches first; then the head, feet, and arms.*

Coccyx Balance with Hip Lift

Beg., Int., Adv.; Seven 3's twice; count at 60–70 B.P.M.

Begin lying prone on the floor, face up, with the legs straight ahead and the arms at the sides of the body.

cts. 1-2-3 Lift the torso and bend both legs gradually until the body is in *Coccyx Balance position;* the arms lift to Middle Parallel.

cts. 2-2-3 Maintaining the Coccyx Balance position, *continue to pull up.*

cts. 3-2-3 *Lift the right hip* so that the right buttock leaves the floor. This causes the weight to shift to the left side; the arms remain in Middle Parallel.

cts. 4-2-3 *Center the weight* by returning the right buttock to the floor.

cts. 5-2-3 *Lift the left hip* so that the left buttock leaves the floor. This causes the weight to shift to the right side; the arms remain in Middle Parallel.

cts. 6-2-3 *Center the weight* by returning the left buttock to the floor.

cts. 7-2-3 *Lower the body to the starting position.* Repeat once more except on counts 3-2-3 lift the left hip and on counts 5-2-3 lift the right hip.

Coccyx Balance with Pietà Position

See Fortification No. 6.

Coccyx Balance with the Legs in 2nd

Int., Adv.; Nine 3's four times; count at 60–70 B.P.M.

Begin lying prone on the floor, face up, with the legs straight and the arms at the sides of the body.

cts. 1-2-3 Lift the torso and bend both legs gradually until the body is in *Coccyx Balance position;* the arms lift to Middle Parallel.

cts. 2-2-3 Maintaining the Coccyx Balance position, *continue to pull up.*

cts. 3-2-3 *Extend both legs* until they are straight, with pointed feet reaching on an upward diagonal. The back remains straight. The arms lift to High Parallel. The torso and legs form a V.

cts. 4-2-3 Maintaining the V position, *continue to pull up.*

cts. 5-2-3 Keeping the back straight, *open both legs to Natural 2nd;* the arms lower to 2nd.

cts. 6-2-3 Return to the V position.

cts. 7-2-3 *Bend both legs* to return to the Coccyx Balance position; the arms lower to Middle Parallel.

cts. 8-2-3 Maintaining the Coccyx Balance position, *continue to pull up*.

cts. 9-2-3 Lower the body to the starting position. Repeat three more times.

Figure 4 Study

Int., Adv.; Count at 55 B.P.M.

Section A

Four 4's twice, six 4's twice, eight 4's twice, Transition No. 1 in 3 counts.

Begin center facing downstage, the feet in Parallel 2nd, the arms in 2nd.

Four 4's

cts. 1-2-3-4 On count 1, lightly accented, *make ¼ turn to the left* on the right leg to face stage left and place the outside of the left anklebone across the front of the right shin. The left leg is turned out fully and the left foot is pointed and slightly off the floor. The right foot is naturally turned out. The right arm lowers to Natural Low. On counts 2-4, slowly slide the left foot up the front of the right leg as high as possible. The legs are forming a *Standing Figure 4 position*. At the same time, the right arm lifts to Middle Parallel, palm facing the ceiling, and bends to Closed Egyptian position. The left arm remains in 2nd.

cts. 2-2-3-4 *Plié* on the right leg and rotate the torso to face the left upstage diagonal. The head and focus move to the left downstage diagonal. The arms remain in place and move with the rotation of the torso.

cts. 3-2-3-4 *Straighten the right leg and rotate the torso to face stage left.* The head and focus move to stage left. The arms remain in place and move with the rotation of the torso.

cts. 4-2-3-4 On counts 1-3, slowly slide the left foot down the front of the right leg until the toes are slightly off the floor and extend the right arm up and lower it forward, palm facing the ceiling, to Natural Low. On count 4, lightly accented, *make ¼ turn* to the right on the right leg and place the left foot in Parallel 2nd. The right foot rotates to Parallel 2nd. The right arm lifts to 2nd.

Repeat the above four 4's to the other side.

Six 4's

cts. 1-2-3-4 Repeat measure 1 of the four 4's phrase above: Make a ¼ *turn* to the left on the right leg and place the outside of the left anklebone across the front of the right shin and slowly slide the left foot up the front of the right leg. The leg is forming a *Standing Figure 4 position*. Both arms remain in 2nd.

cts. 2-2-3-4 Lower the right arm and grasp the top of the left foot. *Pull the left foot up and toward the center of the body.* The left knee continues to press back so that the turnout is maintained or increased in the left hip joint.

cts. 3-2-3-4 Maintaining the position established above, *plié* on the right leg *and rotate the torso* to face the left upstage diagonal. The head and the focus move to the left downstage diagonal.

cts. 4-2-3-4 Maintaining the position established above, *straighten* the right leg *and rotate the torso* to face stage left. The head and the focus move to stage left.

cts. 5-2-3-4 Release the left foot and return the right arm to 2nd.

cts. 6-2-3-4 Repeat measure 4 of the four 4's phrase above: Slide the left foot down the front of the right leg and *turn* ¼ *turn* to the right on the right leg and place the left foot in Parallel 2nd. The right foot rotates to Parallel 2nd.

Repeat the above six 4's to the other side.

Eight 4's

cts. 1-2-3-4 Repeat measure 1 of the four 4's phrase above: Turn ¼ *turn* to the left on the right leg and place the outside of the left anklebone across the front of the right shin and slowly slide the left foot up the front of the right leg as high as possible. The legs are forming a *Standing Figure 4 position*. Both arms lower to Natural Low, lift forward to Middle Parallel (palms facing the ceiling), and bend to Closed Egyptian position.

cts. 2-2-3-4 *Plié* on the right leg and, rounding the torso, *place the elbows on the inside of the lower left leg.* The body lowers as far as possible with the buttocks reaching for the right heel (*Figure 4 Squat position*).

cts. 3-2-3-4 Straighten the right leg and return to *Standing Figure 4 position* with the arms in Closed Egyptian (counts 1 and 2). On counts 3 and 4 both arms reach up and extend forward (palms facing the ceiling), and lower with the palms to the floor (fingers pointing toward stage right). Simultaneously, the torso rounds and lowers forward, with the head reaching toward the right ankle.

cts. 4-2-3-4 *Plié* on the right leg and, rounding the torso, *place the elbows on the inside of the lower left leg.* The body lowers as far as possible with the buttocks reaching for the right heel (*Figure 4 Squat position*).

cts. 5-2-3-4 Repeat counts 3-2-3-4—*Standing Figure 4 position*, ending with the palms on the floor.

cts. 6-2-3-4 Repeat counts 4-2-3-4—*Figure 4 Squat position*.

cts. 7-2-3-4 Straighten the right leg and return to *Standing Figure 4 position* with the arms in Closed Egyptian.

cts. 8-2-3-4 *Slide the left foot* down the front of the right leg and place both feet in *Parallel 2nd*. Both arms reach up and lower forward (palms facing the ceiling) to Natural Low and lift to 2nd.

Repeat the eight 4's above to the other side.

Transition No. 1 in 3 counts

On count 1, turn ½ turn to the left on the left leg to face upstage with both legs in 2nd. On counts 2 and 3, make a Pivotal Descent to the right to sit on the floor in crossed-leg position facing downstage. The arms remain in 2nd. (See Chapter 8, Ascents and Descents.)

Section B

Six 3's, four 3's, four 2's, four 2's accented, transition No. 2 in 3 counts.

cts. 1-2-3   Move both arms forward to Middle Parallel with palms facing the ceiling and bend to *Closed Egyptian position*.

cts. 2-2-3   Maintaining the crossed-leg position, extend both arms up and lower them forward (palms facing the ceiling) and place the palms on the floor with the fingers pointing upstage. At the same time, round the body forward, bend the elbows, lift the buttocks off the floor, and touch the top of the head on the floor. The weight is distributed between the arms and the tops of both knees. Both legs are fully bent so that the lower legs lift off the floor and both feet point as the body rounds forward.

cts. 3-2-3   Return to the seated crossed-leg position with the arms in Closed Egyptian position.

cts. 4-2-3
and 5-2-3   Repeat measures 2 and 3 above.

cts. 6-2-3   Lift both arms to High Parallel and lower them to 2nd position.

Four 3's

> **Note:** *In the seated Laterals described below, both hips must remain on the floor.*

cts. 1-2-3   Bend the right arm to Opened Egyptian and *Lateral to the right side* until the right lower arm touches the floor. The left arm reaches to High Parallel.

cts. 2-2-3   *Center the torso* and return the arms to 2nd position.

cts. 3-2-3
and 4-2-3   Repeat measures 1 and 2 above to the other side.

Four 2's

cts. 1-2   Bend the right arm to Opened Egyptian and *Lateral to the right side* until the lower arm touches the floor. The left arm reaches to High Parallel.

cts. 2-2   *Center the torso* and return the arms to 2nd position.

cts. 3-2   Repeat measures 1 and 2 above to the other side.

and 4-2

Four 2's, Accented

cts. 1-2   On an accented count 1, bend the right arm to Opened Egyptian, *Lateral to the right side,* and touch the lower arm on the floor. *Center the torso* on the "and" count of 2. On count 2, hold the centered position.

cts. 2-2   Repeat measure 1 above—*Lateral to the left side.*

cts. 3-2   Repeat measure 1 above—*Lateral to the right side.*

cts. 4-2   Repeat measure 1 above—*Lateral to the left side.*

Transition No. 2 in 3 counts

Simultaneously, *straighten the left leg* (toes pointing and directed to stage right). Open the right knee to the right side so that the legs form a Figure 4, and place the left palm on the floor to the left of the left hip.

As the left leg straightens, *the weight shifts to the flank of the left leg.* The right leg remains bent and presses the left thigh and the right foot slides along the floor as the right knee opens to the right side. The pelvis presses forward and is aligned with the right leg, which is turned out fully from the right hip joint. The head turns to the right to focus stage right. The right arm remains in 2nd and rests lightly on the top of the right knee. The position described in transition No. 2 is the *Seated Figure 4 position.*

Section C

Three 3's twice, 6 counts accented, Transition No. 3 in 6 counts.

Three 3's

cts. 1-2-3   Keeping the legs in the Figure 4 position, lift the right heel to ¾ relevé and rotate the body to face stage left. The right palm places on the floor alongside the left palm, shoulder width apart, with the elbows straight. Keep the back straight. As the body rotates, the right heel remains touching the left thigh and the right leg continues to turn out. The left leg remains parallel and the top of the left pointed foot rolls onto the floor. The position described in 1-2-3 is the *Push-up Figure 4 position.*

cts. 2-2-3   Slide the top of the left foot back, toward stage right, causing the right heel to slide up the left thigh.

cts. 3-2-3   *Return to the Seated Figure 4 position* established in transition No. 2, maintaining the height of the right leg.

Repeat the above three 3's to the *same* side.

6 cts. accented

cts. 1-2 Keeping the legs in Figure 4 position, *lift the left hip off the floor and drive the left hip diagonally up toward the left elbow*. On count 2 drive the hips down to the right, return the left hip to the floor, and slide the left leg along the floor toward stage right. The right arm slides along the top of the right knee with the hip drive action. The head remains turned to the right, focus stage right.

ct. 3 *Bend the left leg*, and adjust the right leg *to sit in crossed-leg position facing downstage*, focus front. At the same time, bend the right arm to Opened Egyptian position and Lateral to the right side until the lower arm touches the floor. The left arm reaches to High Parallel.

ct. 4 *Center the torso* and return the arms to 2nd position.

ct. 5 *Straighten the left leg* and return to Seated Figure 4 position.

ct. 6 *Place the left palm on the floor* to the left of the left hip and turn the head to the right, focus stage right. The right arm remains in 2nd and rests lightly on the top of the right knee.

Transition No. 3 in 6 counts

cts. 1 and 2 Slide the left hip along the floor toward stage right and rotate the body to face stage left in a *Forward Lunge position* with the right leg forward. Both arms lift to Middle Parallel.

cts. 3 and 4 Straighten the right leg and *turn the body to the left to face upstage* with the legs in Wide Natural 2nd. The arms open horizontally to 2nd position.

cts. 5 and 6 *Pivotal Descent* to the left. The arms remain in 2nd.

Section D

Repeat the six 3's, four 3's, four 2's accented, transition No. 2 in 3 counts, three 3's twice, 6 counts accented, and transition No. 3 in 6 counts to the other side. Repeat transition No. 3 in 6 counts again, transition No. 4 in 3 counts twice, transition No. 5 in 3 counts, final cadence on the upbeat.

Transition No. 4 in 3 counts twice

ct. 1 Slide the right hip along the floor toward stage left and rotate the body to face stage right in a *Forward Lunge position* with the left leg forward. Both arms lift to Middle Parallel.

ct. 2 Straighten the left leg and turn the body to the right to face upstage with the legs in *Wide Natural 2nd*. The arms open horizontally to 2nd position.

ct. 3 *Figure 4 Descent.* Twist the torso ½ turn to the right as the right leg pivots to the right and turns out, and the right knee bends. The left leg remains straight and rotates inward, and the left foot flexes. The inner thighs of both legs are touching. The head turns to the right, with the focus over the right hand. Deepen the plié on the right leg, and slide the left foot along the floor toward stage left. The left arm lowers to a perpendicular line to the floor, to help ease the body down to the floor, and the right arm remains in 2nd and rests lightly on top of the right knee. The left hip touches the floor and the body ends in *Seated Figure 4 position.*

cts. 2-2-3 Repeat to the other side.

Transition No. 5 in 3 counts

ct. 1 Rotate the body to face stage right in a *Forward Lunge position* with the left leg forward. Both arms lift to Middle Parallel.

ct. 2 Straighten the left leg and turn the body to the right to face upstage with the legs in *Wide Natural 2nd.* The arms open horizontally to 2nd.

ct. 3 *Turn to the right* on the right leg to face downstage with the legs in *Wide Natural 2nd.* The arms remain in 2nd.

Final Cadence: upbeat

Move the left leg to *end in Parallel 1st.* Both arms move through Middle Parallel, palms facing up, and end in Closed Egyptian position.

· · · ·
Prelude Studies

Prelude 1

Beg., Int., Adv.; five 2's to each side; count at 75 B.P.M.

Begin center, facing downstage, the feet in Parallel 1st, the arms in Natural Low. (All counts accented except the 4th measure.)

One 2

ct. 1 *Turn out* both feet to Natural 1st.

ct. 2 Keeping the weight on the left foot, *turn the right leg parallel and move it behind you,* with the ball of the foot on the floor as the right arm reaches forward, and the left arm reaches to the side, with both palms facing the floor.

Two 2

ct. 1 *Brush* the right foot on the floor, *and lift the right leg* as high as possible directly forward. Arms remain. (The right arm should be on the outside of the right leg.)

ct. 2 *Return the right leg behind you* as in count 2 of the 1st measure.

Three 2

Same as the 2nd measure. Brush and lift the right leg forward as high as possible and return it behind you.

Four 2

Brush a turned-out right foot into Natural 1st, then *describe a Figure 8.* Smoothly move a pointed right foot diagonally across the body, open it to the side to complete the forward loop of the Figure 8, then brush through Natural 1st and behind the back to move diagonally across the body to complete the back loop of the Figure 8. The right foot ends turned out and pointed to the side. The right arm opens to 2nd at the beginning of the measure. The hips indicate a Figure 8 in coordination with the foot.

Five 2

> ct. 1 *Return the right foot* to Natural 1st.
> ct. 2 The *feet return to Parallel* 1st and the *arms lower* to Natural Low.

Repeat to the other side.

Prelude 2

Int., Adv.; Seven 6's on each side; count at 60 B.P.M.

Begin center, facing downstage, the feet in Wide Natural 2nd, the arms in Natural Low, the head lowered with the focus down.

> ct. 1 *Rotate the arms outward and cup the hands.*
> cts. 2-3-4 *Relevé and raise the arms sideward to form a wide V shape.* The head lifts and the eyes focus to the upward diagonal.
> cts. 5-6 *Release Swing with plié* beginning Lateral right side, going through Lateral left side. *The hands uncup and the arms lift rounded, circling the head. Lift the right leg to Table position* as the arms continue the clockwise circle. The right arm ends in 2nd. The left arm bends and ends with the fingers in front of the sternum.
> cts. 2-2-3 *Extend the right leg and both arms toward stage right.*
> ct. 4 *Step into Deep Forward Lunge with the right foot* facing stage right. The arms are in Middle Parallel.
> cts. 5-6 Keeping the body low, *Release Swing with plié to face stage left and lift the torso erect as the right leg lifts to back attitude.* The arms lift to High Parallel.
> cts. 3-2-3 *Relevé in back attitude with the arms in High Parallel.*
> ct. 4 With a strong accent, bring the right leg forward to *Forward Table.* The arms remain parallel and reach toward the right knee with the palms facing each other.
> ct. 5 *Step forward to stage left with the right foot into Deep Forward Lunge.* The arms reach to Middle Parallel.

ct. 6 *Release Swing with plié* and end with the right leg lifted in back attitude, with the arms in High Parallel facing stage right.

Tempo increases slightly.

cts. 4-2-3 Maintaining the right leg in back attitude, *twist the torso to the right.*

cts. 4-5-6 Maintaining the right leg in back attitude, *twist the torso to the left.*

cts. 5-2-3 Repeat the twist to the right.

cts. 4-5-6 Repeat the twist to the left.

Tempo returns to original meter.

cts. 6-2-3- Leaving the right leg lifted, *circle the torso through Lateral right*
4-5-6 *side, Release Swing (no plié), and Lateral left side, and turn the body ¼ turn to the left to face downstage.* The arms circle a full clockwise circle to the right and lower sideward to 2nd. The right leg remains in Table.

ct. 7- Lower and place the right foot in Wide Natural 2nd and *pull out the body to Flat Back left side.*

2-3-4- *Release Swing with plié, open the torso to Lateral right side with the arms in High Parallel, and bring the body erect as the arms continue to circle to the left and lower to Natural Low.*

5-6 *Circle the left arm across the body, to the right, up, and to the left, and lower again to Natural Low.* Repeat to the other side.

Prelude 3

Beg., Int., Adv.; 12 counts twice, 8 counts twice, 4 counts twice, 12 counts on each side; count at 60 B.P.M.

Begin in High Lateral (see Vocabulary in chapter 3) to the right.

12 cts.

ct. 1 In a circular motion, *drop the left arm* across to the right as an impetus *for a full circle of the arm* ending in High Lateral. The arm is slightly rounded at the bottom of the circle. (Keep the arm extended.)

"and" The *left arm bends sharply,* with the left fingers pointing to the right arm and the palm down.

ct. 2 The *head drops sharply* to the right. Do not permit the head to touch the right arm or shoulder.

cts. 3-8 Maintaining the legs and arms, *gradually lower to Lateral* right side. The hips continue to shift to the left as the upper torso lowers.

ct. 9 *Demi-plié* with both feet in Natural 2nd. The back is straight and the *torso is tilted slightly forward, going into Flat Back Forward.* The right arm rotates in, maintaining the curve; the left arm moves

Figure 27. Prelude 3; begin in High Lateral

across the body, lowers, and opens side. Both arms are slightly rounded and both palms are facing the floor.

cts. 10-12 Shift the weight onto the left bent leg and *turn one full turn to the left,* keeping the back straight and in Flat Back Forward. The arms remain slightly rounded and in 2nd. The right leg straightens and the right big toe traces a complete circle on the floor. The right arm moves diagonally across the body, the left arm lifts, and both the arms and the torso *end in High Lateral to the left.*

Repeat to the other side.

8 cts.

cts. 1-2 Same as 12-count phrase—*circle left arm and drop head.*
cts. 3-5 Same as counts 3-8 in 12-count phrase—*Lateral right side.*

ct. 6 Same as counts 9-10 in 12-count phrase—*plié and turn to the left* in established position.

cts. 7-8 Same as counts 11-12 in 12-count phrase—*pull out to High Lateral to the left.*

Repeat to the other side.

4 cts.

cts. 1-2 Same as 12-count phrase—*circle left arm and drop head.* (Please note: The torso must begin to lower on count 2.)

ct. 3 Same as counts 9-10 in 12-count phrase—*plié and turn to the left* in established position.

ct. 4 Same as counts 11-12 in 12-count phrase—*pull out to High Lateral to the left.*

Repeat to the other side.

12 cts.

After completion of the last turn in 4 counts *the body slowly attenuates into Lateral T for a full 12 counts.*

> **Note:** *The velocity of the turn changes as the counts are reduced.*
>
> **Note:** *The Lateral T is the resolution of the study.*
>
> **Note:** *The entire study should be repeated, beginning in High Lateral to the left.*

Prelude 4

Int., Adv.; Eight 3's and eight 4's to each side; count at 55 B.P.M.

Begin center, facing downstage, the feet in Parallel 1st, the arms in Natural Low.

cts. 1-2-3 *Lift the right knee* forward; the right thigh is parallel to the ceiling, the right foot is pointed directly below the knee. (The leg is forming a right angle.)

on 2-3 of the 1st measure The *right arm lifts* forward to Middle Parallel, palm facing down.

on 3 of the 1st measure The *left arm lifts* forward to Middle Parallel, palm facing down.

cts. 2-2-3 The right palm presses down and reaches back as *the torso tilts forward into Flat Back* and the right leg extends behind the body into *Forward T* position. The right hand is directly below and close to the right thigh.

cts. 3-2-3 Rotate the pelvis ¼ turn to face stage right in *Lateral T* position.

(The standing foot does not move.) The left arm reaches forward to downstage and the palm faces up. The right arm rotates so it is parallel to the leg and the palm is down at the side of the thigh.

cts. 4-2-3   Rotate the pelvis ¼ turn and plié on the left leg; bend the right leg into Standing Stag position (parallel attitude). Simultaneously, the torso lifts erect and twists to face stage left, the upper back arches, and the sternum lifts up and forward. The arms move to Opened Egyptian as the body is twisting. The head moves with the torso and ends with the focus stage left. (The standing foot does not move.)

cts. 5-2-3   *Accent* the first beat of the 5th measure by *dropping the head and the torso straight forward as both legs bend and rotate outward.* The right leg lowers and turns out; the inside of the right pointed foot touches the outside of the left leg below the calf. The arms drop forward with the upper body and are slightly rounded (demi-2nd). Hold counts 2 and 3.

cts. 6-2-3   The *body raises* to a vertical position by rolling up through the spine, *the right knee lifts,* and the right pointed foot touches the inside of the left knee. The arms extend to 2nd.

cts. 7-2-3   The *right leg extends to 2nd* as high as possible. On a breath, *relevé* on the standing leg; the arms round as the palms turn to face the ceiling. The head lifts with the focus on the upward diagonal.

ct 8-   Lower the right leg and the left heel and bend the right knee to *place the ball of the right foot across and on the outside of the standing foot.* Palms face down. Center the head.

2-   Relevé on both legs as you *pivot* to the left, lowering the heels and adjusting the feet to *end in Natural 1st* facing downstage.

3   The arms lower to Natural Low.

Eight 4's, tempo increases; count at 80 B.P.M.

ct. 1   Keeping the right leg straight and turned out, *step to the right downstage diagonal* with the torso tilted slightly forward. At the same time, extend the left leg behind the body with the foot turned out and pointed with the toe touching the floor. Both arms reach diagonally downward, palms facing down.

cts. 2-3-4   Continue to tilt the torso forward and lift the left leg behind the
and   body (as in a cantilever). The wrists pulse down as the fingers move
2-2-3-4   upward on each beat (the fingers are slightly rounded. End in *Forward T position,* the arms in High Parallel, palms facing down.

cts. 3-2-   Continue to *cantilever* and *plié on the standing* leg until the hands
3-4   are reaching to the downward diagonal and the left foot is reaching to the upward diagonal.

cts. 4-2- Straighten the standing leg, rotate the pelvis, lift and rotate the
3-4 torso, and lower and rotate the left leg to end in *Lateral T position*
and *facing downstage.* The standing leg must rotate out fully in order to
5-2-3-4 end facing downstage. The arms remain in High Parallel; the palms
rotate to face each other.

cts. 6-2- *Lifts the torso upright as the left leg rotates out and lifts as high as*
3-4 *possible to the side.* The right arm rotates to 2nd, palm facing
down; the left arm lifts to High Parallel and lowers sideward to 2nd,
palm facing down.

cts. 7-2- *Hold.*
3-4

cts. 8-2- *Lower the left leg to Natural 1st* on the 1st 3 counts. On the 4th
3-4 count, *the toes close inward to Parallel 1st.* The arms lower to
Natural Low using the full measure of 4.

Repeat to the other side.

Prelude 5

Int., Adv.; 10 cts., 6 cts., 8 cts. on each side; count at 55 B.P.M.

Begin center, facing downstage, in High Lateral to the left.

10 cts.

ct. 1 Drop the right arm as an impetus for a *full circle of the arm,* ending
in High Lateral. The arm is slightly rounded at the bottom of the
circle.

"and" *The right arm bends sharply,* forming a right angle.

ct. 2 *The head drops sharply to the left.* Do not permit the head to touch
the left arm or shoulder.

cts. 3 and 4 *Drop to the left and Release Swing* with plié and *turn ½ turn* to the
right on a straight right leg. The left leg is parallel, with the left foot
pointed and touching the inside of the right knee on the ½ turn.
The elbows are in, at the sides of the body, lower arms forward,
forming a right angle, palms facing up. The head is tilted forward,
the focus down.

"and" *Reach into High Lateral to the right.*
(accented)

cts. 5 and 6 Repeat counts 3 and 4 to the other side—*drop, Release Swing* and
turn ½ turn.

cts. 7-10 *The right foot* slides along the inside of the left leg as it *lowers into Natural 1st.*

6 cts.

ct. 1 In a simultaneous action, *the body turns to face the left upstage*
(accented) diagonal by pivoting on the left foot as the arms reach to Middle
Parallel. The head centers and "spots" to the left upstage diagonal.

ct. 2 Step into *Deep Forward Lunge* with the right leg forward.

ct. 3 *Hold.*

ct. 4 Pull the right foot back *into Parallel 1st;* arms lower to Natural Low.

ct. 5 Pivot on the left foot to the right and step with the right foot naturally turned out to the right downstage diagonal; the left foot points and the left leg lifts behind to a very low arabesque. The right palm rotates down and the right arm swings horizontally to the right downstage diagonal. The left palm rotates to face down and reaches behind the body to the left upstage diagonal.

ct. 6 Swing the left arm horizontally to the right downstage diagonal and tap (kiss) the inside of the right wrist (on the "and") with the inside of left wrist. This causes the right arm to swing horizontally to 2nd and the body to turn to the right to face downstage. The left arm remains forward of the body on the turn.

8 cts.

ct. 1 *Turn the body to the left to face upstage.* The standing leg turns out naturally; the left leg remains naturally turned out and in place in the air. Rotate the left hip outward until the hips are squared off. The arms lift to High Parallel. This count ends with the left leg forward, the body facing upstage, and the arms in High Parallel.

cts. 2 and 3 *The upper body rounds over as the extended left leg lifts.* The arms and the torso are parallel to the extended left leg.

ct. 4 *Plié* on the right leg and continue extending the left leg and rounding over.

ct. 5 Open the body to *High Lateral right.*

cts. 6 and 7 Drop to the right and *Release Swing* with plié and turn 1½ turns to the left ending in *High Lateral left.*

ct. 8 Drop to the left and *Release Swing* with plié into *High Lateral right.*

Repeat to the other side.

Prelude 6

Int., Adv.; Two 8's on each side; count at 55 B.P.M.

Begin center, facing downstage, in High Lateral left.

1st 8

ct. 1 Same as Preludes 3 and 5—*circle right arm.*

"and" Same as Preludes 3 and 5—*bend elbow sharply.*

ct. 2 Same as Preludes 3 and 5—*drop head toward left arm.*

cts. 3 and 4 Maintaining the legs and arms, *lower to Lateral* left side. The hips continue to shift to the right as the upper torso lowers.

"and"   Drop the body center, moving through Flat Back left side, opening the right foot wider into a Wide Natural 2nd.

ct. 5   *Roll up through the spine* to Flat Back Back Bend position; both knees are bent, the right foot is in relevé, the arms are in Opened Egyptian, and the focus is diagonally up.

ct. 6   *Hold.*

cts. 7 and 8   Drop to the left and Release Swing with plié (the right foot lowers), moving through Flat Back left side, and ending in High Lateral left.

2nd 8

ct. 1   Shift the weight onto the left foot and *swivel to the left* (the feet do not move) to face the upstage right diagonal. The legs remain straight and the right foot points and pronates slightly. (There is no weight on the right foot). The torso moves to High Lateral left.

ct. 2   *Fall into Side Lunge* on the right foot to the left front diagonal. The torso is tilted to the right on the diagonal. The right elbow cuts to the inside of the right rib cage. The left arm is in 2nd. The focus is to the palm of the right hand and the head is in profile.

ct. 3   Push off the right foot, lift the torso erect, lift the *right leg to back attitude* and *turn left* to face the right downstage diagonal. The right arm extends to 2nd. The head centers and the focus is to the right downstage diagonal.

ct. 4   *Hold.*

ct. 5   Extend the body to Lateral T position.

ct. 6   Moving through Flat Back left, Release Swing into plié, lift the torso erect, and turn 1¼ turns to the right on the right leg to face upstage; the left leg lifts to low arabesque. As the body lifts erect from the Release Swing and turns to the right, the right arm reaches to the right upstage diagonal, palm facing down. The left arm reaches to the left downstage diagonal, palm facing down. Then the left arm swings horizontally to the right and taps (kisses) the inside of the right wrist with the inside of the left wrist, causing the right arm to open to 2nd. The action of the wrist tap motivates the turn. The left arm remains forward of the body on the turn. (The sequence for count 6 is Release Swing, arabesque, tap the wrist, turn.)

ct. 7   Center the torso and lower the left foot to Natural 2nd. Both arms lift to High Parallel.

ct. 8   Moving through High Lateral left, Release Swing with plié into High Lateral right.

Repeat to the other side facing upstage.

• • • • •
Percussive Stroke Study

Preparation No. 1

Beg.; two 4's repeated four times; count at 65 B.P.M.

Begin center stage, facing downstage, the feet in Natural 1st, the arms in 2nd.

cts. 1-2-3-4 Rotate the right arm outward as the torso leans slightly to the right. *The right elbow bends, and lowers to touch the outside of the left knee* as the torso bends forward, through Flat Back, and rounds over and beyond the left leg. The right palm remains up, and the right arm indicates a downward curve. The pelvis rotates back and to the right, to permit the right elbow to touch the outside of the left knee. The left arm rotates inward, and the fingers point straight up toward the ceiling. The head is turned to the left, and is inverted. The focus is upstage.

cts. 2-2-3-4 Lift the torso on an upward curve and return the body to the starting position. The right arm rotates inward and the right elbow opens to 2nd, with the palm facing the floor, as the right arm extends to 2nd. The left arm rotates inward and lifts to 2nd.

Repeat to the other side.

Repeat both sides again.

Figure 28. Percussive Stroke Study, Preparation No. 1, ct. 1

This preparation may be repeated with 2 counts or 1 count for each 4 counts described above.

Preparation No. 2

For first phrase of Percussive Stroke Study

Beg.; 4 cts. repeated four times; count at 65 B.P.M.

ct. 1 *The right elbow strikes to the outside of the left knee,* as described above in counts 1-2-3-4 of preparation No. 1.

"and" *The left arm swoops back, down, and forward* to the left downstage diagonal. The right palm turns to face the floor, and *the right arm reaches toward the left downstage diagonal,* and ends on top of and across the left hand. *The torso lifts* to a high diagonal line with the head erect, and the focus is to the left downstage diagonal. The arms should be parallel to the floor.

ct. 2 *Open the right foot to Natural 2nd* as the right arm slices across the body to 2nd and the torso centers. The right arm remains straight.

ct. 3 Hold the established position.

ct. 4 *Close the right foot to Natural 1st* by pointing it to Natural 2nd and sliding the foot on the floor.

Repeat to the other side.

Repeat both sides again.

Preparation No. 3

For first phrase of Percussive Stroke Study

Beg., Int., Adv.; 18 cts. repeated 4 times; count at 75 B.P.M.

cts. 1 and 2 Same as count 1 in preparation No. 2—*touch the right elbow to the outside of the left knee.*

cts. 3 and 4 Same as "and" in preparation No. 2—*the torso and both arms end reaching to the left downstage diagonal.*

cts. 5 and 6 Same as count 2 in preparation No. 2—*open the right foot to Natural 2nd, and slice the right arm across the body.*

cts. 7 and 8 Without moving the pelvis, *twist the upper torso to the right,* and pull the right elbow back as far as possible, keeping the right arm at shoulder height and parallel to the floor. The left arm remains straight, and the head remains centered on the spine and follows the twist of the torso.

cts. 9 and 10 Without moving the pelvis, *twist the upper torso to the left,* and pull the left elbow back as far as possible, keeping the left arm at shoulder height and parallel to the floor. The right arm remains bent and parallel to the floor. The head remains centered on the spine and follows the twist of the torso.

cts. 11   *Lateral the torso to the right,* allowing the pelvis to shift, as the right
and 12   elbow crosses behind the back, reaching toward the middle of the
         lower spine, with the right palm facing the ceiling. The right
         forearm remains parallel to the floor, and the head turns to the
         right, and down, so the focus is to the palm of the right hand. The
         left arm is in High Parallel.

cts. 13   *Lateral the torso to the left,* allowing the pelvis to shift, as the left
and 14   elbow pulls across the front of the body, reaching toward the navel,
         with the palm facing the ceiling. The left forearm remains parallel to
         the floor, and the head turns to the left, and down, so the focus is to
         the palm of the left hand. The right arm is in High Parallel.

cts. 15   *Lateral the torso to the right,* allowing the pelvis to shift. The left
and 16   arm extends to meet the right arm in High Parallel.

cts. 17   *Lateral the torso to the left,* allowing the pelvis to shift. The arms
and 18   remain in High Parallel.

Repeat to the other side without bringing the torso center, then repeat to both
sides again.

1st Phrase of Percussive Stroke Study

Beg., Int., Adv.; 7 cts. repeated four times; count at 65 B.P.M.

Begin center stage, facing downstage, the feet in Natural 1st, the arms in 2nd.

ct. 1   *Strike the right elbow to the outside of the left knee,* as described
        above.

"and"   *The torso and both arms end reaching to the left downstage
        diagonal,* as described above.

ct. 2   *Open the right foot to Natural 2nd,* as the right arm slices across the
        body to 2nd.

ct. 3   *Twist the upper torso to the right,* and pull the right elbow back as
        far as possible, as described above.

"and"   *Twist the upper torso to the left,* and pull the left elbow back as far
        as possible, as described above.

ct. 4   *Lateral the torso to the right,* as the right elbow. crosses behind the
        back, reaching toward the middle of the lower spine, as described
        above.

ct. 5   *Lateral the torso to the left,* as the left elbow pulls across toward the
        navel, as described above.

ct. 6   *Lateral the torso to the right,* arms in High Parallel, as described
        above.

ct. 7   *Lateral the torso to the left,* arms in High Parallel, as described
        above.

Repeat to the other side, then repeat both sides again.

Preparation

For second phrase of Percussive Stroke Study

Int., Adv.; 18 cts. repeated four times; count at 65 B.P.M.

The starting position is the final position of the 1st phrase.

cts. 1 and 2   *Touch the right elbow to the outside of the left knee* as described above.

cts. 3 and 4   *Lift the torso on an upward curve* and turn to the right on the right leg to face upstage. The left leg lifts to low arabesque, and both arms lift to High Parallel.

cts. 5-8   *Tilt the torso forward and lift the left leg to high arabesque* until both hands are on the floor.

cts. 9 and 10   *Raise the torso erect,* and lift the arms to High Parallel. Lower the left leg, and point.

cts. 11 and 12   *Turn the torso left to face downstage,* and place the left foot on the floor to Natural 4th position.

cts. 13 and 14   Keeping the weight centered, pivot on the balls of the feet, and *turn the body to the right to face upstage.* The arms remain in High Parallel.

cts. 15 and 16   Keeping the weight centered, pivot on the balls of the feet, and *turn the body to the left to face downstage.*

cts. 17 and 18   Point the right foot back, *and close it to Natural 1st,* as the arms lower to 2nd.

Repeat to the other side, then repeat to both sides again.

Preparation

For fourth phrase of Percussive Stroke Study

Int., Adv.; 12 cts. repeated four times; count at 65 B.P.M.

Begin center facing downstage, the feet in Parallel 2nd, the arms in Closed Egyptian.

cts. 1 and 2   *Lower the head forward toward the chest,* and pull both elbows down, back, and up.

cts. 3 and 4   *Center the torso,* and return the arms to Closed Egyptian.

cts. 5 and 6   *Lower the head forward toward the navel,* rounding the back, and pull both elbows down, back, and up.

cts. 7 and 8   *Center the torso,* and return the arms to Closed Egyptian.

cts. 9 and 10   *Lower the head and the torso forward to the knees,* rounding the back, and pull both elbows down, back, and up toward downstage.

cts. 11 and 12   *Center the torso,* and return the arms to Closed Egyptian.

Repeat three more times.

The above preparation may be repeated with reduced counts—with 1 count for each movement described above, or with 1 count for the movement to the chest and a rebound on the upbeat, etc.

Percussive Stroke Study

Int., Adv.; 7 cts. 6 times, 4 cts. 4 times, 4 cts. twice; count at 65 B.P.M.

Begin center, facing downstage, the feet in Natural 1st, the arms in 2nd.

Phrase 1

cts. 1-7 See above—1st phrase of Percussive Stroke Study.

cts. 1-7 Repeat 1st phrase of Percussive Stroke Study to the left side.

Phrase 2

ct. 1 *Strike the right elbow to the outside of the left knee,* as described above in counts 1 and 2 in preparation for the 2nd phrase.

ct. 2 *Lift the torso on an upward curve* and turn to the right on the right leg to face upstage. The left leg lifts to low arabesque, and both arms lift to High Parallel.

ct. 3 *Strike the torso forward,* placing both hands on the floor, and permitting the *left leg to lift to high arabesque.*

ct. 4 *Raise the torso erect* and the arms to High Parallel. The left leg lowers to point back, on the floor.

ct. 5 *Turn the torso to the left to face downstage,* the left foot in Natural 4th. The arms remain in High Parallel.

"and" Keeping the weight centered, pivot on the balls of both feet, and *turn the body to the right to face upstage.* The arms remain in High Parallel.

ct. 6 Keeping the weight centered, pivot on the balls of both feet, and *turn the body to the left to face downstage.* The arms remain in High Parallel.

ct. 7 Point the right foot back and *close it to Natural 1st,* as the arms lower to 2nd.

cts. 1-7 Repeat the 2nd phrase to the other side, except on count 7 the feet end in Parallel 2nd and the arms in Opened Egyptian.

Phrase 3

ct. 1 Holding the pelvis in place, *twist the upper torso to the left,* keeping the arms in Opened Egyptian. The head remains centered.

ct. 2 Holding the pelvis in place, *twist the upper torso to the right,* keeping the arms in Opened Egyptian. The head remains centered.

ct. 3 Holding the pelvis in place, *twist the upper torso to the left,* keeping the arms in Opened Egyptian. The head remains centered.

"and" Bring the arms forward to Closed Egyptian, *strike the torso forward over the left leg,* bringing both elbows back, and keeping them parallel. The head drops toward the left knee.

ct. 4 *Lift the torso erect,* holding the twist of the body to the left. The arms open to Opened Egyptian.

ct. 5 *Hold.*

ct. 6 Holding the pelvis in place, *twist the upper torso to the right,* keeping the arms in Opened Egyptian.

ct. 7 Holding the pelvis in place, *twist the upper torso to the left,* keeping the arms in Opened Egyptian.

cts. 1-7 Repeat to the other side, except on count 7, the torso faces downstage, and the arms move to Closed Egyptian.

Phrase 4 (There is a strike and rebound action for this phrase.)

ct. 1 *Drop the head forward toward the chest,* as the elbows pull down, back, and up.

"and" *Rebound, and center the torso,* as the elbows return to Closed Egyptian.

ct. 2 *Drop the head forward toward the navel,* rounding the back, as the elbows pull up, and back.

"and" *Rebound, and center the torso,* as the elbows return to Closed Egyptian.

ct. 3 *Drop the head and torso forward to the knees,* rounding the back, as the elbows pull down, back, and up toward downstage.

"and" *Rebound, and center the torso,* as the elbows return to Closed Egyptian.

ct. 4 *Hold.*

Repeat three more times. On the last count 4, *open the left foot to Natural 2nd, and the arms to 2nd.*

Phrase 5

ct. 1 *The right knee bends and drops inward,* pivoting on the ball of the
(accented) right foot, as the right elbow pulls across the torso with the palm up.

cts. 2-3-4 *Make an outward circle with the right hip ending with the pelvis center.* The right leg turns outward, and straightens, as the right heel lowers to Natural 2nd. The right hand cuts across the torso, and the arm extends to 2nd by leading with the elbow.

Repeat to the other side.

•• • • •
Deep Floor Vocabulary

Adv.; count at 55 B.P.M.

Section A

(6 cts., 7 cts., 8 cts.) twice, transition No. 1 in 6 cts.

Begin center, facing downstage, with the feet in Natural 2nd, the arms in Natural Low.

Phrase 1

"and" With an accent, *relevé* on both feet with the left arm lifting to 2nd and the right arm lifting with a flexed elbow, with the right hand in front of the sternum, palm down. The right elbow is pointing to stage right.

ct. 1 *Turn right* on the left foot using the right arm opening to 2nd as momentum. Lift the right leg to the side at a 45° angle as the body turns to face upstage. Continue the turn and finish facing the left downstage diagonal with the right leg extended forward on the diagonal. As the body turns, the chest lifts and rotates slightly to the right.

ct. 2 *Begin a Sliding Descent with the right leg forward* on the diagonal, as the torso tilts backward and to the right. The arms are in 2nd. Since the body is tilting to the right, the arms will form a diagonal line. The pelvis presses forward as in a hinge, the left knee bends and turns out, and the left heel lowers slightly to facilitate the hinge.

cts. 3 and 4 *Continue the Sliding Descent* until the right hand touches the floor by count 3. Bend the right leg and place the right shin on the floor and shift the pelvis over the right knee as the left leg lifts to back attitude. The back arches and the pelvis presses forward toward downstage, but not past a straight line at the connection of the thigh to the hip joint. The left arm rounds slightly and circles down and across to the right and lifts upward to frame the head. The head turns to the right and the focus is toward the left foot. (In this position the body feels as if it were wrapping around a column and the head and left foot could meet.)

cts. 5 and 6 *Turn out and extend the left leg sideward and lower the heel to the floor.* The left foot flexes with the toes directed to the ceiling. In a coordinated sequence, *lateral the torso* to the left; the left arm straightens and reaches upward as the right arm lifts through 2nd to meet the left arm in High Parallel and the hips shift to the right, maintaining a flat line at the connection of the thigh to the hip bone (the femoral joint).

Phrase 2

cts. 1-2-3 *Lateral to the right side with the hips shifting to the left. The left heel slides sideward.* Be sure to maintain a flat line at the connection of the thigh to the hip bone (the femoral joint).

ct. 4 Keeping the back straight, *rotate the torso around its axis to the left until it is facing the ceiling.* The left foot points and the right leg rotates inward to parallel in order to maintain the correct alignment of the right hip and the right knee. The focus lifts to the ceiling. The left arm lowers sideward to 2nd and the right arm remains in High Parallel. The body will be on a diagonal line from the head to the left, pointed foot.

ct. 5 Keeping the body in a diagonal line, *rotate the torso around its axis to the right until it is facing the floor.* The left foot stays pointed and the right leg rotates outward in order to maintain the correct alignment of the right hip and the right knee. The focus lowers to the floor. The left arm lifts sideward to High Parallel and the right arm lowers sideward to 2nd.

cts. 6 and 7 In a coordinated sequence, circle the pelvis back and around to the right, as you circle the upper torso forward and around to the left, keeping the back straight until you are in the *Kneeling Lateral left position* described above in counts 5 and 6 in Phrase 1. The right arm lifts overhead to meet the left arm in High Parallel. The left foot flexes with the toes directed to the ceiling.

Phrase 3

cts. 1 and 2 *Repeat the Lateral and the slide* described above in counts 1-2-3 in Phrase 2—Lateral to the right side with the hips shifting to the left. The left heel slides sideward. Be sure to maintain a flat line at the connection of the thigh to the hip bone.

ct. 3 Repeat count 4 of Phrase 2 described above—*rotate the torso around its axis to the left until it is facing the ceiling.*

ct. 4 Repeat count 5 of Phrase 2 described above—*rotate the torso around its axis to the right until it is facing the floor.*

ct. 5 On the "and", drop both arms down and circle them across the front of the body and over the head through High Parallel as an impetus for *a lightly accented rotation of the torso around its axis to the left, ending with the torso facing the ceiling and the arms open to 2nd.* The right leg rotates inward to parallel in order to maintain the correct alignment of the right hip and the right knee.

ct. 6 Maintaining the body position, *tilt the torso to the left until the left hand touches the floor.* The right arm lifts upward to form a diagonal line with the left arm.

ct. 7 Using the inner thigh muscles, the gluteal muscles, and the abdominal muscles, bend the left leg and draw the body forward and upward, shifting the weight to the left leg until you are standing on a straight left leg facing stage left. *As you ascend, the right knee lifts and turns out to back attitude, the body centers, and the arms move to 2nd.*

ct. 8 *Promenade ½ turn to the right* to face stage right.

Repeat Phrase 1 to the other side, except for count 1. *On count 1, lower the right leg to Natural 1st,* then proceed with counts 2-6.

Repeat Phrases 2 and 3 to the other side.

Transition No. 1 in 6 counts

On count 1, lower the left leg to Natural 1st, then repeat counts 2-6 (the Sliding Descent) of Phrase 1.

Section B

Four 4's, four 2's, four 1's, transition No. 2 in 6 cts., four 4's, four 2's, four 1's, transition No. 3 in 6 cts.

On the upbeat of count 1, with a percussive accent, *center the torso and bend the left leg to form a right angle.* The left foot places on the floor and is parallel to the front wall. The left knee is directly over the left ankle and the hips continue to maintain a flat line at the connection of the thigh to the hip bone. The right leg is in natural turnout. Both arms reach overhead; the right arm lowers to 2nd and the left arm lowers with a flexed elbow, the left hand in front of the sternum and the palm down. The left elbow is pointing to stage left.

Phrase 1

cts. 1-2-3-4 Keeping the torso erect and maintaining a flat line at the connection of the right thigh to the right hip bone, *press the pelvis toward the left heel.* The left knee bends; the left heel remains on the floor. As the pelvis is pressing, the arms change to the other side by moving horizontally.

Phrase 2

cts. 2-2-3-4 Keeping the back straight, *move the buttocks and the torso* to the back and around to the right to sit on the floor on the inside of the right foot, and as close as possible to the right heel.

Phrase 3

cts. 3-2-3-4 *Return to the ending position in Phrase 1.* Keeping the back straight, lift the torso and move on a diagonal line to the left to reestablish the position with the pelvis close to the left heel.

Phrase 4

cts. 4-2-3-4 *Return to the starting position.* Press the pelvis to the right and move the arms horizontally to the other side.

four 2's Repeat phrases 1–4 with 2 counts for each phrase.

four 1's Repeat phrases 1–4 with 1 count for each phrase.

Transition No. 2 in 6 counts

cts. 1-2-3-4 Pivot ¼ to the right on the right knee (the lower leg moves forward), invert the left leg, and *sit in Triangle position facing* stage right. The left arm opens to 2nd.

cts. 5-6 *Place the right foot on the floor directly to the side* and lift the torso with a straight back until the left hip is directly over the left knee. Flex the right elbow.

four 4's *Repeat Section B on the other side facing stage right.*

four 2's

four 1's

Transition No. 3 in 6 counts

ct. 1 *Push off and point the right foot to pivot ¼ to the left on the left knee* (the left lower leg moves forward). Place the right big toe on the floor. The right leg is at a right angle. The torso is in High Lateral left. The arms are rounded and framing the head. The focus is front.

cts. 2-6 *Place the right foot on the inside of the left knee and slowly lower the top of the foot and the shin to the floor to sit in Triangle position.* Keep the weight toward the left side by increasing the Lateral. Turn the upper torso, the head, and both arms. Face the left thigh with the back slightly rounded, after the buttocks touch the floor.

Section C

Two 3's, two 2's, two 1's, five 3's, 4 cts., 5 cts, transition No. 4 in 4 cts.

Phrase 1

Two 3's

cts. 1-2-3 *Lift the torso erect and rotate the body to face stage right in Kneeling Stag position.* The arms move horizontally to the right with the left arm reaching stage right and the right arm reaching stage left, both palms down.

cts. 2-2-3 *Retrace* the movement, and return to Triangle position.

Two 2's

Repeat the two measures above in two 2's.

Two 1's

Repeat the two measures above in two 1's.

Five 3's

cts. 1-2-3 *Repeat* counts 1-2-3 above—Kneeling Stag position.

cts. 2-2-3 *Extend the left leg.*

cts. 3-2-3 *Arch the back, and lower the pelvis to the right heel.* This causes the left leg to slide back slightly.

cts. 4-2-3 Continue to arch the back, and *bend the left leg until the left foot touches the head.*

cts. 5-2-3 *Rotate the body to the left and return to Triangle position.* The arms move horizontally to the left, and end rounded and framing the head.

Phrase 2

4 cts.

ct. 1 With a sweeping motion, *circle the upper body forward and around to the right, and lift onto the right knee with the left leg in back attitude.* Place the right hand on the floor to the right and close to the right knee. The pelvis is directly over the right knee and pressing forward toward downstage, but not past a straight line at the connection of the thigh to the hip joint. The left arm circles down, across to the right, and overhead to frame the head. The head turns to the right and the focus is toward the left foot. The body is shaped as if it were wrapped around a column and the head and the left foot could meet.

ct. 2 Drop the left hip, rotate out, and *extend the left leg upward* to the left downstage diagonal. The left arm circles down, across to the left, and reaches upward to the left downstage diagonal parallel to the left leg.

ct. 3 Return to the *wrapped attitude position* on the right knee established in count 1.

ct. 4 Return to *Triangle position.*

5 cts.

cts. 1-2 Repeat count 1, *wrapped attitude,* and count 2, *extend the left leg upward* from Phrase 2.

ct. 3 Keeping the left leg and left arm straight and parallel to each other, describe a *counterclockwise circle* in the air.

ct. 4 Repeat count 3, *wrapped attitude,* from Phrase 2.

ct. 5 Repeat count 4, *return to Triangle position,* from Phrase 2.

Transition No. 4

4 cts.

ct. 1 Swing the body and both arms up and around to the right to High Lateral right, giving impetus to a ½ *turn to the right on the right knee.* The arms are rounded and framing the head. The left leg turns out and moves sideward to form a right angle. The left foot is pointed and is directly under the left knee. Place the left big toe on the floor to stop the ½ turn.

"and" *Place the left foot at the inside of the right knee.*

ct. 2 Lower the top of the foot and shin to *sit in Triangle position.* Keep the weight toward the right side by increasing the Lateral. Turn the upper torso, the head and both arms to face the right thigh with the back slightly rounded, after the buttocks touch the floor.

cts. 3-4 *Describe a full circle of the body:* Circle the torso forward, to the left side, and back onto the floor, and lift the torso off the floor as it circles to the right side; end facing the right thigh. As the torso passes the left knee, the left leg extends sideward; it returns to Triangle position as the torso faces the right thigh. The left arm straightens and the left palm touches the floor on the left upstage diagonal, as the torso circles to the left side. The right arm remains framing the head. The left arm rounds again framing the head, as the torso circles back onto the floor. The arms remain framing the head until the completion of the circle.

Repeat Section C, facing upstage to the other side, with transition No. 5 in 6 cts.; omit transition No. 4.

Transition No. 5

6 cts.

cts. 1-3 Repeat counts 1-3 of transition No. 4 to the other side except instead of returning the right foot to Triangle position, bend the right knee, flex both ankles and *place the ball of the right foot forward* on the floor in line with the center of the body.

cts. 4-6 At the same time, lift the torso erect and open the arms sideward to 2nd. From this seated Natural 4th position, shift the weight onto the right leg and *stand up*. The arms remain in 2nd. Immediately, *turn right ½ turn* to the right with the left leg slightly off the floor in Natural 2nd and end in Natural 2nd facing upstage.

Transition No. 6

4 cts.

cts. 1-4 *Spiral Descent:* Push off with the right foot and lift the right leg to back attitude, giving impetus for a ¾ turn to the right (ending stage right). Simultaneously, tilt the torso forward to Flat Back. The standing leg is bent on the turn and the arms remain in 2nd. Lower the right leg behind to Natural 4th position on count 2; continue to plié on both legs and pivot to sit on the floor in Triangle position with the left leg inverted, facing stage left, on count 3. The right leg is forward, right ankle flexed, with the outside of the right heel on the floor. Immediately, the right hand touches the floor and the head turns to the right in profile. The upper torso circles to the right side, back, and to the left side by count 4. As the upper torso circles, the left arm rounds and circles to the right side, over the head, back, and to the left side; neither the body nor the arm touches the floor. Then the left elbow cuts in toward the torso and ends touching the back of the left rib cage. The left palm faces up and the fingers point upstage. The head moves from profile to the right to profile to the left, as the torso circles and finishes with focus to the left palm.

Section D

Four 6's

Phrase 1

cts. 1-2-3 *Press the left pelvic bone forward* and toward the right, causing the left buttock to lift off the floor and the body to turn to the right as far as possible. The left arm straightens slightly, but remains rounded as it arcs over the head, and the hand lowers so that the little finger of the left hand touches the inside of the right elbow. The head makes the same arc as the left hand; the focus is on the left palm. The right leg extends to the left downstage diagonal by pressing with the heel of the right flexed foot.

cts. 4-5-6 Turn the torso to face the left downstage diagonal and *lift the left rounded arm* overhead and *arch the torso* backward until the head touches the floor. The left arm remains overhead with the focus on the palm.

Phrase 2

cts. 1-2-3 Retrace the movement back to the position established on counts 1-2-3 of Phrase 1.

cts. 4-5-6 Retrace the movement back to the opening position of Section D, except the left arm extends, with palm up, and moves horizontally around to the left and finishes with the elbow touching the back of the rib cage.

Phrase 3

cts. 1-2-3 Repeat counts 1-2-3 of Phrase 1.

cts. 4-5-6 Repeat counts 4-5-6 of Phrase 1, except the torso remains straight as it lowers backward and the head remains straight, in line with the torso, as in a Flat Back Back Bend.

Phrase 4

cts. 1-6 Repeat Phrase 2.

Transition No. 7

11 cts.

ct. 1 *Shift the weight onto the side of the right hip, extend both legs* to the left with the right leg forward and the left leg back, and *place both palms* on the floor to the right with the elbows bent. The legs are opened as wide as possible and slightly off the floor, with both feet pointed. The weight is balanced on the side of the right hip and on both palms. The torso tilts and turns slightly to the right. The head turns to the right with the focus on the floor.

cts. 2-3 *Turn 1 ½ turns to the right in Coccyx Spin* position with extended legs (see Turns, chapter 11).

ct. 4 End the turn in *Triangle position* with the right leg inverted, the left leg forward, left ankle flexed with the outside of the left heel on the floor. The left palm is on the floor behind and to the left of the left hip. The right arm is in 2nd.

ct. 5 *Circle the upper torso* and the right arm forward, to the left, to the back, and around to the right, ending in the opening position of Section D on the other side. The right arm is rounded on the circle. Neither the body nor the arm touches the floor.

ct. 6-8   Rotate the right leg out and extend it forward. Swing it to the left, across the body, and open to the right as impetus for *one full Coccyx Spin* to the right on count 7. The legs continue to swing in the same direction as the torso leans left and forward, ending with the *body prone,* facing the floor. The palms lower to the floor, elbows close to the body.

ct. 9-11   In a simultaneous action, lift, bend, and turn out the left leg, until the left foot touches the floor; the torso turns to face stage right. The body continues to rotate around to the left as the left leg wraps around to the left. The left leg rotates out and lowers to Triangle position with the left foot forward, left ankle flexed with the outside of the left heel on the floor as the right leg bends and inverts. The upper torso and right arm continue to circle around to the left as in count 5, ending in the opening position of Section D on the other side.

Repeat entire Section D and transition No. 7 to the other side.

Transition No. 8

4 cts.

ct. 1   *Press the left pelvic bone forward* and toward the right, causing the left buttock to lift off the floor. Turn the torso to the right to face the left downstage diagonal. Extend the right leg to the left downstage diagonal by pressing with the heel of the right flexed foot. The left arm lifts to High Parallel.

ct. 2   *Tilt the torso forward to Flat Back* position over the right extended leg and point the right foot.

ct. 3   Extend the left leg and *sit in 2nd* position with both buttocks on the floor and swing the torso to Flat Back Forward position. Both arms move to 2nd.

ct. 4   *Swing the torso through Flat Back Forward over the left leg,* through Lateral left side, and finish center. The arms move to High Parallel and open to 2nd as the torso centers.

Section E

Four 4's and two 10's

Four 4's

cts. 1-2-3-4   On the "and", flex the left foot. Rotate the right leg inward and the left leg outward and turn the torso to face upstage in a *full split.* The left arm bends to Opened Egyptian. The head turns to the left to face the forearm.

cts. 2-2-3-4   Return to 2nd position facing stage left and straighten the left arm.
cts. 3-2-3-4   On the "and", flex the right foot. Then repeat the first two measures
and   to the other side.
4-2-3-4

Two 10's

cts. 1-2   Repeat the first measure of Section E in 2 counts.
cts. 3-4   Place both palms on either side of the hips and *lift the buttocks* off the floor. Place the torso close to and inside the left leg, keeping the pelvis centered. The head pulls toward the left ankle. The left leg is parallel and the right leg is in natural turn out.
ct. 5   *Lift the torso to Flat Back Forward* and pivot ¼ turn to the right. The legs turn out to Wide Natural 2nd. The arms lift sideward to 2nd.
ct. 6   Lift the torso erect.
cts. 7-9   Bend the torso forward and place the palms on the floor close to each other, wrists flexed, and fingers facing toward stage right. Flex both feet, slide and lower the body to a *full Russian* split or seated 2nd position.
ct. 10   Lift the torso erect and lift the arms to 2nd.
cts. 1-10   Repeat to the other side.

Section F

One 5, one 12, one 5, one 12

One 5

ct. 1   With a smooth and flowing quality, simultaneously *turn the torso* ¼ to the left to face upstage and bend both legs to Triangle position with the left leg forward, the sole of the foot on the floor, and the right leg inverted. The arms remain in 2nd.
cts. 2-3   *Circle the torso* and the right arm to the left. Place the left hand on the floor and slide the left palm along the floor until the left and then the right shoulder touches the floor. Both arms are rounded and framing the head.
ct. 4   Continuing the torso circle, lift the left and then the right shoulder off the floor until the torso is in a *Lateral to the right*.
ct. 5   Both arms remain rounded and frame the head. *Center the torso* and extend both arms forward to Middle Parallel. Stepping on the left foot, lift the body into a Deep Lunge position with the left foot forward, turned out, and the right leg extended behind, parallel.

One 12

cts. 1-2   Straighten the left knee and press the right heel toward the floor. Place both palms on the floor and place the torso close to and inside the left leg, keeping the pelvis centered. The head pulls toward the left ankle.

cts. 3-4 Lift the torso to Flat Back Forward and pivot ¼ turn to the right. The legs turn out to Wide Natural 2nd. The arms lift to 2nd.

ct. 5 Maintaining the Flat Back Forward position, *pivot ¼ turn to the right*. The legs turn out to Wide Natural 2nd.

ct. 6 *Lift the torso erect.* The arms remain in 2nd.

cts. 7-8 Slide both feet and begin a split to the floor.

ct. 9 With an accent, drop in split position just slightly off the floor. The arms remain in 2nd.

ct. 10 Hold.

ct. 11 Lower to full split on the floor.

ct. 12 Rotate both hips into a Russian split facing stage left as the *torso swings to the left,* passing through Flat Back Forward over the right leg, Flat Back Forward, Flat Back Forward over the left leg, and ends center. As the *torso centers,* both legs bend into Triangle position with the left foot forward, sole of the foot on the floor and the right leg inverted. Both arms move to High Parallel as the torso begins to swing left. The left palm places on the floor close to the left hip and the right arm circles, rounded, over the head as the torso Laterals to the left. The right arm then circles back and around to the right. The right elbow cuts in toward the body and ends touching the back of the right rib cage, the right palm facing up, fingers pointing downstage. Neither the body nor the arm touches the floor (same as the opening position of Section D, to the other side). The head finishes to the right in profile; focus to the right palm. On the "and", straighten both legs and sit in Russian split or seated 2nd position. Both arms move to 2nd.

cts. 1-5 Repeat cts. 1-5 to the other side.

cts. 1-12 Repeat cts. 1-12 to the other side.

Dimensional Tonus (Yawn Stretch)

Int., Adv.; three 8's, two 10's, four 7's, two 4's, two 9's, four 3's, two 9's, 16 cts; count at 45 B.P.M. (very sustained)

Begin center facing downstage, the feet in Natural 1st, the arms in Natural Low.

1st 8

cts. 1 and 2 *Raise the fingertips to the top of the shoulders,* keeping the arms parallel and lifting the elbows as high as possible; turn out the wrists and curl the first joints of the fingers as the elbows begin to open.

cts. 3 and 4 Begin to straighten the arms and stretch them up toward the ceiling, with the wrists flexed and the second and third joints of the fingers curled under. The second knuckles of the center fingers should be touching. *As the arms fully straighten, the face lifts to the ceiling.* Allow the shoulders to lift as the arms straighten. Keep the abdominals lifted to avoid arching the back.

Note: *From this point on the wrists remain flexed and the fingers curled.*

ct. 5 accented   *The head drops,* the chin to the chest, maintaining the body and arm position.

ct. 6 accented   *The shoulders drop down,* maintaining the body and arm position.

cts. 7 and 8   Center the head and *lower the arms forward to Middle Parallel,* keeping the wrists and hands in the position noted above.

2nd 8

cts. 1-4   *Turn the hands* so that the wrists touch (the right hand turns down; the left hand turns up), *lift the right heel off the floor, and pull the right hip back.* Continue to reach forward with the left arm, as the right arm makes a circle by pulling down, reaching back, up, and forward. As the circle of the right arm reaches the highest point, the right hip returns to center, the right heel lowers to the floor, and the torso remains lifted forward. (The torso is permitted to twist and to lean forward slightly.) The head turns to the right and follows the right arm as it circles. End the circle by crossing the right wrist over the left wrist.

cts. 5-8   Repeat to the other side with the left arm circling.

3rd 8

cts. 1 and 2   Simultaneously lift the torso erect, relevé, and step to the side with the left foot into Natural 2nd. The right arm opens horizontally to 2nd. Then *the torso pulls into Lateral left side;* the right arm pulls up and, without turning, reaches into Lateral left side. The left arm remains in place.

cts. 3 and 4   Lift the torso erect and pivoting on both feet, *turn the body to face stage left;* keep the left arm in front of the torso as the right arm lowers forward to cross the right wrist on top of the left wrist. Lower the heels to Natural 4th and open the left arm to 2nd.

cts. 5-8   *Repeat to the right side* by pivoting on both feet and turning the body to face downstage—relevé, pull into Lateral right side, lift the torso erect and pivot to face stage right, cross the left wrist on top of the right wrist, open the right arm to 2nd.

Note: *At this point, the wrists unflex and the hands uncurl.*

Two 10's

1st 10

ct. 1   Pivoting on both feet, turn the body to face downstage as *the fingers of each hand gently touch the tops of the shoulders.* The arms are parallel and bent, and the elbows are pulled up as high as possible. The legs are in 2nd in three-quarter relevé and the focus is on the upward diagonal.

ct. 2 *Straighten the arms to High Parallel* as the face lifts to the ceiling.

ct. 3 Keeping the legs straight and the arms in High Parallel, lower the heels, shift the weight onto the left leg, and *twist the torso to the left to face upstage.* The feet pivot, the legs cross, the thighs touching, and the head centers.

ct. 4 Keeping the legs straight and the arms in High Parallel, release the twist slightly, so the body faces the upstage left diagonal. The weight shifts fully to the left foot, as the right foot points behind the body. Both legs are in natural turnout.

cts. 5-10 *Pull the torso out into Flat Back Forward, and continue to lower the torso in the straight back line,* until the outside of the little fingers of each hand touch the floor. The head remains centered between the arms, the back foot remains pointed, and the knees remain straight. Do not shift the weight off the left foot.

2nd 10

cts. 1-10 *Repeat to the other side* by bringing the torso upright, lowering the arms to Natural Low, and pivoting right to face downstage.

Four 7's

1st 7

ct. 1 Place the left foot on the floor in Natural 4th position, so the body faces stage right. The torso moves to *Lateral left side* with the hip displacement, and the arms go to High Parallel.

ct. 2 Press the pelvis forward and *circle the torso to Flat Back Back Bend.* Arms remain in High Parallel.

ct. 3 *Circle the torso to Lateral right side* with the hip displacement. Arms remain in High Parallel.

ct. 4 *Circle the torso to Flat Back Forward.* Arms remain in High Parallel.

"and" Keeping the arms straight and on the same level, *drop both hands downward from the wrist.* Sharply point the fingers straight down and rotate the hands inward so the palms end facing the body.

cts. 5-7 Leading with the fingers, *pull the hands toward the back heel and extend the torso in Flat Back Forward.* The head is as close to the right ankle as possible. Once the hands have reached beyond the right leg, the wrists straighten, the palms rotate to face each other and continue to reach *down* to the back heel. End count 7 with the torso laying as close to the right leg as possible and the arms pulling diagonally down to the back heel. The arms remain parallel to each other, palms facing each other.

2nd 7

> ct. 1 Keeping the feet in Natural 4th, pull the torso into *Lateral left side* with the hip displacement. The arms lift to High Parallel.
>
> "and" Holding the torso in place, pivot the feet to Natural 2nd facing downstage; the torso will now be in *Flat Back Forward*. Pivot the feet to Natural 4th position facing stage left. *The torso rotates to Lateral right side* with the hip displacement. The arms remain in High Parallel.
>
> cts. 2-7 Continue the movement from the previous seven counts on the other side. *Circle the torso* through Flat Back Back Bend, Lateral left side, and Flat Back Forward, and reach diagonally down to the right heel.

3rd 7

Repeat the second 7 on the first side—*circle the torso.*

4th 7

Repeat the second 7 on the other side—*circle the torso.*

Two 4's

1st 4

> ct. 1 Step forward with the right foot into Natural 4th (the torso is facing stage left) and *Lateral left side* with the hip displacement. The arms are in High Parallel.
>
> ct. 2 Turn the torso to *Flat Back Forward* facing upstage *without moving the feet.*
>
> ct. 3 Holding the torso in place, *pivot the feet to Natural 4th facing stage right; the torso rotates to Lateral right side* with the hip displacement. The arms remain in High Parallel.
>
> ct. 4 *Return the torso upright.* Arms remain in High Parallel.

2nd 4

Repeat to the other side, beginning with the *Lateral to the right.* There is no step forward.

Two 9's

Markedly slower tempo; count at 60 B.P.M.

1st 9

> "and" Step to the left with the left foot into *Wide Natural 2nd* and face upstage. The arms remain in High Parallel.
>
> ct. 1 *Lateral to the left side.*
>
> ct. 2 *Flat Back left side.*

ct. 3 Place the left hand on the floor on the outside and the right hand on the floor on the inside of the left foot and *bend the right knee,* keeping the right heel on the floor. Point the left foot, keeping the toes on the floor. *The torso should stay as close to the left leg as possible* and the head as close to the left ankle as possible. *The pelvis lowers as close to the right heel as possible.*

ct. 4 Keeping the head, the torso, and the hands in place, *straighten the right knee* and relax the pointed left foot.

ct. 5 Keeping the head, the torso, and the hands in place, *bend the right knee,* keeping the right heel on the floor and pointing the left foot with the toes on the floor. The pelvis lowers as close as possible to the right heel.

ct. 6 Keeping the head, the torso, and the hands in place, *straighten the right knee* and relax the pointed left foot.

ct. 7 *Pull the torso out to Flat Back left side.* The arms are in High Parallel.

ct. 8 *Lateral left side.* The arms remain in High Parallel.

ct. 9 *Lift the torso center.* The arms remain in High Parallel.

2nd 9

Repeat to the right side.

Four 3's

Tempo increases; count at 75 B.P.M.

"and" Step with the right foot to stage right into *Deep Forward Lunge,* with both palms on the floor on either side of the right foot.

cts. 1-2-3 Keeping the palms on the floor, take 3 full counts to straighten the right knee. The torso lowers along the right leg and the head is as close as possible to the right ankle.

"and" Keeping the palms on the floor, quickly *bend the right knee* and bring the pelvis down as close as possible to the right heel into *Deep Forward Lunge.* The head lifts to focus forward.

cts. 2-2-3 Repeat counts 1, 2, 3—*straighten the right knee* for three full counts.

Transition No. 1

"and" Keeping both legs straight, pull the torso out to Flat Back, the arms in High Parallel; continue to pull the torso erect; pivot on both feet to face downstage (the legs will be in Wide Natural 2nd), the arms remain in High Parallel; continue to pivot to stage left; bend the left knee into *Deep Forward Lunge* and place the palms on the floor on either side of the left foot.

cts. 3-2-3 Repeat the two 3's above and transition No. 1 on the other side.
and 4-2-3

Two 9's

cts. 1, 2, Keeping the palms on the floor, take 3 full counts to *straighten the*
and 3 *right knee.* The torso lowers along the right leg and the head is as
close as possible to the right ankle.

ct. 4 Keeping both palms on the floor and both legs straight, *arch the
whole back* and lift the head, staying as close as possible to the
extended leg.

ct. 5 *Round the back* as high as possible, keeping both palms on the
floor.

ct. 6 Repeat count 4—*arch the back.*

ct. 7 Repeat count 5—*round the back.*

ct. 8 Return to *Deep Forward Lunge* by bending the right knee, centering
the torso, and lifting the arms to Middle Parallel.

ct. 9 Hold.

Transition No. 2

"and" Straighten the right knee, keep the arms in Middle Parallel, and
pivot on both feet to face stage left. (The legs will pass through Wide
Natural 2nd.) End in Deep Forward Lunge with the left knee bent
and both palms on the floor on either side of the left foot.

cts. 1-9 Repeat on the other side, omitting transition No. 2.

One 16

Tempo returns to opening tempo; count at 45 B.P.M.

ct. 1 Slide the right foot forward and straighten the left knee; *relevé on
both feet in Natural 1st.* Both elbows bend and lift as high as
possible, with arms parallel to each other and the fingertips
touching the tops of the shoulders. The head lifts up, and the focus
is to the upward diagonal.

ct. 2 *Straighten the arms to High Parallel* as the head lifts higher and the
face lifts to the ceiling. The feet remain in relevé.

cts. 3 and 4 Remaining in relevé, *the torso moves to Flat Back Forward,* the
head centers, and the arms remain in High Parallel.

cts. 5-7 *Continue to tilt the Flat Back to a diagonal line toward the floor.*
The arms remain in High Parallel, and the feet remain in relevé.

ct. 8 The heels lower to the floor, *the body releases the Flat Back,* and the
arms drop down. The head is inverted. Exhale.

cts. 9 and 10 On a breath, extend the body into as low a Flat Back as possible and
continue to *lift the body upright* with the arms in High Parallel. The
head is centered between the arms.

ct. 11 *Press the pelvis forward into Flat Back Back Bend.* Bend the arms, keeping the elbows as lifted as possible and the arms parallel to each other.

"and" As the fingertips lightly tap the back of the shoulders, the head drops back slightly and *both the head and the fingertips rebound.*

ct. 12 Center the torso; the arms begin to straighten, and the backs of the hands are pulling up and forward.

cts. 13-16 The arms lower to Middle Parallel, palms facing up.

In silence The arms continue to lower to Natural Low.

•• • • •

Hinge Studies

Preparation for Hinge Study No. 1

Int.; seven 3's; count at 65 B.P.M.

Begin facing downstage in Triangle position, right leg inverted. The torso and the head are rounded over the left knee. Both palms are on the floor on either side of the left knee with the fingers pointing in toward each other. The elbows are bent and pointing sideward of the torso (similar to a push-up position).

ct. 1- *Flex both feet, lift the torso erect and lift both knees, and turn the body ¼ turn to the right* to face stage right. Sit on both buttocks with the feet in Parallel 2nd, both knees bent. The left hand remains on the floor as the left arm straightens and turns out, the fingers point to stage left. The right arm lifts bent and the right elbow places inside and close the right thigh. The right wrist is straight, palm facing downstage, with fingers pointing on the upward diagonal.

2-3 *Press the pelvis upward and forward* and the knees downward *into a deep Hinge* (knees slightly off the floor); extend the right arm to Middle Parallel. The left palm will slide on the floor to stage right.

cts. 2-2-3 Place the right hand on the floor near the right knee, fingers pointing in, as the body turns ¼ turn to the right to face upstage and lowers to *Triangle position, left leg inverted.* The torso and the head round over the right knee as the left hand lifts off the floor and the left arm moves through 2nd and Middle Parallel and lowers rounded with the left hand on the floor, fingers pointing in toward the right hand.

cts. 3-2-3 Repeat phrase 1-2-3 to the other side.

cts. 4-2-3 Repeat phrase 2-2-3 to the other side.

cts. 5-2-3 Repeat phrase 1-2-3 to the first side.

cts. 6-2-3 *Holding the deep Hinge position,* smoothly open the right arm to 2nd and lift the left hand off the floor and move the left arm to 2nd.

cts. 7-2-3 Repeat phrase 2-2-3 to the first side.

Repeat to the other side.

Hinge Study No. 1

Adv.; five 3's four times; count at 65 B.P.M.

Begin center, facing stage right, the feet in Parallel 2nd, the arms in Natural Low.

cts. 1-2-3   *Descend with a hinging action* until the knees are slightly off the floor as the arms lift to 2nd.

cts. 2-2-3   Place the left hand on the floor near the left knee, fingers pointing in, as the body turns ¼ turn to the left to face downstage and lowers to *Triangle position, the right leg inverted.* The torso and the head round over the left knee as the right arm moves through Middle Parallel and lowers with the right hand on the floor, the fingers pointing in toward the left hand.

cts. 3-2-3   *Press directly into a deep Hinge* (the knees slightly off the floor) facing stage right as the arms move horizontally to 2nd.

cts. 4-2-3   Place the right hand on the floor near the right knee, fingers pointing in, as the body turns ¼ turn to the right to face upstage and lowers to *Triangle position, the left leg inverted.* The torso and the head round over the right knee as the left arm moves through Middle Parallel and lowers with the left hand on the floor, the fingers pointing in toward the right hand.

cts. 5-2-3   *Press directly into a deep Hinge* (knees slightly off the floor) facing stage right with both arms in Middle Parallel and ascend with a hinging action as the arms lift to High Parallel and the body becomes erect.

Repeat three more times.

Hinge Study No. 2

Adv.; eight 2's four times; count at 70 B.P.M.

Begin center, facing downstage, the feet in Parallel 2nd, the arms in High Parallel.

cts. 1-2   *Descend with a hinging action* until the knees are slightly off the
and 2-2   floor. The right arm reaches back and diagonally downward to place the right hand on the floor; the left arm lowers to Middle Parallel.

cts. 3-2   *Pivot on the right foot and turn ½ turn to the right, placing the left
and 4-2   foot in Parallel 2nd,* to face upstage. The torso tilts forward to *Flat Back.* The right hand remains on the floor, and the left arm is in High Parallel. The body remains on the same level, or goes lower in Flat Back Forward on the ½ turn.

cts. 5-2   *Press the pelvis forward and tilt the torso back into a deep Hinge*
and 6-2   (the knees slightly off the floor). The left arm circles up, back, and down to place the left hand on the floor as the right arm lifts forward to Middle Parallel. The body remains on the same level.

cts. 7-2 *Ascend with a hinging action.* The left arm circles forward to
and 8-2 Middle Parallel and both arms lift to High Parallel as the body
becomes erect.

Repeat three more times.

> **Note:** *More advanced students may do Hinge Study No. 2 with two counts for each movement.*

Hinge Study No. 3

Adv.; ten 2's on each side; count at 65 B.P.M.

Begin center, facing downstage, the feet in Parallel 2nd, the arms in High Parallel.

cts. 1-2 *Front Fall* (see Falls in chapter 10). The knees touch the floor on cts.
through 4-2.
6-2

cts. 7-2 With an accent, bend the knees and *raise the buttocks toward the ceiling.* The toes stay curled.

cts. 8-2 Pulling the buttocks toward the heels and pushing the left palm into the floor, lift the knees off the floor and *sit in Parallel 2nd Primitive Squat position* with the torso rounded, heels off the floor. The hands are slightly wider than shoulder width apart. The palms slide along the floor and place near the outsides of the feet as the body lifts into the squat position.

cts. 9-2 Keeping the body on the same level, pivot ½ turn to the left on the right foot to face upstage. Place the left foot in Parallel 2nd and *press into a deep Hinge* (the knees slightly off the floor.) The left hand lifts to Middle Parallel and the right hand remains on the floor and adjusts on the pivot if necessary.

cts. 10-2 *Ascend with a hinging action.* The right arm circles forward to Middle Parallel and both arms lift to High Parallel as the body becomes erect.

Repeat on the other side.

Transition from Hinge Study No. 3

Adv.; 4 counts; count at 65 B.P.M.

cts. 1-2-3 *Descend with a hinging action* to the floor with the arms in High Parallel.

4 Center the torso, circle the arms back, down, and forward to Middle Parallel and point the toes.

Hinge Study No. 4

Adv.; five 2's twice, four 2's; count at 65 B.P.M.

The starting position is the final position of the transition from Hinge Study No. 3.

Figure 29. Hinge Study No. 4; to the left

cts. 1-2   As the body *presses back* with a hinging action, circle the right arm
and 2-2   up and over the head and twist the upper torso to the right. Bend the
right arm at a right angle with the elbow reaching toward the center
of the back and the fingers pointing upstage. Continue to press back
with a hinging action until the right forearm places on the floor. The
left arm lifts rounded over the head as the right arm bends at a right
angle. The head turns right with the twist of the upper torso to the
right; the focus is toward the right arm.

cts. 3-2   In a simultaneous action, *swing the torso to the right,* through
Lateral right side, lift the left knee, and *touch the right elbow to the
left knee.* The left arm opens to 2nd.

cts. 4-2   Swing both arms and the torso to *Lateral right side,* as the left knee
returns to the floor, and the torso continues to circle back to Hinge
position on both knees. The arms move to High Parallel.

cts. 5-2   *Center the torso* and circle the arms back, down, and forward to
Middle Parallel. (Do not arch the back.)

Repeat to the other side.

Four 2's

cts. 1-2   Swing both arms up, back, down, and forward to shoulder height,
ending with the arms rounded and the palms facing out and the
elbows lifted higher than the hands. At the same time, *the torso
rounds and tilts back as the knees lift off the floor and the weight
shifts onto the tops of the feet.* The head tilts back with the focus
diagonally upward.

cts. 2-2   *Lower the knees to the floor* and lower the arms and slide the palms
diagonally back along the floor. The arms straighten on the slide
backward and *the torso lowers to the floor with a hinging action.*

cts. 3-2 Swing the arms forward to Middle Parallel, return to both knees as *the torso centers.* (Do not arch the back.)

cts. 4-2 Hold.

Hinge Study No. 5 (Rocking Hinge)

Adv.; 12 cts.; count at 80 B.P.M.

Begin center, facing downstage, on both knees, the legs in Parallel 2nd, the arms in Middle Parallel.

cts. 1 and 2 As the body presses back with a *hinging action,* the right knee lifts and the body leans to the left. The head turns to the right with the focus to stage right. The arms remain in Middle Parallel.

cts. 3 and 4 In a rocking action, lower the right knee and lift the left knee and lean the body to the right. The head turns to the left with the focus to stage left. The arms remain in Middle Parallel. At the same time, the body continues to press back with a hinging action.

cts. 5 and 6 Repeat counts 1 and 2—continues to press back with a hinging action and lift the right knee.

cts. 7 and 8 Repeat counts 3 and 4—continue to press back with a hinging action and lift the left knee.

cts. 9 through 12 Center the torso as the left knee opens and place the left foot on the floor turned out and directly below the left knee. Shift the weight onto the left leg and *stand erect* to face stage left with the feet in Natural 2nd. Then relevé and lift the arms to High Parallel.

Hinge Study No. 6

Adv.; 10 cts.; count at 45 B.P.M.

Follows right after Hinge Study No. 5. The starting position is the final position of Hinge Study No. 5.

ct. 1 *Step out with the left foot to the upstage left diagonal* to Parallel 4th and begin to descend with a hinging action. The right arm lowers to Middle Parallel, palm facing down, and the left arm opens to 2nd. The body should not lower all the way to the floor since the series of hinging swings to follow will get progressively lower to the floor.

ct. 2 Pivot on both feet and *swing the body to face downstage as the body descends further with a hinging action.* The arms swing horizontally to the other side, the left arm to Middle Parallel, the right arm to 2nd.

ct. 3 Pivot on both feet and *swing the body to face the left upstage diagonal as the body descends further* with a hinging action. The arms swing horizontally to the other side, the right arm to Middle Parallel, and left arm to 2nd.

ct. 4   *Repeat the hinging swing as in count 2* and lower the body to
Triangle position with the left leg inverted, facing the right
downstage diagonal. The right hand touches the floor to ease into
Triangle position; then the arms pull to High Parallel, and the torso
is in Flat Back right side.

cts. 5   Turn the body to face stage left and *press into a deep Hinge.* The
and 6   arms lift to Middle Parallel.

cts. 7   *Lower the body to Triangle position* with the right leg inverted,
and 8   facing the left upstage diagonal. The left hand touches the floor to
ease into Triangle position; then the arms pull to High Parallel, and
the torso is in Flat Back left side.

cts. 9   Turn the body to face stage left and *press into a deep Hinge,* the left
and 10   palm on the floor. *Ascend with a hinging action.* The arms lift to
High Parallel as the body becomes erect.

•• • •   •

Torso Language

Int., Adv.; six 4's; count at 60 B.P.M.

Begin center, facing downstage, the feet in Parallel 1st, the arms in Natural Low.

cts. 1-2-3   Step forward on the right leg, *press the pelvis forward and tilt the
torso back into Flat Back Back Bend position* as the left leg lifts to
low attitude back. At the same time, the arms begin to circle
forward, moving through Middle Parallel, palms facing each other
and reaching up. Continue the circle by reaching to the upstage
right diagonal, permitting the left arm to bend as it reaches across
the body. Both palms rotate to face the floor on the diagonal reach.
The head and focus follow the hands as the arms circle. The upper
body turns to the right. The arms remain the same distance apart as
they lower to Natural Low.

ct. 4   Continue to press the pelvis forward and extend the torso back in Flat
Back Back Bend position until the weight shifts so far forward that *the
left foot must step forward to "catch" the weight.* (The feet are in
Parallel Fourth.) As the left foot steps forward, the torso moves
through Flat Back Forward and rotates to Lateral left side to face
stage left. As the torso moves through Flat Back Forward, the arms
pull forward to High Parallel and the head centers between the arms.

cts. 2-2-3-4   Lift the torso erect with the arms in High Parallel and repeat the
movement described above.

ct. 3   Step with the right foot and open the legs to Wide Natural 2nd. At the
same time, twist the torso to the right and *strike the left elbow to the
outside of the right knee* (see Percussive Stroke Study this chapter).
The head turns to the right, focus is upstage. The right arm rotates
outward with the fingers reaching toward the ceiling.

2   *Repeat the torso twist and elbow strike movement to the left knee.*

3   On the "and" count of 3, repeat the *torso twist and elbow strike movement to the right knee.* On count 3, rotate the torso to Flat Back Back Bend position, moving through Lateral right side. Raise the arms to *Diagonal Egyptian.*

4   Keeping the pelvis pressed forward and the torso tilted back, *shift the weight onto the left leg and stretch the right leg to low back attitude.* The arms remain in *Diagonal Egyptian.*

cts. 4-2-3-4   Repeat the third bar—*strike left elbow, right elbow, left elbow, Flat Back Back Bend, pelvic press forward in low back attitude.*

cts. 5-2-3-4   Maintaining the established position, *exert a strong but motionless press for the full four counts.*

cts. 6-2-3-4   *Relevé* with an isometric press of the pelvis and the forearms.

The whole study should be repeated to the other side.

· · · · · ···

Eight

Descents and Ascents

As Horton continued his investigation of level changes in movement, he arrived at several movements that rise and fall. The dramatic quality of these phrases was integral to the movement, not a superficial affectation. The Descents and Ascents require endurance and control, and a demanding development of strength.

Pivotal Descent

Beg., Int., Adv.; 4 cts.; count at 65 B.P.M.

Begin center facing downstage, the feet in Natural 2nd, the arms in 2nd.

cts. 1-4 Shift the weight to the left foot, bend both knees, and *pivot ½ turn to the left to face upstage.* The right foot rolls over as the *body continues to descend to the floor until both buttocks touch.* The right knee is turned out, the left leg is crossed over the right knee with the left foot on the floor. The torso remains erect and the arms remain in 2nd.

Pivotal Ascent

Beg., Int., Adv.; 4 cts.; count at 65 B.P.M.

Begin seated on the floor on both buttocks facing upstage in the final position of Pivotal Descent.

cts. 1-4 *Retrace the path described above to standing.*

Sliding Descent

Beg., Int., Adv.; 4 cts.; count at 65 B.P.M.

Begin stage left facing stage right, or begin upstage, facing downstage. The feet in Natural 1st, the arms in 2nd.

- ct. 1 Slide the right foot diagonally forward across *the body and tilt the torso diagonally backward with the pelvis pressing forward as in a Hinge.* The left leg turns out and the left knee begins to bend and the left heel raises only slightly off the floor.
- ct. 2 Continue to slide and reach with the right hand directly to the floor in line with the right shoulder. At the same time, the body leans to the right. The left arm remains in 2nd. Since the *body is leaning to the right a diagonal line* will be formed with both arms and the shoulders. The left knee continues to bend and turn out.
- ct. 3-4 Continue to slide and place the right palm on the floor. The *pelvis remains pressing diagonally forward until the right buttock touches the floor.* Then the inside of the left bent leg touches the floor and the left foot points.

4th Position Descent

Adv.; 4 cts.; count at 60 B.P.M.

Begin center, facing downstage, the feet in Natural 1st, the arms in Natural Low.

- ct. 1 Step forward on the right foot into Natural 4th. The arms lift to Demi-2nd.
- cts. 2-4 With the weight centered, *grand plié with the feet in ¼ relevé until both buttocks touch the floor.* Point both feet once the buttocks have touched the floor. The torso remains erect.

Figure 4 Descent

Int., Adv.; 4 cts.; count at 60 B.P.M.

Begin center, facing downstage, the feet in Natural 2nd, the arms in 2nd.

- ct. 1 *Twist the torso ½ turn to the right* as the right leg pivots to the right and turns out and the right knee bends. The left leg remains straight and rotates inward, and the left foot flexes. The inner thighs of both legs are touching. The head turns to the right, with the focus over the right hand.
- cts. 2-4 *Deepen the plié* on the right leg, and slide the left foot along the floor toward stage left. The left arm lowers in a perpendicular line to the floor, to help ease the body down to the floor. The left hip touches the floor and the body ends in Seated Figure 4 position.

Side Lunge Descent

Beg., Int., Adv.; 8 cts. on each side; count at 60 B.P.M.

Begin center facing downstage, feet in Natural 1st, the arms in Natural Low.

Preparation

cts. 1 and 2   Step forward with the right foot into *Deep Forward Lunge,* with the arms in Middle Parallel.

cts. 3 and 4   Turn the body ¼ turn to the left to face stage left in *Side Lunge position,* by rotating the left leg outward and the right foot inward. The left foot flexes. The arms remain in Middle Parallel. Place both buttocks on the floor if possible and keep the back straight.

cts. 5 and 6   Return to *Deep Forward Lunge,* facing downstage with the arms in Middle Parallel.

cts. 7 and 8   Keeping the left leg straight, slide the left foot forward into Natural 1st. The arms lower to Natural Low.

Repeat to the other side.

12 ct. Descent and Ascent

Int., Adv.; 12 cts. 2 times; count at 60 B.P.M.

Begin center facing downstage, feet in Natural 1st, the arms in Natural Low.

Descent

cts. 1 and 2   Step forward with the right foot into *Deep Forward Lunge.* The arms lift to Middle Parallel.

cts. 3 and 4   Turn the body ¼ turn to the left to face stage left in seated *Side Lunge position.* The left leg rotates outward, the right foot rotates inward, and the left foot flexes. Both buttocks touch the floor. The arms remain in Middle Parallel and the back remains straight.

ct. 5   Keeping the left foot flexed, slide the left leg and move the hips slightly away from the right heel.

ct. 6   Place the left palm on the floor toward stage right, then place the right palm on the floor as the body *rolls to the left and extends fully.* The front of the body is on the floor. Both arms are bent, and the hands are on the floor, placed directly under the shoulders.

Ascent

cts. 7 and 8   In a simultaneous action, lift, bend, and turn out the left leg, until the left foot touches the floor. The torso turns to face stage right and the body moves to a seated *Side Lunge position.* The arms lift to Middle Parallel.

cts. 9 and 10   Turn the body ¼ turn to the left to face downstage, in *Deep Forward Lunge.* The arms remain in Middle Parallel.

cts. 11 and 12   Keeping the right leg straight, slide the right foot forward into Natural 1st. The arms lower to Natural Low.

Repeat to the other side.

Note: Advanced students may repeat the movement in six counts.

Hinge Descent and Ascent

Beg., Int., Adv.; the Descent can be done in 16 cts., 12 cts., 8 cts., 6 cts., 4 cts., 3 cts., or 1 ct.; count at 60 B.P.M.

Preparation at the barre for beginners.

Begin holding the barre with the left hand, the feet in Parallel 2nd, the other arm in Natural Low.

Descent

Holding onto the barre with the left hand, begin to *press the pelvis forward as the knees bend and the torso tilts back.* The body is in a diagonal line from the knees through the top of the head. Continue to descend with a hinging action until both knees are as close to the floor as possible. Keep the right arm in line with the body throughout the Descent.

Note: The knees drive diagonally downward on the Descent.

Ascent

The Ascent can be done with the same counts as the Descent. Retrace the movement upward and return the heels to the floor as soon as possible.

Note: The heels remain on the floor as long as possible in the Descent and press to the floor as soon as possible on the Ascent.

Note: Intermediate and advanced students can do the Descent center floor, descending with a hinging action until the knees touch the floor.

Crossed Leg Ascent and Descent

Beg., Int.; four 2's five times; count at 55 B.P.M.

Begin sitting on the floor facing the downstage left diagonal with the left knee bent and the right foot crossed over the left knee and placed on the floor. The arms are in 2nd.

Note: The ascent and descent are sequential in movement and smooth and flowing in quality.

Note: The torso remains erect and the arms remain in 2nd throughout the ascent and descent.

Phrase 1

cts. 1-2   Straighten the right leg and open it to 2nd, as the torso turns to the right, passing through downstage, to face the upstage right diagonal. Straighten the left leg, bend the right knee, and bend the left knee in a sequential order. *Place the left foot on the floor, on the outside of the right knee, into a crossed-leg position.* Both buttocks remain on the floor.

cts. 2-2 Repeat to the other side, retracing the movement pattern.

cts. 3-2 and 4-2 Repeat the movement described above in cts. 1-2 and 2-2.

Phrase 2: Ascent to the knee

cts. 1-2 Straighten the right leg and open it to 2nd as the torso turns to the right, passing through downstage, to face the upstage right diagonal. Straighten the left leg, bend the right knee, bend the left knee and place the left foot on the floor on the outside of the right knee and diagonally forward; *lift the body into a kneeling crossed-leg position.* The pelvis lifts forward until it forms a straight line with the femoral joint.

cts. 2-2 Repeat to the other side, retracing the movement pattern.

cts. 3-2 and 4-2 Repeat the movement described above in cts. 1-2 and 2-2.

Phrase 3: Ascent to standing

cts. 1-2 Straighten the right leg and open it to 2nd as the torso turns to the right, passing through downstage, to face the upstage right diagonal. Straighten the left leg, bend the right knee, bend the left knee and place the left foot on the floor on the outside of the right knee and diagonally forward; *stand with the right leg in back attitude.*

cts. 2-2 Repeat to the other side, retracing the movement pattern.

cts. 3-2 and 4-2 Repeat the movement described above in cts. 1-2 and 2-2.

Phrase 4: Ascent with a jump

cts. 1-2 Straighten the right leg and open it to 2nd as the torso turns to the right, passing through downstage, to face the upstage right diagonal. Straighten the left leg, bend the right knee, bend the left knee and place the left foot on the floor on the outside of the right knee and diagonally forward; *stand and jump with the right leg in back attitude.*

cts. 2-2 Repeat to the other side, retracing the movement pattern.

cts. 3-2 and 4-2 Repeat the movement described above in cts. 1-2 and 2-2.

Phrase 5: Ascent with a turning jump

cts. 1-2 Straighten the right leg and open it to 2nd as the torso turns to the right, passing through downstage, to face the upstage right diagonal. Straighten the left leg, bend the right knee, bend the left knee and place the left foot on the floor on the outside of the right knee and diagonally forward; *stand, jump, and turn one full turn to the right in the air with the right leg in back attitude.*

cts. 2-2   Repeat to the other side, retracing the movement pattern.

cts. 3-2   Repeat the movement described above in cts. 1-2 and 2-2.
and 4-2

Nine

Stretches and Strengtheners

It is important to warm up the body thoroughly before executing the Horton stretches. These stretches work the muscles deeply, with the feeling of working from the joint outward. Some of the stretches are stationary, while others use the momentum of the body to greatly increase the stretch.

Triangle Position Stretches and Strengtheners

Starting positions for the following six Triangle exercises are the same. Begin in seated Triangle position, facing downstage, right leg inverted. The arms remain in 2nd throughout this section unless otherwise instructed.

Seated Table No. 1

Strengthens the hip joint and abdominals

Beg.; two 3's 4 times; transition in two 3's; count at 75 B.P.M.

cts. 1-2-3 *Lift the right leg in Seated Table position,* keeping the torso erect.
cts. 2-2-3 *Lower the right leg to the floor.*

Repeat three more times.

Transition

Two 3's

cts. 1-2-3 *Raise the body onto both knees* by bringing the pelvis off the floor and forward, forming a straight line with the femoral joint. *Move the left foot back* to align the legs parallel and hip width apart.

cts. 2-2-3 Move the right foot forward, foreleg parallel to downstage, as *the body lowers to Triangle position with the left leg inverted.*

Repeat on the other side.

Seated Table No. 2

Strengthens the hip joint and abdominals; stretches the side of the body

Beg., Int.; four 3's, four 2's, 4 cts.; count at 75 B.P.M.

Four 3's

cts. 1-2-3 *Lift the right leg to Seated Table position.*
cts. 2-2-3 *Reach the left elbow toward the right inverted knee* by moving the torso to the left and forward.
cts. 3-2-3 *Return the left arm to 2nd and the torso to center* by retracing the movement above.
cts. 4-2-3 *Lower the right leg to Triangle position.* A 4 ct. Coccyx Transition may be used to repeat to the other side (see Turns in Chapter 11). Repeat with 2 counts for each measure and 1 count for each measure.

Seated Table No. 3

Strengthens the hip joint and abdominals; stretches the back and hamstring

Int., Adv.; four 3's four times; count at 75 B.P.M.

cts. 1-2-3 *Lift the right leg to Seated Table position.* Torso remains erect.
cts. 2-2-3 In a simultaneous action, *extend the right leg sideward, keeping it parallel; flex the foot; and tilt the torso to Flat Back Forward.*
cts. 3-2-3 *Return the torso to center and the right leg to Seated Table.*
cts. 4-2-3 *Lower the right leg to Triangle position.* Repeat three more times. A 4 ct. Coccyx Transition may be used to repeat to the other side (see Turns in Chapter 11).

Seated Table No. 4

Strengthens the hip joint and abdominals; stretches the back and hamstring

Int., Adv.; four 3's four times; count at 75 B.P.M.

cts. 1-2-3 *Lift the right leg to Seated Table position.* Torso remains erect.
cts. 2-2-3 In a simultaneous action, *extend the right leg sideward, keeping it parallel; flex the foot; and tilt the torso to Flat Back Forward.*
cts. 3-2-3 *Return the torso to center and the right leg to Seated Table.*
cts. 4-2-3 *Lower the right leg to Triangle position.*

Repeat three more times.

A 4 ct. Coccyx Transition with ¼ turn may be used to repeat to the other side (see Turns in Chapter 11).

Seated Table No. 5 with ¼ Turn

Strengthens the hip joint, abdominals, and quadriceps

Int., Adv.; four 3's four times; count at 75 B.P.M.

cts. 1-2-3 *Lift the right leg to Seated Table position.* Torso remains erect.
cts. 2-2-3 *Turn ¼ turn to face stage right,* as the right leg turns out, lifts up, and extends. The arms reach to Middle Parallel toward stage right, with one arm on either side of the extended right leg. The left foreleg remains on the floor parallel to downstage.
cts. 3-2-3 *Return the torso to face downstage and the arms to 2nd* as the *right leg returns to Seated Table.*
cts. 4-2-3 *Lower the right leg to Seated Triangle position.*

Repeat three more times.

A 4 ct. Coccyx Transition may be used to repeat to the other side (see Turns in Chapter 11).

Seated Table No. 6 with ¼ Turn and Coccyx Balance

Strengthens the hip joint and abdominals

Beg., Int.; three 3's four times; count at 75 B.P.M.

Begin facing downstage in Triangle position, the right leg inverted, the arms in 2nd.

cts. 1-2-3 *Lift the right leg to Seated Table position.* Torso remains erect.
cts. 2-2-3 *Turn the body ¼ turn to face stage right as the weight shifts to both buttocks and the legs lift to Coccyx Balance position.* The arms are in Middle Parallel.
cts. 3-2-3 *Turn the body ¼ turn to the right to face upstage* and lower the legs to Triangle position, the left leg inverted. The right arm opens horizontally to 2nd and the left palm turns to face the floor.

Repeat alternating sides three more times.

Kneeling Triangle

Strengthens the hip joint and stretches the adductors

Int., Adv.; four 3's four times; count at 80 B.P.M.

Begin facing downstage in Triangle position, right leg inverted, the arms in 2nd.

cts. 1-2-3   Keeping the body erect, *press both knees sideward, sliding the legs on the floor.* The left knee will move toward stage left and the right knee will move toward stage right.

cts. 2-2-3   *Raise the body to a kneeling Triangle position* by lifting the buttocks off the floor and moving the pelvis forward over the left shin.

cts. 3-2-3   *Lower the buttocks to the floor,* keeping them as close to the left heel as possible.

cts. 4-2-3   *Press the legs back to Triangle position* by sliding the legs on the floor.

Repeat three more times.

A 4 ct. Coccyx Transition may be used to repeat to the other side (see Turns in Chapter 11).

Hip Press Stretch

Stretches the femoral joint and quadriceps

Beg., Int., Adv.; two 3's four times for each phrase; count at 80 B.P.M.

Phrase 1

Begin facing downstage in Triangle position, the right leg inverted. The torso is tilted back, the elbows bent, and the forearms on the floor behind the hips.

cts. 1-2-3   *Press the right hip bone diagonally to the left,* without disturbing the torso or twisting the shoulders. The right buttock will lift off the floor. Keep both knees down.

cts. 2-2-3   *Center the pelvis and return the right buttock to the floor.* Keep both knees on the floor.

Repeat three more times.

Phrase 2

Begin with the left leg extended on the floor, as far to the side as possible, the left foot pointed. The torso is tilted back, the elbows bent, and the forearms on the floor behind the hips.

cts. 1-2-3   *Press the right hip bone diagonally to the left,* without disturbing the torso or twisting the shoulders. The right buttock will lift off the floor. Keep the right knee on the floor.

cts. 2-2-3   *Center the pelvis and return the right buttock to the floor.* As the buttock returns to the floor, the left foot flexes. Keep the right knee on the floor.

Repeat three more times.

Phrase 3

Begin with the left leg extended on the floor, as above. The torso is stretched out on the floor, the right armpit as close to the inverted right foot as possible, and the arms in 2nd, the palms on the floor.

cts. 1-2-3   *Press the right hip bone diagonally to the left* without disturbing the torso or twisting the shoulders. The right buttock will lift slightly off the floor. Keep the right knee on the floor.

cts. 2-2-3   *Center the pelvis and return the right buttock to the floor.* As the buttock returns to the floor, the left foot flexes. Keep the right knee on the floor.

Repeat three more times.

Repeat the entire sequence on the other side.

Straight Back Descent with Circular Recovery

Stretches the quadriceps

Begin facing downstage in Triangle position; the right leg is inverted, the arms are in 2nd.

Int., Adv.; 8 cts. three times; 4 ct. transition; count at 65 B.P.M.

cts. 1 and 2   Tilt the torso back to *Flat Back Back Bend.*

cts. 3 and 4   *Slide the palms on the floor* with each hand pointing to the upstage diagonal. Keeping the back straight, lower the back to the floor.

cts. 5 and 6   *Turn the torso to the left to face stage left and place the weight on the left forearm, the elbow bent, the palm up, the fingers pointing to the upstage diagonal.* The right arm is rounded and over the head. The focus is to the palm of the left hand.

ct. 7   Swing the torso to the right to finish *in Flat Back Forward, arms in 2nd.*

ct. 8   *Center the torso.*

Repeat twice more.

A 4 count Coccyx Transition may be used to repeat to the other side.

Variation

Same sequence may be repeated in 4 counts.

"and"   Tilt the torso to *Flat Back Back Bend.*

ct. 1   *Slide the palms on the floor.*

ct. 2   *Turn the torso to face stage left, weight on the forearm.*

ct. 3   Swing the torso *to Flat Back Forward.*

ct. 4   *Center the torso.*

Percussive Hip

Stretches quadriceps and adductors; strengthens the abdominals

Int., Adv., 2 cts. four times, 16 cts. twice, 4 ct. transition; count at 60 B.P.M.

Preparation

Begin facing downstage in Triangle position, the right leg inverted, arms in 2nd.

ct. 1   *Press the right hip toward the left downstage diagonal.* The right buttock will lift off the floor.

ct. 2   *Center the pelvis* and return the right buttock to the floor.

Repeat three more times.

A 4 ct. Coccyx Transition may be used to repeat to the other side.

16 ct. Phrase

ct. 1   *With a percussive action, press the right hip toward the left downstage diagonal.* The right buttock will lift off the floor.

cts. 2-4   *Turn the torso to face the downstage left diagonal* as the arms lift to Diagonal Egyptian (see Vocabulary in chapter 3). The head is lifted up toward the high diagonal, the hands approximately ten inches from the face, and the focus through the fingers.

cts. 5-8   *Flat Back Back Bend the torso to the floor, as the left leg extends along the floor with a pointed foot, as far back as possible.* Keep the right buttock off the floor and the arms in place.

cts. 9-12   On a breath, *lift the torso erect* (the body is still facing the downstage left diagonal), *and return the left leg to Triangle position.* The arms lift and press open to 2nd.

cts. 13-15   *Turn the upper torso to face downstage,* keeping the right buttock off the floor.

ct. 16   With an accented motion, *center the pelvis and return the right buttock to the floor.*

Repeat once more.

A 4 ct. Coccyx Transition may be used to repeat to the other side.

Variation

The same sequence may be done in seven counts.

ct. 1   *Percussive hip action* toward the left downstage diagonal.

"and"   *Turn the torso* to face downstage left diagonal, and *raise the arms to Diagonal Egyptian.*

ct. 2   *Hold.*

cts. 3-4   *Flat Back Back Bend, and extend the left leg.*

cts. 5-6   *Lift torso erect, and bend the left leg to Triangle position.*

ct. 7 *Percussive hip action to turn the torso to face downstage, return the right buttock to the floor.*

•• • •   •
Wide Natural 2nd Stretch

Int., Adv.; eight 3's four times; count at 65 B.P.M.

Begin center, facing downstage, the feet in Wide Natural 2nd, the arms remain in 2nd throughout.

    cts. 1-2-3 *Press into grand plié,* keeping the back straight and the torso centered.

    cts. 2-2-3 As the left leg straightens, *shift the weight onto the right leg,* keeping the pelvis on the same level.

    cts. 3-2-3 *Shift the weight back to center* as the left leg bends, keeping the pelvis on the same level.

    cts. 4-2-3 *Straighten both legs.*

Repeat to the other side.

Increase the width of the Wide Natural 2nd, and repeat the stretch three more times, increasing the width of the Wide Natural 2nd after each set.

Variation

On 2-2-3, lift the right heel off the floor as the left leg straightens, and *shift the pelvis as close as possible to the right heel.* The torso must remain upright. On 3-2-3, as the weight shifts back to center, *keep the pelvis as low as possible in the grand plié.*

•• • •   •
Strike Stretch

Stretches the hamstrings and lengthens the back muscles

Begin stage left, facing stage right, the feet in Natural 1st, the arms in Natural Low.

Variation No. 1

Beg., Int., Adv.; 8 cts.; count at 55 B.P.M.

    cts. 1-2 Step forward with the left foot, and *lift the right leg forward with the right knee bent at a right angle and parallel.* The arms raise to Middle Parallel, with the palms facing the floor.

    cts. 3-4 *Step forward onto the right foot,* reach forward with both arms, *and begin to tilt the body forward to Flat Back Forward.*

    cts. 5-6 Place both palms on the floor *as the left leg lifts to Strike position.*

cts. 7-8 *Hold the Strike position,* and continue to lift the leg and pull the head down.

Repeat, progressing across the floor alternating legs and stepping on the "and" beat.

Variation No. 2

Beg., Int., Adv.; 8 cts.; count at 55 B.P.M.

Repeat counts 1-6 as described above; on counts 7-8, *extend the left leg.*

Variation No. 3

Int., Adv.; 8 cts.; count at 55 B.P.M.

cts. 1-2 Same as above—*lift the right leg forward.*
cts. 3-4 Same as above—*tilt the torso forward to Flat Back Forward,* and bring the left leg to Natural 1st.
cts. 5-6 Place both palms on the floor and raise the *left leg to Lateral T, with the torso as close to the standing leg as possible.*
cts. 7-8 *Hold the Lateral T position.*

Repeat, progressing across the floor, alternating legs and stepping on the "and" beat.

Variation No. 4

Int., Adv.; 16 cts.; count at 55 B.P.M.

cts. 1-2 Same as above—*lift the right leg forward.*
cts. 3-4 Same as above in Variation No. 1—*tilt the body forward to Flat Back.*
cts. 5-6 Same as above in Variation No. 1—place the palms on the floor and *lift the left leg to Strike position.*
cts. 7-8 Same as above in Variation No. 1—hold the Strike position.
cts. 9-12 For the full four counts, bring the left leg forward to *Lateral T position,* keeping the hands on the floor. Simultaneously, the left foot flexes on count 9, points on count 10, flexes on count 11, and points on count 12.
cts. 13-14 *Lift the torso erect as the left leg rotates outward to 2nd,* as high as possible. The arms raise to High Parallel.
ct. 15 *Bend the left knee,* keeping the arms in High Parallel.
ct. 16 Keeping the left knee bent at a right angle, *bring the left leg forward, and the arms to Middle Parallel.*

Repeat, progressing across the floor alternating legs and stepping on the "and" beat.

• • • • •
Deep Forward Lunge Stretches

Stretches the hip joint, Achilles tendon, adductors, and hamstring

Begin center, facing downstage, in Deep Forward Lunge position, with the right knee bent, both palms on the floor on either side of the right foot.

Deep Forward Lunge Stretch No. 1

Int., Adv.; (16 cts., 4 ct. transition) twice; count at 45 B.P.M.

ct. 1   On a down beat action, *press the pelvis diagonally forward toward the right heel.*

Repeat 16 times. Do not bounce.

Transition

cts. 1-4   Straighten the right knee and place the ball of the right foot behind the body, parallel and close to the left foot. *The hands remain on the floor, and the body is extended in a diagonal line.* Do not lift the buttocks too high. Bring the left leg forward, with a bent knee, to *Deep Forward Lunge position.*

Repeat 16-count pelvic press action and transition on the left side.

Deep Forward Lunge Stretch No. 2

Int., Adv.; (Three 4's four times, 4 ct. transition) twice; count at 45 B.P.M.

cts. 1-4   On the down beat, *press the pelvis diagonally forward toward the right heel,* four times.

cts. 2-4   Keeping the hands on the floor, *straighten the right knee, as the left heel presses toward the floor.* The left heel should not be able to touch the floor. (Increase the length of the lunge if the heel is able to touch.) The body lengthens along the inside of the right leg, with the head pulling toward the right ankle.

cts. 3-4   Maintaining the established position, continue to *stretch the left heel toward the floor and to lengthen the back. Continue to pull the head toward the right ankle.*

"and"   Bend the right knee, and raise the torso to *return to Deep Forward Lunge position,* with the hands remaining in place on the floor.

Repeat three more times.

Transition

Same as above—in 4 counts, *straighten the right leg behind and form a diagonal line with the body. Bring the left leg forward with a bent knee to Deep Forward Lunge position.*

Deep Forward Lunge Stretch No. 3

Int., Adv.; (five 4's four times, 4 ct. transition) twice; count at 45 B.P.M.

cts. 1-4 Same as above—*pelvic press action toward the right heel.*

cts. 2-4 Same as above—*straighten the right knee, lengthen the torso, and press the left heel toward the floor.*

cts. 3-4 Same as above—*maintain the position established and continue to stretch.*

cts. 4-4 Keeping both palms on the floor and the body as low as possible, *arch the back.*

cts. 5-4 Keeping both palms on the floor, *return the back to the stretched-out position close to the inside of the right leg.*

"and" Return to *Deep Forward Lunge position.*

Repeat three more times.

Transition

Same as above—in four counts, *straighten the right leg behind and form a diagonal line with the body. Bring the left leg forward with a bent knee to Deep Forward Lunge.*

Deep Forward Lunge Stretch No. 4

Int., Adv.; (16 cts., 4 ct. transition) twice; count at 45 B.P.M.

cts. 1-16 In Deep Forward Lunge position, place the outside of the right shoulder on the inside of the right knee. *Walk forward with both hands* as the body continues to stretch forward and the pelvis lowers toward the right heel, which must remain on the floor.

Transition

Same as above—in 4 counts, *straighten the right leg behind and form a diagonal line with the body. Bring the left leg forward with a bent knee to Deep Forward Lunge position.* Repeat to the other side.

The following *Studies* from Chapter 7 may also be used as *Stretches and Strengtheners:*

> Deep Floor Vocabulary
>
> Fortification Study Nos. 4, 5 and 6
>
> Figure 4 Study

Ten

Falls

The falls display the most dynamic and spectacular motion in this technique. Horton designed the falls to assure the dancer of control and support while giving the illusion of momentary collapse promptly followed by a recovery. He explored the aspects of balanced and off-balance positions to initiate many of the fall sequences. He used the floor as an extension of space, and thus increased the dancer's sensitivity to it.

Front Fall

Int., Adv.; 12 cts., 8 cts., 5 cts., and 3 cts. (7 measures of 4/4); count at 60 B.P.M.

Begin center, facing downstage, the feet in Parallel 2nd, the arms in Natural Low.

12 cts.

ct. 1   With an accent, relevé; arms move through Middle Parallel to High Parallel.

cts. 2-3   Begin to *descend with a hinging action.*

ct. 4   Continue to hinge until the *knees touch the floor.* The toes remain curled.

"and"   *The pelvis presses forward as the back arches.*

ct. 5   The arms reach back in a circular motion and come down to the sides of the body, as *the pelvis continues to press forward* and the back continues to arch.

ct. 6   Staying in arched position, *fall forward,* bracing the fall with bent arms, elbows close to the body, hands at the pelvis. As the hands touch the floor, the right arm straightens and slides forward on the little finger side of the hand; the head looks left.

"and"   Pull back the pelvis and bend the knees so that *the buttocks lift toward the ceiling;* the toes stay curled.

cts. 7-8   Continue to pull back the pelvis and push the left palm into the floor; lift the knees off the floor and *squat,* ending with the torso

152

rounded over, heels off the floor, legs parallel and hip width apart, and both hands on the floor, near the outsides of the feet.

ct. 9   Pivot on the right foot as the left foot opens and the *body makes ½ turn* to the left. Simultaneously, begin to press the pelvis forward in Hinge position, and face back in *deep Hinge* position (knees two inches from the floor). The left arm lifts to Middle Parallel as the turn begins; the right hand remains on the floor.

cts. 10-12   The right arm lifts to Middle Parallel, and both arms lift to High Parallel as *the body ascends with a hinging action. The body comes erect and the heels lift simultaneously into relevé.* Do not arch the back.

Begin facing upstage.

8 cts.

cts. 1-2   *Begin to descend with a hinging action.*

ct. 3   End in *Hinge position, knees on the floor;* the pelvis presses forward as back arches and the arms reach back in a circular motion and come down to the sides as pelvis continues to press forward.

ct. 4   Staying in arched position, *fall forward* as in count 6.

"and"   Pull back the pelvis and bend the knees so that the buttocks lift toward the ceiling.

ct. 5   *Pull back to Squat position* as in counts 7 and 8.

ct. 6   Pivot on the right foot; the left foot opens as the *body turns ½ turn to the left* as in count 9.

cts. 7-8   *Ascend with a hinging action* as described in counts 10-11-12.

Begin facing downstage.

5 cts.

ct. 1   *Begin to descend with a hinging action.*

ct. 2   *End in Hinge position, knees on the floor;* pelvis presses forward as back arches and arms reach back in a circular motion.

ct. 3   *Fall forward* as described above.

"and"   *Pull back to Squat position* as described above.

ct. 4   Pivot on right foot; left foot opens as *body makes ½ turn to the left* as above.

ct. 5   *Ascend with a hinging action* as described in counts 10-11-12.

Markedly slower tempo; count at 50 B.P.M.

Begin facing upstage.

3 cts.

"and"   *Begin to descend with a hinging action.*

ct. 1   *End Hinge,* knees on the floor; *pelvis presses forward as back arches* and arms reach back in a circular motion.

"and"   *Fall forward* as described above.

ct. 2   Pull back to Squat position as described above.

"and"   Pivot on right foot; left foot opens as body turns ½ *turn to left* as described above.

ct. 3   Ascend with a hinging action as described above.

•• • •
Back Fall

Int., Adv.; 12 cts. twice, 8 cts. twice, and 4 cts. twice; count at 60 B.P.M.

Begin center, facing downstage, the feet in Parallel 2nd, the arms in Natural Low.

12 cts.

ct. 1   With a slight accent, *relevé,* and lift both arms through Middle Parallel to *High Parallel.*

cts. 2-3   Descend with a hinging action, lowering the heels to ½ relevé, and simultaneously reach the right arm back in a circular motion as the left arm lowers forward to Middle Parallel. *The side of the right hand touches the floor and slides back on a straight arm.* Maintain the Hinge position.

ct. 4   *Touch right shoulder to the floor,* and continue to slide back on the right hand (the upper back may arch, if necessary). The pelvis is still pressing up, with the knees as close to the floor as possible without touching.

cts. 5-6-7-8   *The body slides to a supine position on the back,* as the left arm lowers to the floor close to the body.

cts. 9-10-11-12   *Front Recovery;* see the end of this chapter.

Repeat to the left side.

8 cts.

ct. 1   Same as count 1 above—*relevé, arms lift to High Parallel.*

ct. 2   Same as counts 2 and 3 above—*descend with a hinging action; the side of right hand touches the floor.*

ct. 3   Same as count 4 above—the right *shoulder touches floor.*

ct. 4   Same as counts 5-8 above—body slides to supine position.

cts. 5-6-7-8   *Front Recovery;* see the end of this chapter.

Repeat to the left side.

4 cts.

"and"   Same as 12-count phrase above in counts 1-3—*relevé and descend*

ct. 1   *with a hinging action;* the side of the right hand touches the floor.

"and"   Same as 12-count phrase above in count 4—the right *shoulder touches floor.*

ct. 2 Same as 12-count phrase above in cts. 5-8—*the body slides to supine position.*

cts. 3-4 *Front Recovery;* see the end of this chapter.

Repeat to the left side.

Preparation for Side Fall

Beg.; 4 cts.; count at 60 B.P.M.

Begin center, facing downstage, kneeling, with the legs in Parallel 2nd, the arms in Natural Low.

cts. 1-3 *Both arms reach to the right, lift up to High Parallel, and continue the circle to Lateral left side.* The pelvis pulls to the right on the Lateral left side to act as a counterbalance.

ct. 4 *Side Fall* to the right as the body continues to Lateral to the left. In a succession, the side of the right thigh (the flank) touches the floor, then the right hip, then the arms circle down to the sides, then the little finger side of the hand touches the floor and slides sideward on a straight arm. The side of the rib cage then touches the floor, with the head resting on the right arm. End lying on the right side in a straight line, the left leg straight and the right knee bent, the right big toe touching the left knee, the left palm on the floor in front of the sternum.

Front Recovery or Rib Cage Recovery; see the end of this chapter.

Side Fall

Beg.; 12 cts.; count at 60 B.P.M.

Begin center, facing downstage, the feet in Parallel 2nd, the arms in Natural Low.

ct. 1 With an accent, relevé, and lift both arms to High Parallel, moving through Middle Parallel.

cts. 2-3-4 *Bend both knees, press into a shallow Hinge and shift the weight to the left leg, and begin to lower the body to the floor;* Lateral the upper body to the left; the arms remain in High Parallel.

ct. 5 Continue to lower the body to the floor, Lateral to the left, and *place the top of the right foot on the floor* (there is no weight on the foot), and lightly place the shin on the floor.

ct. 6 *Side Fall to the right:* As the body continues to Lateral to the left, in a succession the side of the right thigh (the flank) touches the floor, then the right hip, then the arms circle down to the sides, then the little finger side of the right hand touches the floor and slides sideward on a straight arm. The side of the rib cage then touches the floor. Continue to slide until the entire right side of the body touches the floor, with the head resting on the right arm. End lying on the right side in a straight line, the left leg straight and the right knee bent, the right big toe touching the left knee, the left palm on the floor in front of the sternum.

"and" Simultaneously, *lift the left side of the rib cage* toward the ceiling and the right side of the rib cage off the floor and pull the left elbow diagonally upward to the left until the hand lifts slightly off the floor.

cts. 7-8 In a succession, lift the torso, then the head erect, then lift the left arm on an upward diagonal to the left; the left leg stays parallel, and the left foot slides sideward on the floor (the left buttock is off the floor); the right arm slides toward the body and lifts to 2nd.

ct. 9 Rotate the left leg out, and lift the leg diagonally forward at a 45° angle (the left buttock touches the floor); the arms reach to Middle Parallel.

cts. 10-11-12 *Front Recovery;* see the end of this chapter.

Repeat to the other side.

Side Fall with a Jump

Beg., Int.; 2 cts.; count at 65 B.P.M.

Begin stage left, facing downstage, the feet in Natural 1st, the arms in Natural Low.

ct. 1 *The left foot takes a wide step across to the right and pushes off the floor to jump* as the right leg bends and turns parallel. Both arms reach to the right, lift up to High Parallel, and continue to circle to Lateral left side.

ct. 2 Land on the left foot and continue to plié and to lower the body toward the floor until the right shin touches the floor, keeping the right foot pointed. *Continue the Side Fall as described above.*

Front Recovery or Rib Cage Recovery; see the end of this chapter.

⋅⋅ ⋅ ⋅ ⋅ Spiral Fall

Int., Adv.; 24 cts.; count at 55–60 B.P.M.

Begin facing downstage, standing, the feet in Parallel 2nd, the arms in Natural Low.

ct. 1 *Relevé and step forward with right foot to Parallel 4th position;* the arms lift in opposition to the feet; the left arm lifts forward

Figure 30. Spiral Fall

to Middle Parallel, the palm facing down, the right arm lifts to 2nd.

cts. 2-3-4   *Begin to Hinge,* and lower the heels to two inches off the floor.

cts. 5-6-7-8   As the body continues to descend lower with a hinging action, *pivot left ¼ turn;* the legs rotate out slightly; the left arm opens to 2nd position.

cts. 9-10-   Continue to hinge lower; *pivot left ¼ turn to face upstage;* the legs
11-12   continue to turn out and the body continues to descend lower with a hinging action.

cts. 13-14-   The pelvis continues to press upward as the *left arm reaches behind*
15-16   *and diagonally downward toward the floor;* right arm moves to Middle Parallel, the palm facing down.

ct. 17   Keeping the buttocks off the floor, *place the left palm on the floor;* the head turns left and the focus is to the left hand.

ct. 18   Keep the buttocks lifted and slide back on the left arm keeping it straight until *the back of the shoulder touches the floor.*

ct. 19   Point both feet and *lower the body to the floor.*

ct. 20   The right arm circles back, picking up left arm as both arms circle overhead; the body moves laterally to the right, the head turns to the right.

Figure 31. Spiral Fall; final position

cts. 21-22- The body continues to circle to the right. The right inverted leg turns
    23-24 out and straightens forward as the torso lifts erect and both arms
reach into Middle Parallel for *Front Recovery.*

> **Note:** *The movement should be a continuous circular motion.*

> **Note:** *The action of a Spiral Fall is the combination of a Hinge and a pivotal turn.*

•• • •   •
Lateral Side Twist Fall

Adv.; six 3's twice, eight 3's twice, twelve 3's, four 3's; count at 60 B.P.M.

Begin facing downstage, the feet in Natural 2nd; the arms in 2nd.

Phrase 1

cts. 1-2-3 *Bend knees and rebound out of the plié* without fully straightening
the knees; both arms drop, bend, and cross in front of the sternum,
the palms facing upward, with the left arm always crossing in front
of the right.

cts. 2-2-3 *Repeat the plié and rebound action* in knees as both arms drop and
open to 2nd position.

cts. 3-2-3 Repeat 1-2-3 as described above—*bend knees and rebound.*

cts. 4-2-3 Repeat the plié and rebound action, but as arms open, shift the
weight onto the right foot into High Lateral position. The torso tilts
to the right as both arms open to High Parallel. The left leg turns
parallel and the toes point slightly off the floor. A diagonal line
should be formed from the fingertips through the torso and the left
leg and the left foot.

cts. 5-2-3 *Hold High Lateral position.*
   and
   6-2-3

Repeat phrase 1 to the left side.

Phrase 2

cts. 1-2-3 *Repeat opening phrase (phrase 1) to the right side.*
through
6-2-3

cts. 7-2-3 Holding the body in the same position, change the axis to form a
Lateral T position.

cts. 8-2-3 *Hold Lateral T position.*

Repeat phrase 2 to the other side.

Phrase 3

cts. 1-2-3 *Repeat phrase 2 to the right side.*
through
8-2-3

cts. 9-2-3   *Relevé* in Lateral T position.

cts. 10-2-3   Keeping the arms in High Parallel, and the torso in Lateral right, *step with the left foot directly side,* across and past the right foot, to a *wide Cross Lunge* position with the torso facing forward and in Lateral right. The arms remain in High Parallel.

cts. 11-2-3   Maintaining the Cross Lunge position described above, turn the
and   torso to face the ceiling with the feet adjusting to accommodate the
12-2-3   ½ turn to the right. The weight remains on the left foot; the extended right foot slides slightly forward as *the body lowers to the floor;* the arms reach diagonally back as both hands touch the floor first, then the shoulders touch the floor, and lastly the buttocks and the inverted knee.

cts. 1-2-3   *Front Recovery;* see the end of this chapter.
through
4-2-3

·· · · ·
Back T Fall

Back T Fall Preparation

Int., Adv.; 4 cts. progressing across the floor; count at 60 B.P.M.

Begin stage,left facing stage right, the feet in Parallel 1st, the arms in Natural Low.

Standing Stag position (see Vocabulary in chapter 3)

ct. 1   *Step forward* onto slightly turned out right leg; the left leg is straight, parallel, and directly behind, the foot pointed and slightly off the floor; both arms lifted forward to shoulder height, with the right hand approximately two inches above the left, the palms facing down.

cts. 2-3-4   Slowly plié on the right leg and descend into *Standing Stag position;* the right arm passes through 2nd and reaches directly behind the right shoulder.

"and"   Step through on left leg; the arms lower to Natural Low.

Repeat the 4-count phrase progressing across the floor.

Standing Stag Position with Single Turn

ct. 1   Repeat count 1 as above—*step forward.*

cts. 2-3-4   Open the right arm to the back in one accented motion as impetus for *a sustained turn to the right in Standing Stag position.*

"and"   Step through on left leg; the arms lower to Natural Low.

Repeat the 4-count phrase progressing across the floor.

Standing Stag Position with Single Turn and Single Turn in Lateral T position

cts. 1-4 Repeat the *single Stag turn* as described above.

cts. 5-8 Continue to turn and simultaneously circle the torso to the right and extend the left leg, bringing it in line with the torso to *Lateral T position;* the standing leg slowly straightens; the arms remain straight and move to High Parallel.

cts. 9-11 Stop turning, but continue to circle the torso to the right and bring the left leg forward to *Back T position;* the standing leg bends, the heel lifts slightly off the floor; the left arm circles back and to 2nd.

"and" *Maintain the Back T position* and inhale deeply, causing the T position to raise up slightly.

ct. 12 Descend with a hinging action as deeply as possible on the right leg to fall forward onto the left foot, out of the Back T position, and step forward on the right foot. (This is a preparatory movement for the actual Back T Fall.)

Repeat the 12-count phrase progressing across the floor.

Back T Fall

Repeat cts. 1-11 as described above, ending in Back T position with the arms in 2nd.

ct. 11 Relevé slightly on the right leg, lift the right metatarsal off the floor,
"and" and rise to the tips of the toes and *over the top of the foot, with the foot fully pointed.*

ct. 12 Lower onto the lower part of the right leg as you fall to the floor in the *Back T position.* Both arms reach back and down; the fingers touch the floor and slide back as the shoulders, then the back, then the buttocks and the left foot touch the floor.

Note: *This fall is only for advanced students.*

•• • •   •
Lateral T Fall

Int., Adv.; 4 cts.; count at 50 B.P.M.

Begin facing downstage, the feet in Natural 1st, the arms in Natural Low.

ct. 1 Step with the right foot turned out and *lift the left leg* to High Lateral position. The left leg lifts parallel and slightly off the floor, the foot pointed. Simultaneously, circle both arms to the left, then up to High Parallel, then Lateral right.

ct. 2 Continue to stretch the body and *change the axis into Lateral T position.*

ct. 3 Continue to stretch the body and *change the axis into a low Lateral position* until the right hand touches the floor. Try to keep the front of the body parallel to downstage as the hand touches.

ct. 4 Place the left hand on the floor in front of the sternum and bracing the fall with the left hand, slide the right hand sideward on the floor and slowly lower the left leg as the body descends onto the floor. End lying on the right side, the right arm extended sideward, the left hand in front of the sternum.

Note: *This fall is done in a smooth and continuous phrase.*

Shoulder Fall (Roll)

Beg., Int.; 4 cts.; count at 60 B.P.M.

Begin stage left, facing downstage, the feet in Parallel 2nd, the arms in Natural Low.

ct. 1 Bend both knees and *lower the body as low as possible,* passing through Primitive Squat position (see Vocabulary in chapter 3). Begin to tilt the torso to the right as the torso rounds inward, and the upper part of the back, then the right shoulder, touches the floor.

cts. 2 and 3 *Roll over on the back,* keeping the body and arms rounded inward and the legs bent, continuing to roll until the left palm and the left shin touch the floor. The chest will be facing the floor.

ct. 4 *Lift the torso erect* and step up on the right foot and place the left foot in Parallel 2nd.

Variation

As the body is rolling over onto the back, in a sequential motion the left leg straightens and the right leg straightens so both legs are stretched in 2nd position in the air. Both legs bend sequentially as the roll continues on count 3. Continue count 4, the same as described above.

Front Recovery

Beg., Int., Adv.

This recovery is used with any of the falls described in this chapter. It can be done in the number of counts that best suits the fall that precedes it.

Lift the torso off the floor, and center the weight onto both buttocks. The right knee is bent with the outside of the leg touching the floor, and the left leg is turned out and extended diagonally forward at a 45° angle.

The buttocks leave the floor as the pelvis lifts *upward and forward, over the right knee,* keeping the left leg straight and at hip level. Both arms reach to Middle Parallel.

Bend the left leg, and place the left foot forward on the floor; as you shift the pelvis forward, simultaneously flex the right foot and place the ball of the right foot on the floor. Both arms open to 2nd.

Lift the torso erect, and pull the left foot back to Parallel 1st, as the arms lower to Natural Low.

Note: *Front Recovery can be done on either side.*

.. . . .
Rib Cage Recovery

Beg., Int., Adv.

Begin with the right side of the body stretched out on the floor, as in Side Fall. The right arm is straight and the left arm is bent with the hand in front of the sternum. The counts are suited to the fall that precedes it.

Simultaneously *lift the left side of the rib cage toward the ceiling* and the right side of the rib cage off the floor and *pull the left elbow diagonally upward to the left* until the hand lifts slightly off the floor.

In a succession, lift the torso then the head erect, then lift the left arm on an upward diagonal to the left. The left leg stays parallel, and the left foot slides sideward on the floor, (the left buttock is off the floor). The right arm slides toward the body and lifts to 2nd.

Step sideward onto the left foot, and shift the weight onto the left leg. Bring the right foot to Natural 1st, and the arms to Natural Low.

Note: *Rib Cage Recovery can be done on either side.*

• • • • • • • ••

Eleven

Turns

This section of the book is one of the most extensive and varied. The turns are initiated by using different parts of the body, and many of the turns do not "spot" in the conventional sense of snapping the head and focusing the eyes. The torso is seldom erect, an aspect that poses a challenge to most students of dance. Almost all of the turns can be used as progressions.

•• • • •

Table Turn

Beg., Int., Adv.; 3 cts.; count at 55–60 B.P.M.

Begin stage left, facing stage right, the feet in Natural 1st, the arms in 2nd.

Preparation

> ct. 1 Step forward onto a straight right leg, the right foot turned out, and *lift the left leg to Table position* (see Vocabulary in chapter 3).
> 2 Hold.
> 3 Keeping the left knee bent, lower the left leg and *step forward onto a turned-out left foot.*

Repeat this three-count phrase progressing across the floor.

Repeat to the other side.

Preparation (no turn) with Arm Movement I

> ct. 1 Step forward onto a straight right leg, the right foot turned out, and *lift the left leg to Table position.*
> 2 *Hold the left leg in Table position* and, in a smooth, flowing motion, reach back with the right arm as far as possible, bend the elbow and bring the back of the hand close to the right cheek, straighten the right arm to the ceiling (palm remains facing outward), and tilt the head back, focus to the ceiling.

3 Keeping the left knee bent, lower the left leg forward and *step onto a turned-out left foot;* lower the right arm to 2nd, return the head to the center, and focus stage right.

Repeat this three-count phrase progressing across the floor.

Repeat to the other side.

Table Turn with Arm Movement I

The left arm remains in 2nd throughout.

ct. 1 Step forward onto a turned-out right foot and plié (as preparation for one turn to the right) and *lift the left leg to Table position.*

2 Straighten the right knee and rise to a ¾ relevé for *one turn to the right* as the head and right arm repeat the movements described in ct. 2 above. The left leg remains in Table position during the turn.

3 Same as count 3 above—*step forward onto a turned-out left foot.*

Preparation (no turn) with Arm Movement II

The left arm remains in 2nd throughout.

ct. 1 Step forward onto a straight right leg, the right foot turned out, and *lift the left leg into Table position;* reach back with the right arm as far as possible, bend the elbow and bring the right palm (facing the ceiling) directly in front of the sternum.

2 *Hold the left leg in Table position* and, in a smooth, flowing motion, straighten the right arm and reach forward with the right palm, open the arm to 2nd (palm is still facing up), reach back as far as possible, bend the elbow, and, turning the palm to face down, bring the hand overhead. At the same time, Lateral to the left with the upper body as far as possible.

3 Keeping the left knee bent, lower the left leg and *step forward onto a turned-out left foot;* center the upper body and cut the right arm across the body and open to 2nd.

Repeat the 3-count phrase progressing across the floor.

Repeat to the other side.

Table Turn with Arm Movement II

The left arm remains in 2nd throughout.

ct. 1 Step forward onto a turned-out right foot and plié (as preparation for one turn to the right), *lift the left leg to Table position,* and bend the right elbow and bring the right palm (facing the ceiling) directly in front of the sternum.

2 Straighten the right knee and rise to ¾ relevé for *one turn to the right* as the upper body and right arm repeat the movements described in count 2 above. The left leg remains in Table position during the turn.

3 Same as count 3 above—*step onto a turned-out left foot.*

Stag Turn

Beg.; 4 cts.; smooth and flowing quality; count at 60 B.P.M.

Begin stage left, facing stage right, the feet in Parallel 1st, the arms in Natural Low.

Preparation

ct. 1 *Step forward onto a slightly turned out right leg; the left leg is straight,* parallel, and directly behind, foot pointed and slightly off the floor. Both arms are lifted forward to shoulder height, with the right hand approximately two inches above the left hand; the palms are facing down.

cts. 2-4 *Slowly plié on the right leg and descend into Standing Stag position* (see Vocabulary in chapter 3). The right arm passes through 2nd, and reaches directly behind the body.

"and" *Step forward with the left leg,* the arms lower to Natural Low.

Repeat on the same side, progressing across the floor.

Repeat on the other side.

Preparation with Turn

ct. 1 Same as above—*step forward on the right foot, the left foot pointed behind.*

cts. 2-4 Open the right arm to the back in one *accented* motion, as impetus for *one sustained turn to the right in the Standing Stag position.*

"and" Same as above—*step through with the left leg and lower the arms to Natural Low.*

Standing Stag Turn with Lateral T Turn

cts. 1-4 Same as above—*single turn in Standing Stag position.*

cts. 5-8 *Continue to turn and simultaneously circle the torso to the right and extend the left leg, bringing it in line with the torso into Lateral T position.* The standing leg straightens and the arms move to High Parallel. Continue to circle the torso to the right and bring the left leg forward to Back T position. The standing leg bends and the heel lifts off the floor slightly. The left arm circles back and opens to 2nd.

"and" Same as above—*step forward on the left leg and lower the arms to Natural Low.*

```
•• • •   •
```
Lateral T Turn

Variation No. 1

Beg.; three 3's; slow and flowing quality; count at 60 B.P.M.

Begin center stage facing downstage, the feet in Natural 1st, the arms in Natural Low.

cts. 1-2-3 *Step side to stage right on the right foot in plié,* as both arms begin to reach across the body, to the right on an upward diagonal.

2-2-3 Both arms continue to reach into High Parallel as the left leg and the
and 3-2-3 body move to *Lateral T position and the body makes a single turn to the right.* The standing leg straightens on the turn. Either step immediately with the left leg sideward to repeat to the left, or bring the left leg down to Natural 1st on the upbeat and repeat the right side again.

Variation No. 2

Beg.; three 3's; slow and flowing quality; count at 60 B.P.M.

Begin stage left facing downstage, the feet in Natural 1st, the arms in Natural Low.

cts. 1-2-3 Slide the right foot into *2nd position plié;* the arms reach sideward to 2nd position.

2-2-3 *The left leg and the torso move to Lateral T position, and the body*
and 3-2-3 *makes a single turn to the right.* As the arms move to High Parallel, the palms gradually turn to face each other. The right leg straightens on the turn. Bring the left leg down to Natural 1st on the upbeat, and repeat to the same side, progressing across the floor.

Variation No. 3

Int.; 4 cts.; strong quality; count at 60 B.P.M.

Begin center stage, the body in Flat Back right side, the legs in Wide Natural 2nd, the arms in High Parallel.

ct. 1 *Horizontal Swing* to Flat Back left side.
ct. 2 *Horizontal Swing* to Flat Back right side.

ct. 3 *Horizontal Swing* to left side, *opening the body into Lateral T position* as the body makes a *single turn to the left.* Both arms remain in High Parallel.

ct. 4 Bring the right leg down to Wide Natural 2nd and return the torso to Flat Back left side to begin to the other side.

Variation No. 4

Int.; eight 3's; flowing quality; count at 55 B.P.M.

Begin center stage, the body in Flat Back right side, the legs in Wide Natural 2nd, the arms in High Parallel.

cts. 1-2-3 *Release Swing* to Flat Back left side.
and 2-2-3
cts. 3-2-3 *Release Swing* to Flat Back right side.
and 4-2-3
cts. 5-2-3 *Release Swing* to Flat Back left side, *opening the body into Lateral*
and 6-2-3 *T position* as the body makes a *single turn to the left.* Both arms remain in High Parallel.
cts. 7-2-3 *Hold Lateral T position.*
and 8-2-3
upbeat *Lower the right foot to Wide Natural 2nd,* and return the torso to Flat Back left side to begin to the other side.

Note: *More advanced students may do a double or triple turn in any of the Lateral turns described above.*

Hip Twist Turn

Variation No. 1

Beg.; 3 cts; count at 55–60 B.P.M.

Begin stage left, facing stage right, the feet in Natural 1st, the arms in Natural Low.

ct. 1 *Step forward with the right foot to a shallow Lunge position.* The arms remain in Natural Low.

cts. 2 and 3 With an accent emanating from the hip, *twist the torso ¼ turn to the right, keeping the right knee bent.* The torso is in a high diagonal to the left. The right foot pivots and turns out. The left leg remains straight and rotates inward as the left foot flexes. The inner thighs of both legs are touching. Both arms reach across the body in a downward diagonal, parallel to each other and parallel to the extended leg. Sustain the position on count 3.

Repeat to the other side by stepping forward with the left foot.

Note: *This movement may also be repeated with a full turn.*

Variation No. 2

Beg.; 3 cts.; count at 55–60 B.P.M.

Begin stage left, facing downstage, the feet in Natural 2nd, the arms in 2nd.

ct. 1   Bend the right knee and *twist the torso ½ turn to the right.* The
(accented)   torso moves to a high diagonal line to the left. The right foot pivots
and turns out. The left leg remains straight and rotates inward as
the left foot flexes. The inner thighs of both legs are touching. The
left arm bends, the palm facing the ceiling, and the left elbow slices
across toward the center of the body.

cts. 2 and 3   *Lift the left hip,* as if pulled by a string from above, and begin to
(smooth)   straighten the right leg. *Slide the left foot past the right heel* and
rotate the left leg outward and place the left foot in 2nd and *center
the torso.* The left elbow lifts sideward to shoulder height, and the
lower arm unfolds to 2nd.

Repeat to the other side, progressing across the floor.

> **Note:** More advanced students may do one and a half or more turns.

. . . . .
Hip Press Turn and Hip Pull Turn

Hip Press Turn

Beg.; 2 cts.; smooth quality; count at 50 B.P.M.

Begin stage left facing downstage, the feet in Natural 2nd; the arms remain in 2nd throughout.

ct. 1   Push off with the left foot, *press the pelvis forward, and pivot ½
turn to the right on the right foot.* (The action of the forward pelvic
press causes the torso to tilt back into Flat Back Back Bend.) The left
leg remains in Natural 2nd as the left knee flexes and the toes lift
pointed and slightly off the floor.

ct. 2   *Return to Natural 2nd;* permit the torso to tilt slightly forward as
the pelvis pulls back. There should be a rocking action.

Repeat, alternating sides and progressing across the floor.

Hip Pull Turn

Beg.; 2 cts.; smooth quality; count at 50 B.P.M.

Begin stage left facing downstage, the feet in Natural 2nd, the arms remain in 2nd throughout.

ct. 1   Push off and flex the left foot; *pull the left hip up and back and pivot*

½ *turn to the left on the right foot.* (The action of the hip pull causes the torso to tilt forward.) Both legs remain straight.

ct. 2 *Return to Natural 2nd.*

Repeat, alternating sides and progressing across the floor.

> **Note:** Alternate the right hip press turn and the left hip pull turn, to make continuous ½ turns progressing across the floor.
> **Note:** The right hip press turn and the left hip pull turn may be done as a continuous full turn remaining stationary.

•• • • •
Pencil Turn

Beg., Int.; 2 cts.; smooth quality; count at 60 B.P.M.

Begin stage left, facing downstage, the feet in Natural 1st, the arms in Natural Low.

ct. 1. Slide the right foot sideward and simultaneously *plié on both legs, ending in 2nd position plié.* (The plié should be deeper than a demi-plié, but not as deep as a grand plié.) Both arms lift sideward to 2nd.

ct. 2 Straighten both legs; the left foot flexes and closes to Natural 1st; *and turn ½ turn to the right on the right foot.* The right heel lifts to ¼ relevé. Both arms lower to Natural Low. The head "spots" to focus upstage.

Repeat, alternating sides and progressing across the floor.

> **Note:** This turn may also be done as a full turn, 1 ½ turns, 2 turns, and 2 ½ turns for more advanced students.

•• • • •
Hip Turn

Int., Adv.; 4 cts.; smooth and flowing quality; count at 50 B.P.M.

Begin stage left facing stage right, the feet in Natural 1st, the arms in Natural Low.

(This ½ turn pivots around the stationary leg.)

Variation No. 1

ct. 1 *Step forward with the right foot turned in and bend the right knee.* The right arm opens side, the left arm reaches forward, both arms are shoulder height, and both palms are down.

ct. 2 The right knee straightens; *lift the left leg into turned-out back attitude, tilt the torso to Flat Back Forward,* and turn the body ½

Figure 32. Hip Turn, Variation No. 1

turn to the left in the established position. The left arm opens to 2nd.

ct. 3 *The left leg turns out, straightens, and lowers toward the floor,* with the left foot reaching forward. *The right leg pivots ½ turn to the left as the left leg is straightening.* The torso rotates to face the ceiling.

ct. 4 *Place the left foot on the floor reaching forward with it, ending in plié in natural turn-out.* The torso lifts erect, and the arms remain in 2nd.

Both arms lower to Natural Low before repeating to the same side to progress across the floor.

Repeat to the other side.

Variation No. 2

ct. 1 Same as above—*step forward with the right foot.*

ct. 2 Same as above—*lift the left leg into turned-out back attitude.* As the leg lifts and the torso lowers to Flat Back Forward, *the right arm remains on a horizontal plane as it begins a counterclockwise circle around the head.*

ct. 3 Same as above—*the left leg turns out, straightens, and lowers to the floor and the right leg pivots ½ turn to the left. The torso rotates to face the ceiling.* The right arm continues the counterclockwise circle around the head and returns to 2nd position with the palm up.

ct. 4 Same as above—*place the left foot on the floor, lift the torso erect, and turn the right palm to face the floor.*

Both arms lower to Natural Low before repeating to the same side to progress across the floor.

Repeat to the other side.

Figure 4 Turn

Beg.; 2 cts. smooth and accented quality; count at 55 B.P.M.

Begin stage left facing downstage, the feet in Natural 1st, the arms in Natural Low.

Preparation

ct. 1 smooth Step sideward with the right foot into *Side Hip Push* (see Progressions in Chapter 13).

ct. 2 accented *Figure 4 Squat* by pressing into plié on the right leg and placing the left ankle on the right thigh slightly above the knee. The left foot is flexed. The *torso changes to Lateral right side*. The right arm bends, the palm faces the ceiling, and the elbow slices across toward the center of the body.

Repeat on the same side, progressing across the floor.

Repeat to the other side.

Figure 4 Turn

ct. 1 smooth Same as above—*Side Hip Push*.
    ct. 2 Same as above—*Figure 4 Squat* with one turn to the left. The elbow
accented slicing across acts as the impetus for the turn. The left thigh pressing open and the left arm reaching diagonally up contribute to the smooth continuation of the turn.

Repeat on the same side, progressing across the floor.

Repeat to the other side.

•• • • •
Back T Turn

Int., Adv.; 3 cts. smooth quality; count at 65 B.P.M.

Begin stage left, facing stage right, the feet in Natural 1st, the arms in Natural Low.

Preparation

    "and" *Step forward with the right foot parallel.*
    ct. 1 *Left foot steps forward into Parallel 4th position Hinge* (see Vocabulary in Chapter 3), arms remain straight and lift in opposition to the legs (the right arm forward and parallel to the floor, the left arm side and parallel to the floor, both palms facing the floor).
    ct. 2 Tilt the torso back and lift the left leg into *Back T position* (see Vocabulary in chapter 3). The standing leg continues to bend and turns out slightly for support and balance. The right arm opens to 2nd.
    ct. 3 *Bring the torso erect and step forward on the left foot, as the arms lower to Natural Low.*

Repeat to the same side, progressing across the floor.

Repeat to the other side.

Back T turn

    "and" Same as above—*step forward with the right foot parallel.*
    ct. 1 Same as above—*step forward with the left foot to Parallel 4th position Hinge.*

ct. 2   The *body turns ½ turn to the right on the left foot, as the torso tilts back and the right leg lifts to Back T position.* Maintain the *Back T position,* and continue the turn until facing stage right. The standing (left) leg continues to bend and turns out slightly for support and balance. The right arm opens to 2nd.

ct. 3   *Bring the torso erect and step forward on the right foot, as the arms lower to Natural Low.*

Repeat alternating sides and progressing across the floor.

Lateral–Back–Lateral Turn

Beg., Int.; two 3's; accented and smooth quality; count at 45 B.P.M.

Begin stage left facing stage right, the feet in Natural 1st, the arms in Natural Low.

Preparation No. 1

cts. 1-2-3   Beginning on the left foot, *Unaccented Runs with the arms in Natural Low* (see Elevation in chapter 14).

cts. 2-2-3   Step onto high relevé on the right foot with the right leg straight; *the left leg lifts* behind the back, to *arabesque.* Both arms raise forward through Middle Parallel to High Parallel.

Repeat same side, progressing across the floor.

Repeat to the other side.

Preparation No. 2

cts. 1-2-3   Same as above—*Unaccented Runs with the arms in Natural Low* (see Elevation in chapter 14).

cts. 2-2-3   Step onto high relevé on the right foot with the right leg straight; *the left leg lifts* to *arabesque.* As the torso moves to Lateral right side, both arms cut a diagonal path from Natural Low to High Parallel into Lateral right side (the arms remain parallel to each other, palms facing each other). The torso circles back to Flat Back Back Bend with the arms remaining in High Parallel. The torso continues to circle around to Lateral left side. The arms remain parallel to each other throughout the circle, with the palms facing each other, and the head remains centered between the arms. The lifted leg maintains its high position. The arms return to Natural Low on the upbeat.

Repeat same side, progressing across the floor.

Repeat to the other side.

Lateral-Back-Lateral Turn

cts. 1-2-3   Same as above—*Unaccented Runs with the arms in Natural Low* (see Elevation in chapter 14).

cts. 2-2-3   Same as preparation No. 2, but as the torso and arms are circling, the *body turns to the right one full turn.*

Repeat same side, progressing across the floor.

Repeat to the other side.

> **Note:** *This turn may also be done in plié on the standing leg and attitude on the lifted leg.*

Leg Fan with ½ Turn

Beg., Int.; four 3's smooth and flowing quality; count at 60 B.P.M.

Begin center stage, facing downstage, the feet in Wide Natural 2nd, the right leg in plié, the left leg straight, the arms in 2nd.

> **Note:** *The leg fan action may be done at three different levels, low (one foot off the floor), medium (hip height), or high (as high as possible).*

Preparation

cts. 1-2-3

ct. 1   Push off the right foot, straighten the right leg, and *brush the right foot turned out across the body to the left.*

ct. 2   *Open and lift the right leg side,* describing a fan shape in the air.

ct. 3   *Place the right foot in 2nd, and plié on the right leg as in the starting position.*

cts. 2-2-3   Repeat same as above—brush across, open, and lift the leg; place the foot back in starting position.

cts. 3-2-3   Repeat same as above—brush across, open, and lift the leg; place the foot back in starting position.

cts. 4-2-3   Transition—*Shift the weight to the left leg* by straightening the right knee and bending the left knee. The arms remain in 2nd throughout.

Repeat to the other side.

Preparation with Arm

cts. 1-2-3

ct. 1   The leg fan action remains the same as described above. The left arm (the opposite arm to working leg) describes a complete circle. As the right foot brushes across, the left arm curves as it lowers and reaches to the right.

ct. 2   As the right leg opens and lifts, the left arm raises up over the head, still rounded.

ct. 3   As the right foot places in 2nd in plié, the left arm straightens and return to 2nd with the palm down.

cts. 2-2-3   Same as counts 1-2-3 immediately above.

cts. 3-2-3   Same as counts 1-2-3 immediately above.

cts. 4-2-3   Same transition as described above.

Leg Fan with ½ Turn

cts. 1-2-3   Repeat the leg fan and arm circle action described above.

"and"   *Pivot ½ turn to the right on the right foot* to face upstage and *step with the left foot to 2nd on straight leg.* The arms remain in 2nd on the turn.

cts. 2-2-3   Repeat the leg fan and arm circle action described above, facing upstage.

"and"   *Pivot ½ turn to the right on the right foot* to face downstage and *step with the left foot to 2nd on a straight leg.* Arms remain in 2nd on the turn.

cts. 3-2-3   Repeat the leg fan and arm circle action described above, facing downstage.

cts. 4-2-3   Same transition as described above.

Repeat to the other side.

Note: *The leg fan may also be done with a jump.*

Pivotal Turns

Beg., Int., Adv.; 1 ct., the feet accented quality, the arms smooth quality; count at 65 B.P.M.

Note: *These turns are done in place, and although the knees remain in plié, there is a constant "down" beat action.*

Begin center stage, facing downstage, standing on the right foot, which is extremely turned out; the left foot is in ¾ relevé placed directly behind the right ankle; both knees are bent.

Basic Foot Action (the arms remain in Natural Low):

"and"   Keeping both knees bent, *shift the weight to the ball of the left foot* and *pick the right foot off the floor slightly.*

ct. 1   *Shift the weight and place the turned-out right foot on the floor.* Accent the "down" beat.

Pivotal ¼ Turns

cts. 1-2-3-4   Repeat the *basic foot action* four times, facing downstage.
  "and"   *Pivot on the left foot ¼ turn to the right* to face stage right.
cts. 2-2-3-4   Repeat the *basic foot action* four times, facing stage right.
  "and"   *Pivot on the left foot ¼ turn to the right* to face upstage.
cts. 3-2-3-4   Repeat the *basic foot action* four times, facing upstage.
  "and"   *Pivot on the left foot ¼ turn to the right to face stage left.*
cts. 4-2-3-4   Repeat the *basic foot action* four times, facing stage left.

> **Note:** The pattern may be continued with two basic foot actions in each direction, and then with one basic foot action in each direction.

Transition No. 1

  "and"   *Straighten the right leg and relevé on the right foot* as the left leg opens to the side low.
  ct. 1   Bring the left foot underneath you into the *starting position on the left side.*

Transition No. 2

  "and"   *Straighten the right leg and relevé on the right foot.*
  ct. 1   Bring the left foot forward, keeping the knee bent and the foot slightly off the floor, and *place it into the starting position on the left side.*

¼ Pivotal Turns with Torso Circle

Variation No. 1

Four 4's

Starting position: the same as for the basic foot action.

cts. 1-2-3-4   As the *basic foot action* continues, *accent the torso to Lateral* right side with both arms in High Parallel.
cts. 2-2-3-4   Continue the *basic foot action, pivot ¼ turn to the right to face stage right, and accent the torso into Flat Back Forward,* the arms in High Parallel.
cts. 3-2-3-4   Continue the *basic foot action, pivot ¼ turn to the right to face upstage, and accent the torso to Flat Back Back Bend,* the arms in High Parallel.
cts. 4-2-3-4   Continue the *basic foot action, pivot ¼ turn to the right to face stage left, and accent the torso to Flat Back Forward,* the arms in High Parallel.

Repeat with 2 counts in each direction and 1 count in each direction twice.

Use transition No. 1 to repeat to the left side.

Variation No. 2

Four 4's

Begin Flat Back Forward, facing downstage, the feet in the basic foot action position, the arms in High Parallel.

cts. 1-2-3-4 *Pivot ¼ turn to the right to face stage right and accent the torso to Lateral right side, the arms in High Parallel,* as the *basic foot action continues.*

cts. 2-2-3-4 Continue the *basic foot action, pivot ¼ turn to the right to face upstage, and accent the torso to Flat Back Back Bend, arms in High Parallel.*

cts. 3-2-3-4 Continue the *basic foot action, pivot ¼ turn to the right to face stage left, and accent the torso to Lateral left side, the arms in High Parallel.*

cts. 4-2-3-4 Continue the *basic foot action, pivot ¼ turn to the right to face downstage, and accent the torso to Flat Back Forward, the arms in High Parallel.*

Repeat transition No. 2, keep the torso in Flat Back Forward.

Repeat with two counts and transition No. 2 on both sides.

Repeat with one count and transition No. 2 on both sides.

Pivotal Turns with Torso and ½ Turns

Begin Flat Back Forward, facing downstage, the feet in basic foot action position, the arms in High Parallel.

ct. 1 *Pivot ½ turn to the right to face upstage. The torso moves through Lateral right side to Flat Back Back Bend, the arms in High Parallel, as the basic foot action continues.*

ct. 2 *Pivot ½ turn to the right to face downstage. The torso moves through Lateral left side to Flat Back Forward, the arms in High Parallel, as the basic foot action continues.*

Repeat the phrase above once more.

Transition No. 1 or No. 2 may be used to repeat to the other side.

Full Pivotal Turn with Torso

ct. 1 *Pivot one full turn to the right as the torso moves through Lateral right side, Flat Back Back Bend, Lateral left side, and Flat Back Forward, the arms in High Parallel, as the basic foot action continues.*

ct. 2 *Repeat the basic foot action as the torso remains in Flat Back Forward.*

Repeat three more times.

Transition No. 1 or No. 2 may be used to repeat to the other side.

•• • • •
Accented Run with Turn

See Runs in chapter 14.

•• • • •
Cross Slide Step Turn

Beg.; 3 cts.; count at 55 B.P.M.

Begin stage left, facing downstage, the feet in Natural 2nd, the arms in Natural Low.

Preparation (no turn)

ct. 1 The left foot is fully turned out as it *steps across in plié, past the right foot.* The arms cross at the wrists in front of the hips.

ct. 2 *Brush a turned-out right foot sideward and slightly off the floor, as the left foot slides sideward toward stage right along the floor.* The torso leans slightly to the left as the slide occurs. The head turns to focus to stage right, and the arms open to 2nd on the slide.

ct. 3 *Center the torso, and step on the right foot to Natural 2nd,* as the arms lower to Natural Low. The head returns to focus to downstage.

Repeat on the same side, progressing across the floor.

Repeat to the other side.

Cross Slide Step Turn

ct. 1 Same as above—*step across the right foot with the left foot fully turned out.*

ct. 2 Same as above—*brush the right foot and slide the left foot sideways along the floor.*

ct. 3 As you step on the right foot in plié, *the left foot pulls into low Figure 4 position of the legs, the toes skim the floor, the body centers, and the body turns one turn to the left.* The head "spots" downstage on the turn. The arms are in Natural Low on the turn.

Repeat on the same side, progressing across the floor.

Repeat on the other side.

•• • •   •
Coccyx Transition (Coccyx Spin)

Beg., Int.; 4 cts., smooth or accented quality; count at 55 B.P.M.

Begin facing downstage in Triangle position, the right leg inverted, the arms in 2nd.

> ct. 1 *Shift the weight onto the outside left hip and place both palms on the floor* to stage left, keeping the elbows bent. Both legs straighten, stay close to the floor, and open apart from each other as far as possible. The right leg opens back, the left leg opens forward. The torso leans to the left and twists to face the floor as much as possible. The focus is to the floor.
>
> ct. 2 *Swing the legs and the torso to Coccyx Balance position* with both legs extended and place the hands on either side of the buttocks.
>
> ct. 3 As both arms extend to 2nd, bend and turn out the right leg and place the little toe of the right foot on the floor.
>
> ct. 4 Rotate the left leg inward to *return to Triangle position on the other side.*

Repeat three more times.

Coccyx Transition with ½ Turn

Beg., Int.; 4 cts.; count at 55 B.P.M.

Begin facing downstage in Triangle position, the right leg inverted, the arms in 2nd.

> ct. 1 Same as count 1 in *Coccyx Transition described above.*
>
> ct. 2 Swing the right leg forward as impetus for a ½ *turn to the left in Coccyx Balance position with extended legs.* The arms are in Middle Parallel.
>
> ct. 3 Same as count 3 in *Coccyx Transition described above.*
>
> ct. 4 Same as count 4 in *Coccyx Transition described above.*

Repeat three more times.

> **Note:** Coccyx Transition may also be done with 1 full turn, 1 ½ turns, and 2 turns.

•• • •   •
Barrel Turn

Int., Adv.; 2 cts.; count at 60 B.P.M.

Begin stage left, facing downstage, the feet in Natural 2nd, the arms in 2nd.

"and" Turn ½ turn to the right on the right foot and *step with the left foot into plié in Natural 2nd*. The upper body rounds forward as the arms curve forward, as if wrapping around a barrel.

ct. 1 With a suspended quality, *turn ½ turn to the right* on the left foot. The right foot lifts slightly off the floor and opens sideward as the torso tilts to Flat Back Back Bend and continues to curve back as if lying back on a barrel. The right arm opens sideward and both arms are reaching up to the upstage diagonal. The body and arms are forming a curved X in space.

ct. 2 *Turn ½ turn to the right, place the right foot in Natural 2nd, keeping the body in the curved position.*

Repeat on the same side, progressing across the floor.

Repeat on the other side.

Jumping Barrel Turn

Int., Adv.; 2 cts.; count at 70 B.P.M.

"and" Same as above—*½ turn and step into plié 2nd.*
ct. 1 Same as above—*jumping in the curved X position.*
ct. 2 *Land in plié.*

Repeat on the same side, progressing across the floor.

Repeat on the other side.

Twelve

Isolations

Horton was fascinated with isolated actions. The majority of these isolations have a percussive quality and should be executed by placing the feet flat on the floor, with the knees bent and the rest of the body absolutely still.

Isolations

Beg., Int., Adv.; 1 ct. step, progressing across the floor; count at 65 B.P.M.

> **Note:** *Do not move any other part of the torso while working the isolated part.*

Begin stage left, facing stage right, the knees in plié, the feet in Parallel 1st, the arms in Natural Low or Demi-2nd.

Basic One-Count Step

ct. 1 Remaining in plié, *step forward by placing the whole left foot on the floor.*

ct. 2 Remaining in plié, *step forward by placing the whole right foot on the floor.*

Continue the basic one-count step, progressing across the floor.

Phrase 1: Head Isolations

Section A

ct. 1 *Step forward with the left foot,* as described above in the basic one-count step, and *sharply turn the head to the left.*

ct. 2 *Step forward with the right foot,* as described above in the basic one-count step, and *sharply turn the head to the right.*

Section B

ct. 1 *Step forward with the left foot,* as described above in the basic one-count step, and *sharply lift the head to the ceiling,* without dropping the head on the spine.

ct. 2 *Step forward with the right foot,* as described above in the basic one-count step, and *sharply tilt the head down to focus to the floor.*

Note: Section A and B may be combined to form a longer phrase.

Phrase 2: Shoulder Isolations

Section A

ct. 1 *Step forward with the left foot,* as described above in the basic one-count step, and *sharply lift up both shoulders.*

ct. 2 *Step forward with the right foot,* as described above in the basic one-count step, and *sharply lower both shoulders.*

Section B

ct. 1 *Step forward with the left foot,* as described above in the basic one-count step, and *sharply press both shoulders forward.*

ct. 2 *Step forward with the right foot,* as described above in the basic one-count step, and *sharply pull both shoulders back.*

Section C

ct. 1 *Step forward with the left foot,* as described above in the basic one-count step, and *smoothly move both shoulders forward and up.*

ct. 2 *Step forward with the right foot,* as described above in the basic one-count step, and *smoothly move both shoulders back and down.*

Section D

ct. 1 *Step forward with the left foot,* as described above in the basic one-count step, and *smoothly move both shoulders back and up.*

ct. 2 *Step forward with the right foot,* as described above in the basic one-count step, and *smoothly move both shoulders forward and down.*

Note: Sections C and D may be alternated progressing across the floor.

Section E

ct. 1 *Step forward with the left foot,* as described above in the basic one-count step, and *smoothly circle the right shoulder forward and up, as the left shoulder is circling back and down.*

ct. 2 *Step forward with the right foot,* as described above in the basic one-count step, and *smoothly circle the right shoulder back and down, as the left shoulder is circling forward and up.*

Section F

Reverse the circles described in Section E.

Phrase 3: Rib Cage Isolations

Section A

    ct. 1 *Step forward with the left foot,* as described above in the basic one-count step, and *sharply move the rib cage to the left.*

    ct. 2 *Step forward with the right foot,* as described above in the basic one-count step, and *sharply move the rib cage to the right.*

Section B

    ct. 1 *Step forward with the left foot,* as described above in the basic one-count step, and *sharply move the rib cage forward.*

    ct. 2 *Step forward with the right foot,* as described above in the basic one-count step, and *sharply move the rib cage backward beyond center.*

Section C

    ct. 1 *Step forward with the left foot,* as described above in the basic one-count step, and *smoothly move the rib cage forward.*

    ct. 2 *Step forward with the right foot,* as described above in the basic one-count step, and *sharply move the rib cage to the right.*

    ct. 3 *Step forward with the left foot,* as described above in the basic one-count step, and *smoothly move the rib cage backward beyond center.*

    ct. 4 *Step forward with the right foot,* as described above in the basic one-count step, and *smoothly move the rib cage to the left.*

Section D

    ct. 1 *Step forward with the left foot,* as described above in the basic one-count step, and *smoothly circle the rib cage diagonally forward to the right, side, back, and center.*

    ct. 2 *Step forward with the right foot,* as described above in the basic one-count step, and *smoothly circle the rib cage diagonally forward to the left, side, back, and center.*

Phrase 4: Hip Isolations

Section A

    ct. 1 *Step forward with the left foot,* as described above in the basic one-count step, and *sharply move the hips to the left.*

ct. 2 *Step forward with the right foot,* as described above in the basic one-count step, and *sharply move the hips to the right.*

Section B

ct. 1 *Step forward with the left foot,* as described above in the basic one-count step, and *sharply move the hips forward.*

ct. 2 *Step forward with the right foot,* as described above in the basic one-count step, and *sharply move the hips back beyond center.*

Section C

ct. 1 *Step forward with the left foot,* as described above in the basic one-count step, and *sharply move the hips forward.*

ct. 2 *Step forward with the right foot,* as described above in the basic one-count step, and *sharply move the hips to the right.*

ct. 3 *Step forward with the left foot,* as described above in the basic one-count step, and *sharply move the hips back beyond center.*

ct. 4 *Step forward with the right foot,* as described above in the basic one-count step, and *sharply move the hips to the left.*

Note: *Begin with the same foot, and reverse the circle of the hips.*

Section D

ct. 1 *Step forward with the left foot,* as described above in the basic one-count step, and *circle the hips diagonally forward to the left, side, back, and center.*

ct. 2 *Step forward with the right foot,* as described above in the basic one-count step, and *circle the hips diagonally forward to the right, side, back, and center.*

•• • • •
Foot Isolations and Strengtheners

Beg.; 4 cts.; count at 65 B.P.M.

Begin center, facing downstage, seated on both buttocks, the knees bent, and the feet placed on the floor in Parallel 1st. The arms wrapped around the knees.

Phrase 1

ct. 1 *Lift all the toes off the floor,* keeping the metatarsals on the floor.

ct. 2 *Lower the toes.*

ct. 3 *Lift the metatarsals and the longitudinal arches off the floor,* keeping the pads of the toes and the heels on the floor.

ct. 4 *Lower the metatarsals and the longitudinal arches to the floor.*

Phrase 2

ct. 1 *Lift the big toes off the floor.*
ct. 2 *Lower the big toes to the floor.*
ct. 3 *Lift all the other toes, not the big toes, off the floor.*
ct. 4 *Lower the toes to the floor.*

Phrase 3

ct. 1 *Lift all the toes off the floor.*
cts. 2-4 *Lower each toe of each foot sequentially, beginning with the little toes.*

Phrase 4

ct. 1 *Lift all the toes off the floor.*
cts. 2-4 *Lower each toe of each foot sequentially, beginning with the big toes.*

Phrase 5

cts. 1-2-3 Keeping the toes on the floor, *spread all the toes apart, accentuating the little toes.*
ct. 4 Close the toes and return to starting position.

Thirteen

Progressions

When progressions are presented in class, the students move across the floor through space. After the warm-up, the floorwork, and the stretches and strengtheners, the dancer's body is thoroughly warmed up and prepared to move with full range of movement. Many of the movements included in this chapter can be combined to create longer and more exciting phrases of movement.

Side Hip Push

Beg.; 3 cts., progressing across the floor; count at 70 B.P.M.

Begin stage left, facing downstage, the feet in Natural 1st, the arms in Natural Low.

cts. 1 and 2 *Step sideward, to stage right, shift the weight onto the right foot, and push the hips to the right as far as possible.* This causes the upper torso to bend to the left. The right leg remains straight, and the right heel remains on the floor. The left leg is extended to a pointed foot, and parallel. The right arm lifts sideward, passing through the upward right diagonal, with the palms facing the floor. The left arm pulls out sideward, and makes a diagonal line parallel to the left leg.

ct. 3 Continue to push the hips to the right, which causes the left foot to catch the weight, *by stepping across in plié, in front of the right foot. The right arm turns over, and curves over the head, then circles down and across the front of the torso to end in Natural Low.*

Repeat to the same side, progressing across the floor.

Repeat to the other side.

Forward Hip Push

Beg.; 3 cts., progressing across the floor; count at 70 B.P.M.

Begin stage left, facing stage right, the feet in Natural 1st, the arms in Natural Low.

cts. 1 and 2   *Step forward, and shift the weight onto the right foot as the pelvis pushes down and forward.* The right leg remains straight, the right foot in natural turnout. The pelvis is pushing so far forward that it is forward of the supporting foot, shaping a curved line from the head to the standing heel. The left arm reaches forward, and up to the upward diagonal, with the palm facing the floor. The left leg is extended directly behind with the foot pointed, and turned out naturally. The right leg remains straight, and the right heel remains on the floor.

       ct. 3   *Continue to push the pelvis down and forward, causing the left foot to catch the weight by stepping forward in plié.* The pelvic push also causes the left arm to rotate and continue a full circle to the back, passing through the back diagonal and ending in Natural Low.

Repeat to the same side, progressing across the floor.

Repeat to the other side.

> **Note:** Side Hip Push and the Forward Hip Push may be done alternating across the floor.

•• • • •
Left–Right Series

Beg.; 2 ct. phrase progressing across the floor; count at 60 B.P.M.

Begin stage left, facing stage left, the feet in Parallel 1st, the arms in Natural Low.

     "and"   *Step back with the left foot with both knees bent, and place the whole left foot on the floor in Parallel 4th.* The arms remain in Natural Low.

       ct. 1   With an accent, *tilt the torso slightly forward and step back with the right foot into a shallow lunge. Place the whole right foot on the floor, in Parallel 4th.* The arms remain in Natural Low.

       ct. 2   *Hold.*

Repeat the 2-count phrase progression across the floor.

Repeat to the other side.

Left-Right Series with Turn

     "and"   Same as above—*step left foot back, with bent knees.*

       ct. 1   Same as above—*step right foot back into shallow lunge, place the right foot in Parallel 4th.*

       ct. 2   *Turn one full turn to the right.* The turn begins as a pivotal turn; then turn out both feet on the second half of the turn. Allow the left foot to adjust by sliding around to complete the full turn, and permit the body to end facing stage left. The arms remain in Natural Low.

Repeat progressing across the floor.

Repeat to the other side.

> **Note:** *This may also be done as a 3-count phrase, holding count 3. The extra count may be useful for beginning students, or a place to add a dramatic accent, such as raising the head to the ceiling.*

Left–Right Series with Horizontal Swing

Beg.; 3 cts., progressing across the floor; count at 60 B.P.M.

Begin stage left, facing stage left, the feet in Natural 1st, the arms in Natural Low.

> **Note:** *This movement includes Flat Back Forward, Horizontal Rib Cage Isolation, and a Turn.*

"and"   Repeat the same foot pattern described above —*step back with the left foot.* Both arms bend and lift up with the palms facing the sternum.

ct. 1   Repeat the same foot pattern described above—*step back with the right foot.* Extend both arms to High Parallel as the torso bends forward to Flat Back.

ct. 2   *Rib Cage Isolation, as the torso swings horizontally to Flat Back right side.* The right elbow and the right side of the rib cage lead as the torso swings to the Flat Back right side.

ct. 3   *Turn ½ turn to the right, as described above, and adjust the left foot to pivot to face stage left.* Both feet turn out. The torso remains in Flat Back Forward, and the arms remain in High Parallel throughout the turn. The arms lower, and the torso centers itself just before the "and" to begin again.

Repeat progressing across the floor.

Repeat to the other side.

Left–Right Series with Squat

Int.; 2 cts., progressing across the floor; count at 60 B.P.M.

"and"   Same as above in Left–Right Series With Horizontal Swing—*step back with the left foot and raise the arms with the palms facing the sternum.*

ct. 1   Same as above in Left–Right Series With Horizontal Swing—*step back with the right foot, and extend the arms in High Parallel* as the torso tilts to Flat Back Forward.

ct. 2   *Turn ½ turn to the right, and squat with both feet in Parallel 4th and both hands on the floor near the feet.*

Stand erect, *turn ½ turn to the right to face stage left, with the arms in Natural Low.*

Repeat progressing across the floor.

Repeat to the other side.

Left–Right Series with Forward and Back T

Int.; 4 cts. progressing across the floor; count at 60 B.P.M.

"and"   Same as above in Left–Right Series With Horizontal Swing—*step left, and raise the arms with the palms facing the sternum.*

ct. 1   Same as above in Left–Right Series With Horizontal Swing—*step right and extend both arms to High Parallel and Flat Back Forward.*

"and"   *Lift the torso erect and the arms to High Parallel and turn right, passing through 2nd, to face stage right.*

ct. 2   *Lift the left leg to Forward T position.*

ct. 3   *Step back on the left foot, and lift the right leg to Back T position.* The standing knee is bent.

ct. 4   *Step onto the right foot, and turn ½ turn to the right to begin again.* The arms lower to Natural Low.

Repeat on the same side to progress across the floor.

Repeat to the other side.

Knee Crawl

Int.; 4 cts., progressing across the floor; count at 45 B.P.M.

Begin upstage, facing downstage, in Triangle position, the left leg inverted, the arms in 2nd.

ct. 1   *Raise up onto the right knee.* The pelvis moves forward over the right knee. The right foot remains pointed.

ct. 2   *Extend the left leg,* moving it forward through Parallel 2nd to turned out 2nd. The left leg moves to the downstage left diagonal, keeping the leg turned out and the foot pointed.

ct. 3   *Flex the left foot and simultaneously lower the pelvis and place both buttocks on the floor. Press the pelvis forward and slide the left leg toward the left downstage diagonal.*

ct. 4   *Bend the left knee, point the left foot, and move it inward to Triangle position. The right leg remains inverted.*

Repeat progressing forward, alternating sides.

Variation with Arms

ct. 1 Same leg action as described above. *The arms circle down, forward, and up to High Parallel as the body lifts up to the right knee.*

ct. 2 Same leg action as described above. *The arms remain in High Parallel.*

ct. 3 Same leg action as described above. *Both arms open to 2nd with the palms facing up as the pelvis presses and the leg slides.*

ct. 4 Same leg action as described above. *Both palms turn down as the body returns to Triangle position.*

Repeat progressing forward, alternating sides.

All of the following are also Progressions.

Leg Swings (chapter 6)

Turns, except Pivotal (chapter 11), and Coccyx Transition (chapter 11)

Isolations (chapter 12)

Preparation for 5/4 Swing Variation (chapter 6)

Runs (chapter 14)

Elevation (chapter 14)

• • • • • • ••

Fourteen

Elevation

Elevation is always the final part of the class. It lends itself to drama and excitement and allows the dancer great freedom. It also requires the most concentrated outlay of energy.

Elevation Preparations

Metatarsal Press (see Fortification No. 15)

Int., Adv.; 8 cts.; count at 85 B.P.M.

Begin center, facing downstage, the right leg extended back and parallel, with the ball of the foot on the floor; the left knee is bent, the left foot naturally turned out; the right arm is forward, the left arm in 2nd, both palms down.

> ct. 1 *Press the right heel toward the floor, and increase the plié in the left knee.*
> "and" *Release the press of the right heel.*
> cts. 2-6 Repeat the movement described above—*press the right heel toward the floor, and release the press.*
> cts. 7 and 8 *Change legs* by moving the left foot back through Natural 1st to extend back and turn the leg parallel.

Repeat to the other side.

> **Note:** *This metatarsal press or Achilles tendon stretch can be done as a progression; the transition to the other side then becomes a jump taking off from both feet and landing with the position of the feet reversed. The heel of the working foot should press down and lift up as fully as possible to maximize the stretch of the achilles tendon.*

Plié and Relevé

Beg.; 8 cts.; count at 70 B.P.M.

Begin center, facing downstage, the feet in Natural 2nd, the arms in 2nd.

Phrase 1

cts. 1 and 2 *Plié on both legs.*
cts. 3 and 4 *Straighten both legs.*
cts. 5 and 6 *Relevé on both legs.*
cts. 7 and 8 *Lower the heels.*

Phrase 2

cts. 1 and 2 *Plié on both legs.*
cts. 3 and 4 *Maintaining the plié, raise both heels off the floor.*
cts. 5 and 6 *Straighten both legs.*
cts. 7 and 8 *Lower the heels.*

Phrase 3

cts. 1 and 2 *Relevé on both legs.*
cts. 3 and 4 *Plié, keeping the heels off the floor.*
cts. 5 and 6 *Lower both heels to the floor.*
cts. 7 and 8 *Straighten both legs.*

These phrases may be combined for more advanced students.

Jumps and Skips

Stag Jump

Int., Adv.; 4 cts.; count at 135 B.P.M.

Begin stage left, facing stage right, the feet in Natural 1st, the arms in Natural Low.

ct. 1 *Step forward with the right foot* toward stage right.
"and" *Spring up into the air; lift the right leg forward and the left leg to Stag position.* Both knees are bent in the air. The upper torso twists to the right to face upstage, and the arms lift sideward to Opened Egyptian.
ct. 2 *Land on the right foot* in plié on the right leg.
ct. 3 Maintaining the twist in the upper torso, *step forward to stage right on the left foot.*
ct. 4 Maintaining the twist in the upper torso, *step forward to stage right on the right foot.*

Repeat on the other side, and alternate progressing across the floor.

2nd Position Jump

Int., Adv.; 2 cts.; count at 65 B.P.M.

Begin stage left, facing downstage, the feet in Natural 1st, the arms in 2nd.

Preparation

> ct. 1 *Step across in plié toward stage right with the left foot* as the left arm lowers. The left arm is slightly rounded. The right arm remains in 2nd.
>
> "and" *Brush the right foot sideward, and lift the right leg to 2nd as high as possible* as the left leg straightens. The left arm continues to circle by reaching across the body to the right, and then overhead. The left arm is slightly rounded, and the right arm remains in 2nd.
>
> ct. 2 *Lower the right leg and step on the right foot* as the left arm opens to 2nd.

Repeat to the same side, progressing across the floor.

> **Note:** To alternate sides, step sideward on the left foot, and turn ½ turn to the right.

2nd Position Jump

> ct. 1 Same as above—*step across in plié toward stage right with the left foot.*
>
> "and" *Jump on the left foot as the right foot brushes sideward and lifts to 2nd. The left leg straightens in the air. The left arm continues to circle by reaching across the body, to the right, and overhead.*
>
> ct. 2 *Land in plié on the left foot, lower the right leg, and step on the right foot, as the left arm opens to 2nd.*

Repeat to the same side and alternate as described above.

Barrel Turn Jump

See Turns in chapter 11.

Angel Jump

Int., Adv.; 2 cts.; count at 60 B.P.M.

Begin stage left, facing downstage, the feet in Natural 1st, the arms in Natural Low.

Preparation

> ct. 1 *Step sideward in plié toward stage right with the right foot.*
>
> "and" *Straighten the right leg, tilt and arch the back to the right, and lift the left leg in attitude.* The back and the left leg should feel as if they were wrapping around a column. Both arms lift parallel to each other, across the body, and on the right upward diagonal.
>
> ct. 2 *Lower the left leg, turn to the left, and step with the left foot*

through Natural 2nd facing upstage. Continue to turn to the left to begin the movement again.

Repeat progressing across the floor.

Angel Jump

ct. 1 Same as above—*step sideward in plié with the right foot.*
"and" *Spring into the air in the position described above in the preparation.*
ct. 2 *Land in plié on the right foot,* lower the left leg, turn to the left, and step with the left foot through Natural 2nd facing upstage. Continue to turn to the left to begin again.

Skips

Beg., Int., Adv.; varying tempi

Begin stage left, facing stage right, the feet in Natural 1st, the arms in Natural Low.

The body position for skips is the left leg lifted forward and parallel, with the knee bent at a right angle. The left foot is pointed toward the floor. The right leg is straight and turned out naturally. The right arm is extended forward, parallel to the floor, the left arm is in 2nd, and both palms are facing down.

The legs alternate consecutively.

Skips may be done *traveling forward for breadth,* or *moving up and down for height.*

Skips may be done with ½ or full turns.

Strike Hop

Adv.; 2 cts.; count at 50 B.P.M.

Begin stage left, facing stage right, the feet in Natural 1st, the arms in Natural Low.

ct. 1 *Step forward and jump on the left foot as the right leg lifts forward into Skip position* as described above. Both arms lift to High Parallel.
ct. 2 *Step onto and hop on the right foot, tilt the torso forward, place both hands on the floor, and lift the left leg into Strike position.*

Repeat on the same side, progressing across the floor.

Repeat to the other side.

Single-Foot Arch Springs

Beg., Int., Adv.; count at 100 B.P.M.

Single-foot arch springs are done parallel, and the landing of the spring is always accompanied by a plié. The spring occurs on the upbeat and the landing is on the beat.

Begin stage left, facing stage right, legs parallel, the right knee is bent with the toes pointed and slightly off the floor.

Plain Spring

1 ct. 4 times

      ct. 1 *Spring up into the air* from the left foot and straighten both legs in the air with both feet fully pointed. Land in plié on the right foot. The left leg bends, left foot pointed, and slightly off the floor.

   cts. 2-4 *Alternate the arch spring* to progress to stage right.

Spring Right, Spring Left, Feet Together, Up Down (or single, single, double, double)

4 cts.

      ct. 1 *Spring up into the air* from the left foot and land on the right foot as described above.

      ct. 2 *Repeat the arch spring,* landing on the left foot.

      ct. 3 *Repeat the arch spring and land in Parallel 1st* with both legs in plié.

      ct. 4 *Spring up into the air* from both feet and land in Parallel 1st with both legs in plié.

Repeat by springing from both feet and landing on the right foot to progress to stage right.

Variation

  cts. 1 and 2 Same as above—*spring right and spring left.*

      ct. 3 Repeat the arch spring and *land in Natural 1st* with both legs in plié.

      ct. 4 *Spring up into the air* from both feet and *land in Natural 1st* with both legs in plié.

Spring Right, Spring Left, Feet Together with Variations

Variation No. 1

Beg.; 4 cts.

      ct. 1 *Spring up into the air* from the left foot and land on the right foot.

ct. 2 *Repeat the arch spring,* landing on the left foot.

ct. 3 *Repeat the arch spring and land in Parallel 1st* with both legs in plié.

ct. 4 *Spring up into the air* from both feet and *bring both knees up and forward* so the back and the upper thighs are forming a right angle in the air. The heels are as close to the buttocks as possible. The hands slap the thighs at the height of the jump (the "and" count of 4). Land in Parallel 1st with both legs in plié.

Variation No. 2

Beg.; 4 cts.

cts. 1-3 Same as above—*spring right and spring left, spring feet together.*

ct. 4 *Spring up into the air* from both feet and *turn out and bend both legs.* Bring the pointed toes together, keeping the feet fully pointed, so that the legs are forming a *diamond shape.* Both arms lift sideward and the hands clap overhead at the height of the jump. Land in Parallel 1st with both legs in plié.

Variation No. 3

Int.; 4 cts.

cts. 1-3 Same as above—*spring right and spring left, spring feet together.*

ct. 4 *Spring up into the air* from both feet and *tilt and arch the back to the left.* The left leg bends and the left foot points. Lift the right leg back in attitude. The back and the right leg should feel as if they were wrapping around a column. Both arms lift, parallel to each other, across the body to the left on an upward diagonal. Both arms round slightly and rotate so that the palms are facing the body as they lift. Land in Parallel 1st with both legs in plié.

Variation No. 4

Beg.; 4 cts.

cts. 1-3 Same as above—*spring right and spring left, spring feet together.*

ct. 4 *Spring up into the air* from both feet and *bring both knees up and forward to the chest.* The back remains straight and tilts slightly forward. The heels are as close to the buttocks as possible. The arms lift to 2nd at the height of the jump. Land in Parallel 1st with both legs in plié.

Variation No. 5

Int.; 4 cts.

cts. 1-3 Same as above—*spring right and spring left, spring feet together.*

ct. 4 *Spring up into the air* from both feet and lift the right knee forward and the left knee back in *Stag position*. The right arm lifts to 2nd and the left arm lifts to Middle Parallel, palm facing down. Land in Parallel 1st with both legs in plié.

Variation No. 6

Int.; 4 cts.

cts. 1-3 Same as above—*spring right and spring left, spring feet together.*
ct. 4 *Spring up into the air* from both feet and lift the legs in *Triangle position* with the right leg forward, the left leg inverted to the back. The arms lift to 2nd. Land in Parallel 1st with both legs in plié.

Variation No. 7

Beg., Int.; 4 cts.

cts. 1-3 Same as above—*spring right and spring left, spring feet together.*
ct. 4 *Spring up into the air* from both feet and *open the legs to 2nd.* The arms open sideward with the hands reaching toward the feet. Land in Parallel 1st with both legs in plié.

Variation No. 8

Adv.; 4 cts.

cts. 1-3 Same as above—*spring right and spring left, spring feet together.*
ct. 4 *Spring up into the air* from both feet and lift the right leg straight forward and the left leg straight back in a *split position*. The right arm lifts to 2nd and the left arm lifts to Middle Parallel, palm facing down. Land in Parallel 1st with both legs in plié.

Variations 1 to 8 can be combined into a sequence of consecutive jumps.

• • • •
Elevation Study No. 1

Adv.; six 4's; count at 75 B.P.M.

Begin stage left, facing downstage, the feet in Natural 1st, the arms in Natural Low.

cts. 1-2 Plié on the left leg; brush the right leg slightly off the floor to stage right to jump onto the right foot, into *Cross Lunge position*. The right leg is bent, with the right foot turned out naturally. The left leg is straight and crossed behind the right leg. The left foot is in ¾ relevé with the heel reaching toward stage right. Both feet are on the same line. The torso is in High Lateral to the left, forming a diagonal line of the body from the head to the left heel. The arms remain straight and parallel to each other, palms facing, and make a full counterclockwise circle to the right, up, and left, and end reaching across the body, on a downward diagonal, parallel to the back left leg. The head stays in line with the torso, focus front.

ct. 3 Center the torso and turn to face stage left. Step to stage left with the left leg turned out naturally and in plié. *Simultaneously, swing the right leg forward in attitude passing through Natural 1st, to stage left.* Drop the right arm, slightly rounded, down to Natural Low and forward to Middle Parallel. The left arm lifts to 2nd on count 3.

ct. 4 *Spring from the left foot, straighten the left leg in the air, toes pointed, and turn ½ turn to the left* to face stage right. The right leg rotates to back attitude as the ½ turn occurs in the air. The right arm, slightly rounded, lifts overhead. Plié on the left leg to land.

cts. 2-2 *Straighten and brush the right leg forward, through Natural 1st, and spring from the left foot.* At the same time, the torso bends slightly to the left, and both arms lower sideward and reach forward to Middle Parallel.

cts. 3-4 Plié on the left leg and spring to *Cross Lunge position* with the right leg forward, facing downstage, as in counts 1 and 2 of the 1st measure. The arms make the same counterclockwise circle.

cts. 3-2-3-4 *Four leaps downstage with straight legs,* beginning with the left leg, landing in plié each time. The arms swing in opposition to the forward leaping leg.

ct. 4 *Spring up from the right foot and land with both legs, in plié, in Natural 1st.* Both arms lower, slightly rounded, to Natural Low.

ct. 2 *Spring from both feet and turn ¼ turn in the air to the right to face stage right, landing on the right leg in plié.* The left leg lifts to Stag position. The left arm lifts, slightly rounded, through the center, overhead. The right arm lifts sideward to 2nd.

ct. 3 *Spring from the right foot, turn ¼ in the air to the left to face downstage, and lower the left leg to land in Natural 1st, in plié.* The right arm lowers, slightly rounded, to Natural Low. The left arm lowers, slightly rounded, through the center to Natural Low.

ct. 4 *Spring from both feet and turn ¼ turn in the air to the left to face stage left, landing on the left leg in plié.* The right leg lifts to arabesque. The right arm lifts to Middle Parallel, palm facing down, and the left arm lifts sideward to 2nd.

cts. 5-2 Traveling on the upstage right diagonal, turn to the left and on the "and" of count 1, *step right.* On count 1 *step left.* On the "and" of count 2, *hop on the left foot,* landing on count 2. As the left leg steps forward on count 1, the right leg brushes forward, through Natural 1st, and extends slightly off the floor. On the "and" of count 2, as the hop occurs on the left leg, the right knee bends, right foot pointed, and passes the inside of the left anklebone, extending back to low arabesque on the landing. The arms remain in 2nd.

cts. 3-4 and 6-2 Repeat the action of counts 5-2—on the "and" *step right; on count 3, step left. On the "and" hop on the left foot,* landing on count 4. Repeat once more. The arms remain in 2nd.

ct. 3 On the "and" of count 3, *step right.* On count 3, *step left, and brush the right leg forward,* through Natural 1st, slightly off the floor.

ct. 4 Spring from the left foot, and turn to the left to face downstage with both *feet in ballet 5th position, the right foot forward, in ¾ relevé.* At the same time, *Lateral the torso to the right* and lower both arms to Natural Low and lift slightly rounded, through the center, overhead.

•• • • • Leg Slice Series

Int.; 3 ct. phrase, progressing across the floor; count at 75 B.P.M.

Begin stage left, the feet in Natural 1st, the arms in 2nd, facing stage right.

Phrase 1

ct. 1 Step diagonally forward with the left foot to the right downstage diagonal, and plié on the left leg. Keeping the shoulders and hips square, *brush the right leg across the body with the leg turned out, foot pointed, and leg slightly off the floor.* The arms remain in 2nd.

ct. 2 Straighten the left leg and "slice" the right leg *open, toes reaching to the right upstage diagonal.* As the right leg opens waist high, the weight shifts forward and to the right. The arms remain in 2nd.

ct. 3 Continue to shift the weight and *place the right foot on the floor to the right upstage diagonal,* with the right leg bent. Arms remain in 2nd.

Continue progressing across the floor with the right leg "slicing."

Repeat to the other side.

Phrase 2

ct. 1 Same as count 1 above—*brush the right leg across the body with the leg turned out, foot pointed, and leg slightly off the floor.*

ct. 2 *Straighten the left leg and spring into the air as the right leg "slices" open, toes reaching to the right upstage diagonal.* The weight remains centered. The arms remain in 2nd.

"and" *Land on the left leg in plié.*

ct. 3 Shift the weight forward and to the right *and place the right foot on the floor to the right upstage diagonal, with the right leg bent.*

Continue progressing across the floor with the right leg "slicing."

Repeat on the other side.

Runs

Unaccented Runs

Beg.; varying tempo

Begin stage left, facing stage right, the right leg in natural turnout; the left leg turns out, the foot in natural turnout to the back and the ball of the foot is on the floor. The arms in 2nd. The run is done with both legs in plié and on the balls of both feet. The body remains on the same level.

Moving forward, run left foot, right foot. Repeat to progress to stage right.

Accented Runs in 3

Beg.; 3 cts.; count at 180 B.P.M.

Begin stage left, facing stage right, the right leg in natural turnout; the left leg is in natural turnout; the foot to the back and the ball of the foot on the floor. The arms remain in Natural Low throughout.

cts. 1-2-3   Moving forward, *run left foot, right foot, left foot,* with both legs in plié. On the first run, the whole foot is on the floor. The plié is increased to create an accent. The second and third runs are on the balls of the feet.

Repeat the 3-count phrase, alternating sides, to progress to stage right.

Accented Runs in 3 with a Turn

Beg.; two 3's; count at 180 B.P.M.

cts. 1-2-3   Moving forward, *run left foot, right foot, left foot* as described above.
cts. 4-5-6   Moving forward, *run right foot, left foot, right foot,* and turn ½ turn to the right on the left foot on the 2nd run and ½ turn to the right on the right foot on the 3rd run. The legs remain in plié throughout in the runs.

Repeat the 6-count phrase to progress to stage right, alternating the forward run with the turning run.

Repeat to the other side.

Accented Runs on Every 2nd Beat

Beg.; 6 cts.; count at 180 B.P.M.

cts. 1-2 Moving forward, *run left foot, right foot* with both legs in plié. On the first run, the plié is increased to create an accent.

cts. 3-4 Repeat 1-2 above—*run forward* with accent on count 3.

cts. 5-6 Repeat 1-2 above—*run forward* with accent on count 5.

Repeat the 6-count phrase to progress to stage right.

Repeat to the other side.

Accented Runs in 5

Beg.; 5 cts.; count at 180 B.P.M.

cts. 1-5 Moving forward, *run left foot, right foot, left foot, right foot, left foot* with both legs in plié. On the 1st and 3rd runs, the plié is increased to create the accents.

Repeat the 5-count phrase, alternating sides, to progress to stage right.

Accented Runs in 6

Beg., Int.; 6 cts.; count at 180 B.P.M.

cts. 1-6 Moving forward, *run left foot, right foot, left foot, right foot, left foot, right foot* with both legs in plié. On the 1st and 4th runs, the plié is increased to create the accents.

Repeat the 6-count phrase to progress to stage right.

Repeat to the other side.

Accented Runs in 7

Beg., Int.; 7 cts.; count at 180 B.P.M.

cts. 1-7 Moving forward, *run left foot, right foot, left foot, right foot, left foot, right foot, left foot* with both legs in plié. On the 1st, 4th, and 6th runs the plié is increased to create the accents.

Repeat the 7-count phrase, alternating sides, to progress to stage right.

> **Note:** *For rhythmic training, accented runs in 2, 3, 5, 6, or 7 may be combined into a single progression across the floor.*

Elongated Runs

Beg., Int.; four 4's; count at 75 B.P.M.

Begin stage right, facing stage left, the left leg in natural turnout, the right leg in natural turnout, the foot to the back and the ball of the foot on the floor. The right arm in Middle Parallel, palm facing down, the left arm in 2nd.

cts. 1-2-3-4 Moving forward, *run right foot, left foot, right foot, left foot.* The arms swing in opposition to the forward running leg. Both legs extend fully. Do not jump.

Repeat the 4-count phrase to progress to stage left.

Repeat to the other side.

Leaps

> **Note:** *The following leaps have a forward, darting action with the legs splitting and the body moving forward on a horizontal plane.*

Step, Leap

Beg., Int.; 2 cts.; count at 90 B.P.M.

Begin stage right, facing stage left, the left leg in natural turnout, the right leg in natural turnout with the foot to the back and the ball of the foot on the floor, the right arm in Middle Parallel, palm facing down; the left arm in 2nd.

cts. 1-2 *Step forward on the right leg, brush the left foot forward, and leap.* Both legs are straight in the air. Land in plié on the left leg on count 2. The arms swing in opposition to the forward leg, palms facing down.

Repeat to progress to stage left.

Repeat to the other side.

Leap, Step

Beg., Int.; 2 cts.; count at 90 B.P.M.

Begin stage right, facing stage left, the left leg in natural turnout, the right leg in natural turnout with the foot to the back and the ball of the foot on the floor, the right arm in Middle Parallel, palm facing down; the left arm in 2nd.

cts. 1-2 On the "and", *brush the right foot forward and leap.* Both legs are straight in the air. Land in plié on the right leg on count 1. Step forward on the left leg on count 2. The arms swing in opposition to the forward leg, palms facing down.

Repeat to progress to stage left.

Repeat to the other side.

Run, Run, Leap

Beg., Int.; four 4's; count at 165 B.P.M.

Begin stage right, facing stage left, the left leg in Natural turnout, the right leg in natural turnout with the foot to the back and the ball of the foot on the floor, the right arm in Middle Parallel, palm facing down; the left arm in 2nd.

cts. 1-2   Moving forward, *run right foot, left foot.* The arms do not change.

cts. 3-4   *Brush the right foot forward and leap.* Both legs are straight in the air. The arms swing in opposition to the forward leg, palms facing down. Land in plié on the right leg on count 4.

Repeat, alternating sides, to progress to stage left.

Repeat to the other side.

Leap, Run, Run

Beg., Int.; four 4's; count at 165 B.P.M.

Begin stage right, facing stage left, the left foot in natural turnout, the right leg in natural turnout with the foot to the back and the ball of the foot on the floor, the right arm in Middle Parallel, palm facing down, the left arm in 2nd.

cts. 1-2   *Brush the right foot forward and leap.* Both legs are straight in the air. The arms swing in opposition to the forward leg, palms facing down. Land in plié on the right leg on count 2.

cts. 3-4   Moving forward, *run left foot, right foot.* The arms do not change on the runs.

Repeat, alternating sides, to progress to stage left.

Repeat to the other side.

A Final Word

Each of the three authors came to study the Horton technique in very different ways. Marjorie Perces, having been a student, teacher, and dancer at the Horton School in Los Angeles during the middle years of his work, brings a direct link. Ana Marie Forsythe inherited the legacy from the late Joyce Trisler and from James Truitte. Mr. Truitte was also the major influence for Cheryl Bell's training in Horton technique. But no matter how this technique was learned, we all agree that there is an inherent uniqueness that distinguishes Horton's work from any other modern technique. This is the gift that Lester Horton gave us, directly or indirectly, and this is the gift we want to pass on to the next generation.

The volume of material that Horton created in such a short time is impressive. He was enormously inventive and was constantly working and reworking his movements. He expected that his students would continue in this creative spirit.

Everyone who studied with Horton loved him and felt his strong commitment. His enthusiasm was contagious. He made the lives of all who worked with him so rich because he lived his art and generously shared it. He created a living technique that perpetuates those feelings of optimism and love.

We hope the magic of Lester Horton and his technique has been transposed to these pages.